10-3-74

The
SEABIRDS
of Britain and Ireland

The
SEABIRDS
of Britain and Ireland

Stanley Cramp · W. R. P. Bourne

David Saunders

TAPLINGER PUBLISHING CO., INC.
NEW YORK

First published in the United States in 1974 by
TAPLINGER PUBLISHING CO., INC.
New York, New York

Library of Congress Catalog Card Number: 74-106
ISBN 0-8008-7013-1

Contents

Colour Plates

BY ROBERT GILLMOR

Plate 1   A Manx Shearwater (*from above and below*); B Fulmar; C Storm Petrel; D Leach's Storm-petrel; E Guillemot (*winter and summer*); F Razorbill (*winter and summer*); G Black Guillemot (*winter and summer*); H Puffin (*winter and summer*)

Plate 2   A Gannet (*adult and immature*); B Great Skua; C Arctic Skua (*light and dark phase*); D Cormorant (*adult and immature*); E Shag (*adult and immature*)

Plate 3   A Great Black-backed Gull; B Lesser Black-backed Gull; C Herring Gull (*adult and immature*); D Black-headed Gull (*summer and winter*); E Kittiwake (*adult summer and immature*); F Common Gull (*adult summer and immature*)

Plate 4   A Sandwich Tern; B Common Tern; C Arctic Tern (*adult and immature, left*); D Roseate Tern; E Little Tern

Maps

CRISPIN FISHER

Photographs

Acknowledgments

This book would not have been possible without the strenuous labours of more than a thousand observers who surveyed all the coastal breeding seabirds of Britain and Ireland during 'Operation Seafarer' in 1969-70. It is unfortunately not practicable to mention them all individually, but deserving of particular thanks are the regional organisers and those who led the major expeditions. The former include E. Balfour, W. A. Burridge, Dr J. J. M. Flegg, Dr J. A. Gibson, J. J. D. Greenwood, J. Grey, D. E. B. Lloyd, A. Macdonald, I. Maclean, N. D. McKee, O. J. Merne, G. Noonan, J. L. F. Parslow, N. R. Phillips, K. Preston, E. I. S. Rees, F. R. G. Rountree, M. J. Seago, M. Shrubb, D. J. Slinn, J. Stafford, D. M. Stark, A. J. Stewart, Mrs F. le Sueur and J. G. Young, while the major expedition leaders were J. Blatchford, the Brathay Exploration Group, M. de L. Brooke, W. Cooper, P. G. H. Evans, A. Ferguson, J. N. Ford, J. E. Fowler, R. G. Gibbs, N. Hammond, R. W. Hansford, J. Keys, J. E. McCarthy, J. Oakshatt, J. R. Pinder, R. W. Powell, A. D. K. Ramsay, P. Stanley, D. J. Steventon, D. Swann, I. Thomas, P. Watson, R. G. Wheeler, P. R. Williams, D. R. Wilson, and R. W. Woods. We realise that there may well be other field workers who expended just as much of their time and energy on the survey and we hope they will forgive us if space precludes mentioning them all by name.

We are also grateful to others who helped in organising the survey in various ways, including D. G. Andrew, Dr J. Morton Boyd, M. J. Everett, F. R. Hamilton, C. G. Headlam, R. Hudson, J. Temple Lang, A. T. Macmillan, R. J. O'Connor (who did much of the preliminary work), D. Scott and Dr J. T. R. Sharrock and to the Ministry of Defence who arranged for many colonies to be examined and photographed from aircraft on training flights and the Irish Air Corps who gave similar assistance in Ireland.

David Saunders acted as full-time organiser of the field work from 1968 to 1971. He then extracted and analysed the thousands of record cards to prepare the basic data on which the species maps and tables are based. He has been mainly responsible for writing the accounts of the regular breeding species in this book, except for the Kittiwake, for which we are indebted to Dr J. C. Coulson. Our thanks are also due to P. F. Bonham for much valuable editorial advice and to the following who gave us expert assistance on particular species or problems:– Dr R. S. Bailey, C. J. Bibby, N. Brown, P. E. Davis, J. J. D. Greenwood, N. Langham, Dr J. B. Nelson, D. Nettleship, J. Parsons, Dr G. R. Potts, Major R. F. Ruttledge, A. J. M. Smith, G. J. Thomas, W. E. Waters, and D. R. Wilson.

'Operation Seafarer' was planned by the Executive Committee of the Seabird Group and directed by them and a specially appointed Census Committee.

Those who served on these bodies include C. J. Bibby, W. R. P. Bourne, Dr. James Cadbury, Dr J. C. Coulson, Stanley Cramp, J. Crudass, T. R. E. Devlin, Professor G. M. Dunnet, the late James Fisher, D. Lea, O. J. Merne, R. J. O'Connor, J. L. F. Parslow, Dr C. M. Perrins, R. G. Pettitt, E. I. S. Rees and George Waterston. They have all devoted many hours to the project, but we feel sure that the others would agree that special thanks are due to Professor G. M. Dunnet, the first Chairman of the Seabird Group, and to the late James Fisher who was Chairman of the Census Committee until his tragic death in 1969.

The appointment of David Saunders as full-time organiser was made possible by a most generous grant from the three bodies concerned with the *Torrey Canyon* Appeal Fund – the Royal Society for the Protection of Birds, the Royal Society for the Prevention of Cruelty to Animals and the World Wildlife Fund. Others who have given welcome financial assistance are the British Ornithologists' Union, the British Trust for Ornithology, A. M. Jacob, the Royal Irish Academy, the Scottish Ornithologists' Club and the West Wales Naturalists' Trust. Finally, we extend our thanks to Bruce Coleman Limited, Arthur Gilpin, Eric Hosking, S. C. Porter, the late Niall Rankin, and R. J. Tulloch, who have made their excellent photographs available without charge, to Robert Gillmor for his fine paintings and line drawings, and to Crispin Fisher for his attractive maps.

Preface

In recent years attention has been focused on seabirds in many parts of the world: huge numbers have been killed in oil spills at sea off America, South Africa, Europe and elsewhere; the guano-producing seabirds of the Peruvian coast have been declining; hundreds of thousands of auks are caught and killed each year in nets off the Greenland coast; DDT residues have been recorded in Antarctic penguins. Nearer home the spectacular increase in Fulmar numbers and breeding range has been well documented while the recent apparent decline in the Puffin, especially on our western seaboard, has not. Increasing numbers of Herring Gulls have led to drastic control measures being taken on some of our islands, while species like the Little Tern become scarcer. To detect these changes and assess their magnitude we require a base-line of information against which the necessary comparisons can be made, and also continuing surveillance to record the geographic extent and size of fluctuations in numbers which are occurring 'naturally' as well as in response to exploitation or environmental crises.

Britain and Ireland provide the most important breeding places for seabirds in the north-east Atlantic, and our seabird colonies are of outstanding international importance, and a great tourist attraction. We also are situated in part of the world where many of the current threats to seabirds are manifestly destructive. The development of the North Sea oilfield, the discharge to the sea of industrial effluents, sewage and refuse from the cities of Western Europe, the impact on on-shore breeding colonies of changing land-use and holiday crowds, the pesticide problem, and the development of commercial fisheries – all of these are at this very moment having their effect on the distribution and numbers of seabirds. Further, these birds, by their conspicuousness and the general interest taken in them, often provide the first indication that things are going wrong in the marine environment, as shown by the massive mortality in the Irish Sea in the autumn of 1969, leading to concern about the discharge of PCBs into the sea.

It therefore seemed appropriate to the Seabird Group, established in 1965, to take on as one of its primary tasks a census of breeding seabirds in Great Britain and Ireland, and this book embodies the results of this mammoth undertaking. Planned by a committee under the chairmanship of the late James Fisher, organised by David Saunders, and financed mainly by a generous grant from the three bodies associated with the Torrey Canyon

Appeal Fund (the Royal Society for the Protection of Birds, the Royal Society for the Prevention of Cruelty to Animals and the World Wildlife Fund), the work was carried out by a large number of amateur and professional ornithologists who spent long hours and travelled far to record the location and size of seabird colonies round the entire coastline. The preparation of this book has been carried out by Stanley Cramp, Chairman of the Seabird Group and outstanding ornithologist, Bill Bourne, Secretary and Director of Research of the Group and world authority on seabirds, and David Saunders who worked so successfully as co-ordinator of the census. Yet, no one will feel that this is the last word on censusing seabirds: apart from the fact that distributions and numbers will change necessitating continuing routine observations at least at sample sites, the project highlighted a whole series of problems associated with the counting of breeding seabirds. Kittiwakes and Cormorants on the one hand may prove relatively easy, but the nocturnal burrowing shearwaters and storm petrels, and the Puffin, are almost impossible to census in terms of breeding pairs. Most species pose some problems and before specific methods can finally be adopted for each species much research is still needed on breeding behaviour, and breeding biology generally. It is important that this work will be undertaken and that the Seabird Group will continue to play its role both in research and in co-ordinating the surveillance of selected species and breeding colonies. The Group is to be congratulated on the successful completion of its first major project.

Professor G. M. Dunnet

Introduction

LYING on the western edge of the great land mass of Europe and Asia, Britain and Ireland cannot compete in the variety of their breeding birds with many of the countries farther east. Yet for one group of species, the seabirds, they are justly renowned, with few countries in this area able to surpass them in richness of species or in the sheer numbers which gather to breed each summer around their coasts. Many people in these islands may, perhaps, not fully appreciate this, for to them, especially if they live in the south, the only seabirds are gulls, either the Herring Gulls which frequent the popular seaside resorts or the smaller Black-headed Gulls which range over the built-up areas in winter, penetrating even into the heart of major cities. There are, however, no less than 24 species of seabird which breed regularly on the coasts of Britain and Ireland, but to see them in their full glory one must travel to the great bird-cliffs of the north and west where they gather in bustling thousands, and to observe the nests of all of them would entail excursions also to noisy tern colonies or hazardous voyages to remote islets to track down the nocturnal petrels and shearwaters.

Human interest in our seabirds has a long history. For our early ancestors this was, perhaps, largely utilitarian, as seabirds and their eggs provided sustenance for many coastal settlements and were indeed an essential basis of life on such island outposts as St Kilda. Yet they had a less practical appeal too, for James Fisher (1966a) argued eloquently that the poem 'The Seafarer', composed perhaps 1300 years ago, must refer to one of the most famous of the seabird colonies of Britain and Ireland, the Bass Rock. Certainly the poet described vividly seabirds which now breed there or close by – the Gannet, Kittiwake and a tern, as well as the White-tailed or Sea Eagle, once widespread around our coasts, but which has not nested in Britain since about 1916. It was much later before more precise accounts became available, but for a number of the main colonies there are records by ornithologists going back 300 years or more, while within the last century the great majority of seabird sites around the coasts of Britain and Ireland have received some mention in regional or county avifaunas. Even these, however, rarely did more than list the species nesting and for any indication of numbers we are left tantalised by vague expressions such as 'incredible number', 'a marvellous multitude', 'obscure the sun' and so on.

Credit for the first attempt to assess the breeding numbers of any seabird over a wide area is due to J. H. Gurney (1913). His survey covered the Gannet over the whole of its range in the North Atlantic. The Gannet is large and conspicuous, breeding in a limited number of colonies, but even so, this was a bold effort. Some 20 years later the great period of seabird censuses began, appropriately enough with a more sophisticated attack on the world Gannet population by V. C. Wynne-Edwards and his colleagues (1936). Around this time the steady growth in the numbers of amateur observers of birds began, which has accelerated so remarkably in the last 20 years. This led in 1934 to the formation of the British Trust for Ornithology, which has played a major part in organising co-operative inquiries of many kinds. There followed a number of seabird censuses, many organised by the Trust. James Fisher continued the Gannet surveys and added regular censuses of the Fulmar, a species which was showing an almost unparalleled expansion and increase, while others carried out surveys covering the whole or considerable proportions of Britain and Ireland for such species as Leach's Storm-petrel, Great Black-backed Gull, Black-headed Gull, Kittiwake and Cormorant. There was also a steady growth of information available on the numbers of nesting birds at individual colonies for a variety of other species, including terns, skuas and auks, although these were rarely comprehensive enough to make possible any accurate assessment of population trends. (References for all these surveys and inquiries are given later in the appropriate species accounts.) This was regrettable, for some of these species were showing signs of decline over at least some part of their ranges and, with the growing fears of environmental pollution added to other threats, the need for full surveys was becoming pressing.

The challenge was taken up by the Seabird Group, a new body formed to co-ordinate co-operative research into seabirds, following the initiative of Dr W. R. P. Bourne in 1965. The Seabird Group soon decided that it was essential from both the scientific and conservation aspects to find out precisely where all our seabirds were nesting and to estimate as accurately as possible their present numbers. This information could then be used in the light of the often limited historical data to find out how the various species have fared in recent years and, perhaps even more important, to provide a base-line to measure future changes. The basic conception was simple and daring, but its execution proved formidable. It involved visiting and surveying every site likely to include nesting seabirds, including miles of cliffs, often precipitous and difficult of access, and innumerable islands, some far from land or guarded by treacherous currents. After trial surveys in 1967, the summer of 1968 was devoted to a preliminary reconnaissance of the less well-known areas, together with attempts to refine the techniques for assessing the numbers of the more difficult species such as auks. The main census took place in 1969, when a gratifying 95 per cent coverage was obtained and the summer of 1970 was devoted to filling the gaps. The task of organising this major combined operation fell to David Saunders, formerly Warden of Skomer in South Wales and lifelong enthusiast for seabirds. He stumped the country appealing for volunteer observers, guided them to key areas and wrestled with crises when sickness struck observers or the weather hindered visits to remote islands. After this, he faced the perhaps more daunting task of gathering in all the reports from over 1,000 observers and collating and analysing them to provide the maps and the statistics which form the basis of this book.

The result is, I believe, unique. It is the first time that all the coastal seabird colonies of any large country in the world have been mapped and an attempt made, successful for most species, to estimate their total numbers accurately enough to make possible assessments of future changes. Indeed, we now know more about our seabird numbers than we do for all but a handful of our more familiar landbirds. The core of this book is therefore the maps which show where all the seabirds nesting round the coasts of Britain and Ireland are to be found and the tables giving national and county totals with, for key species, details of many individual colonies. The full results, running to several volumes, will be available to serious research workers. However, this book aims to do more than present such bare, but vital facts. It tries to set the seabirds of Britain and Ireland in perspective – to describe their appearance, behaviour, food, nesting habits and migrations; to assess the threats and opportunities which face them and to outline what is known of their past and present numbers and distribution.

This book will, I hope, be of value and interest to the reader who desires a general survey of what is known about our seabirds, whilst providing the enthusiast with an accurate summary of all aspects of current knowledge, including fully documented accounts of earlier studies. I trust it will also appeal to all who care for the natural heritage of these islands and the manifold threats presented by modern man's impact upon his environment. Many believe that the oceans of the world are being recklessly and dangerously over-exploited, whilst others argue that once again the prophets of doom are here displaying an equally reckless panic. If the pessimists are right, our seabirds will provide one of the earliest and best indicators of environmental damage which, unchecked, could harm man and his food supplies. For our own future, as well as for the pleasure these free and so far long-lived birds bring to many, we need a much greater understanding of their lives and their place in nature. The pages which follow make clear how inadequate in many respects is our knowledge of the seabirds of these islands; yet equally we have a foundation of information which is surpassed for few other groups of living creatures anywhere in the world. I hope this book will convey that knowledge and its limitations to all who are interested and, no less important, something of the beauty and marvels of the many species of seabirds which have sought the summer shelter of our coasts and islands down the centuries.

CHAPTER I

The Biology of Seabirds

BIRDS as a group have achieved most of their success through the development of the power of flight as a means of dispersal in search of food, to avoid enemies, and on migration. Only in exceptional circumstances have the larger forms and those occurring on undisturbed oceanic islands succeeded in surviving in a flightless state, despite the advantage this confers in allowing them to reach a larger size. Overland they encounter only a limited amount of competition for food from bats and insects, as bats have not obtained the same mastery of flight, so that their distribution and the times of day at which they find activity successful are limited, while the anatomy of insects (especially that of their breathing apparatus) imposes limits on their size. Out at sea birds have the air almost entirely to themselves, if we exclude the flying-fish who use it only as an emergency means of escaping predators.

In the past there has always been an ample supply of food to support large populations of birds somewhere out at sea, though from time to time it becomes inaccessible because of its movements, notably into deep water, or because of bad weather. Therefore once seabirds, either as species or as maturing individuals, achieve a satisfactory adaptation to the marine environment, including powers of endurance in the face of local food shortage and bad weather, a capacity for wide dispersal in search of food, and powers of accurate navigation at sea, they are commonly very safe and live long, for decades or even scores of years in the case of the larger species. On the other hand, as a result of their extreme specialisation for a life at sea they may prove very vulnerable to additional threats arising from human activity in the form of new types of predation or pollution affecting them or their food-supply, or when they come ashore to breed, since the external or internal carriage of an egg or foetus has proved incompatible with such advanced development of the powers of flight.

It seems likely that birds were originally terrestrial animals, but some certainly took to the sea very early in their existence. There they have tended to show one of two contrasting types of adaptation for marine conditions, either as aerial types with small, light legs which save weight, adapted to feed by picking food from the vicinity of the sea surface from the air, or as aquatic types with short, strong legs set well back for efficient propulsion, which dive for their food, often to remarkable depths; thus Cormorants have been caught in nets down to 20 metres and Guillemots to 140 metres, while Emperor Penguins *Aptenodytes forsteri* have carried depth recorders down to 265 metres (Balfour *et al.* 1967; Holgersen 1961; Kooyman *et al.* 1971). These two types of specialisation are to some extent mutually exclusive since long or broad wings with a large surface area adapted for sustained effortless gliding flight are a serious encumbrance if the bird takes to the water, while short, narrow wings suitable for use as flippers in the water are relatively inefficient in air, requiring disproportionate expenditure of effort to keep even the smaller species airborne. It may be noted that in different ways, but especially because of the modification it involves for the legs, either type of adaptation also renders the bird clumsy on land.

Hence most seabird families have tended to develop one type of adaptation, either for aerial hunting over vast distances where the food-supply is dispersed or very patchy, as it is in the centre of the oceans and along some coasts, or for deep-diving in areas where food is denser, so that the birds do not need to travel so far, but it may be hard to catch, as in the areas with a high marine productivity in summer in high latitudes and where upwelling occurs along the coasts in lower latitudes, e.g. Peru, California, west and south-west Africa and Arabia (Cushing 1971). The shearwaters are remarkable for showing both types of adaptation (Kuroda 1954; Ashmole 1971). The birds' behaviour is further modified to take advantage of that of their prey, since marine animals may behave differently at different stages of their life-cycles, seasons, or times of day. Many fish adopt a pelagic way of life at sea during their first summer, moving inshore or into deeper water afterwards, while many pelagic animals make marked vertical movements towards the surface at night and into deep water by day. Some of these movements may also be associated with the animals assembling into dense shoals at some times and scattering at others, in the way reported by Raitt *et al.* (1970) during sonar investigations off west Africa. Comparatively little is known yet about how bird feeding routines are adapted to the behaviour of their prey, except that whereas most coastal species appear to be mainly active by day, often feeding where marine predators force fish-shoals to the surface, many pelagic species are clearly also very active at night, and it is notable that two of our most pelagic seabirds, the Kittiwake and Fulmar also leave their colonies then, possibly to feed at sea (Myres 1963, Coulson and Horobin 1972).

Since extreme aquatic adaptations of the limbs render seabirds, especially the larger ones, extremely clumsy in the air, and the sea is a comparatively safe environment, aquatic birds have shown a repeated tendency throughout their history to develop into large, flightless forms. However, possibly owing to their extreme vulnerability when they have to come ashore to breed, these seldom appear to have lasted long on a geological time-scale except in the special case of the penguins, which live in the far south where there was originally little hostile life on land. The normal fate of large flightless or near-flightless species elsewhere is illustrated only too clearly by the story in our own times of the Great Auk *Pinguinus impennis* in the North Atlantic and Pallas's Cormorant *Phalacrocorax perspicillatus* in the North Pacific which were exterminated by fishermen in the first half of the last century just before their vulnerability was realised (Greenway 1958). The more successful trends of adaptation shown by modern seabirds are illustrated by considering the manner of development of the four surviving orders, which between them show a wide variety of types of specialisation for the marine way of life within the limits already discussed.

The Charadriiformes appear to have developed originally as a group feeding along the shore, though they have proved so successful that some have now moved inland and others out to sea, while a variety of species commute between the land and sea at different seasons. A number of families of more or less ground-feeding waders frequent open muddy, sandy or rocky ground, often between the tidelines or along river margins, especially in winter, though some have colonised deserts, plains, marshes and tundra, especially to breed, and one family, the phalaropes, has taken to feeding on the water surface upon zooplankton, breeding by tundra pools but spending the winter out at sea in the tropical upwelling areas (Meinertzhagen 1925). Several other families of gulls, terns, skuas and skimmers are adapted to feed in much the same places from the air upon more mobile prey, though the gulls in particular have also recently emerged as important predators upon the invertebrates of farmland and scavengers exploiting human wastes. Some of these, notably the smaller skuas, Sabine's Gull *Larus sabini* and Black Tern *Chlidonias niger*, also winter at sea far to the south of their north temperate or Arctic breeding grounds, while some species such as the kittiwakes *Rissa spp.* and Sooty Tern *Sterna fuscata* have become entirely pelagic.

The Pelecaniformes include another six families showing a high degree. of adaptation for catching large aquatic prey. Two of these, the darters and pelicans, show differing types of adaptation for fishing in inland waters, the first by solitary stalking, the second by communally rounding up shoals of fish, while the Brown Pelican *Pelecanus occidentalis* also hunts by diving on its prey out at sea. The cormorants are more marine, most species feeding by diving from the water surface along the shore, though some also exploit inland waters. The gannets and boobies, frigatebirds and tropicbirds feed entirely at sea, the first group by diving from the air, the second by hawking over the water and parasitising other species (though, as with the skuas, the extent to which they carry out this highly conspicuous activity may have been exaggerated), and the third by catching prey at the water surface in the centres of the tropical oceans.

A much higher degree of marine adaptation is shown by the four families of Procellariiformes. The albatrosses are huge birds with long wings which feed from the air, probably largely upon cephalopods, though they also catch fish and scavenge when they are given the opportunity. Most of them occur in the southern ocean, but they were also widespread in the intercommunicating northern seas of the tertiary period, and their fossils have been found in Britain, though they now breed north of the equator only in the Pacific. It is not clear why they died out in the North Atlantic; they might have been exterminated by man, but the evidence which might have been expected for this (and which is abundantly available where primitive men hunted albatrosses in the Pacific) has not been found in the North Atlantic yet, so it seems more likely that they were unable to adapt to some change in ecological or meteorological conditions affecting either their food-supply or hunting techniques during the Pleistocene. Representative examples of two main divisions of the true petrels, an aerial fulmar and a diving shearwater, still breed with us, though, and one or more examples of the cephalopod-catching gadfly-petrels of the genus *Pterodroma* have wandered here, though no representative of the fourth main group, the plankton-eating prions of the genus *Pachyptila*, has yet been found far north of the equator. Two members of the northern division of the fourth family, the storm-petrels, characterised by a relatively swooping type of flight, also breed with us, while a typical example of the pattering southern species, Wilson's Storm-petrel *Oceanites oceanicus*, regularly approaches as close as the Bay of Biscay as a migrant from the Antarctic.

The eighteen species of Sphenisciformes (penguins) are of course restricted to the southern hemisphere, one reaching the equator at the Galápagos in the cool-current area off Peru. Their character is well known, and they are chiefly of interest from our point of view in providing an indication of the likely way of life of the most remarkable North Atlantic seabird, the lost Great Auk. It would appear from comparisons that the loss of the power of flight by aquatic seabirds tends to be associated with a rapid increase not only in size but also in swimming ability, as the wing becomes completely adapted for use as a flipper. In consequence the penguins at least have become outstandingly successful, with colonies holding millions of large birds all round the Antarctic. It seems likely that the Great Auk in its day may also have been a highly successful species in the North Atlantic, since its remains have been found very widely in the middens left by prehistoric man from the Arctic breeding grounds south to Florida and the Mediterranean, where it may have occurred as a winter visitor, doubtless feeding on the larger herring, mackerel and pilchards, whose immature stages are taken by the smaller auks. These remains also, of course, provide a clue to its fate, since it must have been utterly defenceless once men built boats seaworthy enough to reach its breeding islands. It was only the inaccessibility of some of their breeding sites which saved the penguins in their turn from extermination by whalers in search of oil later in the last century, and some populations are still only just beginning to recover again after a century of respite.

Within the general framework of adaptive radiation to exploit the marine environment represented by the four main orders of seabirds it is possible to distinguish some interesting examples of ecological replacement by different groups in different parts of the world. In addition to the way in which the Great Auk developed as a northern equivalent of the penguins, the Little Auk *Alle alle* shows an equally remarkable convergence in form, habits and markings with the southern diving-petrels of the genus *Pelecanoides* (Murphy and Harper 1921; Kuroda 1967), and the Ivory Gull *Pagophila eburnea* of the Arctic pack-ice with the Snow Petrel *Pagodroma nivea* of the same habitat in the Antarctic; the evolutionary pressures leading unrelated species to adopt such similar forms in similar but widely-separated habitats at opposite ends of the earth must be very strong. Besides the strong similarities, marked differences may also be found between comparable seabird communities in different parts of the world; thus, while the northern North Pacific tends to have a generally richer biology than the North Atlantic, it is notable that it has fewer large auks, but many more smaller ones (and also more storm petrels), and while it has three albatrosses it lacks a gannet. It seems possible that, while the vast expanse of shallow seas communicating freely with the Arctic Ocean has favoured the development of large, fish-eating species in the North Atlantic, the more intense oceanic circulation in a wider, deeper ocean which during much of its history has been cut off from the Arctic Ocean by a landbridge across the Bering Strait has favoured instead the establishment of an avifauna composed of more plankton- and cephalopod-eaters in the North Pacific.

All these birds show a common tendency to develop a distinct type of life cycle, commented upon by Wynne-Edwards (1955, 1962) among others, including a high adult survival rate and hence long life, retarded maturity, and a naturally low reproductive rate, a trend which becomes increasingly marked among the more pelagic species. It would appear that while the more extreme forms of marine adaptation enable birds to survive well, they are then less successful in breeding, doubtless because they are clumsy on land, few safe sites are available where they can come ashore to breed, and these tend to become overcrowded so that competition for nest-space and food close to the colony tends to become extreme (Ashmole 1963). Seabirds have therefore tended to develop particular breeding adaptations associated with their way of life, discussed by Lack (1967), including the adoption of particularly safe types of nest-site close to a good food-supply, a long period of immaturity during which they learn to survive at sea before they return to land, then a long period of prospecting a suitable breeding site before they attempt to breed, often strong territorial behaviour when they do take up a nest-site so that they can retain it in the face of competition (Nelson 1970), and finally a prolonged breeding-cycle during which they rear few or only one chick which grows rather slowly so that the minimal demands are made on a potentially limited and irregular local food-supply.

Within these limits, seabirds are also surprisingly variable in their breeding adaptations. Most of them nest near the sea, but species feeding in estuaries commonly select sandbanks for nest-sites, those feeding off stormy coasts may favour cliffs, those feeding far out to sea may choose uninhabited islands or rocks, while some species may fly inland to nest by rivers and lakes, in the middle of wild open spaces such as shingle-beds, deserts, moors, marshes or the Arctic tundra, or, in less stormy climates than ours, in trees, which are favoured by many tropical species. Some species are rather specialised in their choice of nest-site, notably the many small ones and especially the smaller petrels and auks, which nest in holes, perhaps chiefly to avoid aerial predators, but also for protection from the weather, and also the northern cliff-nesting species such as the Kittiwake (Cullen 1957) and tropical tree-nesters such as the White or Fairy Tern *Gygis alba* which lays its single egg on an unadorned twig or rock ledge (Dorward 1963). Others are extremely plastic, including some of the gulls which will nest almost anywhere, or the petrels, some of which are quite prepared to use impartially suitable nest-sites all the way from small offshore islets to the tops of inland mountains thousands of feet above sea-level as does the Manx Shearwater in Britain (Bourne 1957a).

The main limiting factors for seabird breeding-sites in fact appear to be the availability of a good food-supply close to a safe site, and these Britain affords in abundance. In general, with us, the smaller pelagic species such as the petrels and Puffin nest in holes on the outer islands facing the Atlantic, the larger pelagic species which have difficulty in finding enough suitable holes tend to take refuge on inaccessible rocks and cliffs, the terns use inshore islands and inland waters and especially a habitat increasingly disturbed by man, the sandbanks which tend to form off the mouths of estuaries, and the gulls use all these sites and shingle-banks, moors, marshes and recently (Cramp 1971) buildings as well, though individual species often feed together on the same superabundant small fish, which may vary from one area to another, sand-eels *Ammodytes* often being prominent off the north-east coast of England for example (Pearson 1968) though in the north and west young Clupeoid and Gadoid fishes are at least equally important (W. R. P. Bourne, personal observation).

Within the broad outline of adaptations for a marine way of life represented by the higher levels of classification from orders through families down to genera, the more successful types have often broken up into large groups of more or less similar species and races adapted to exploit many different regions, climates, or habitats in much the same way. This widespread phenomenon is particularly prominent among marine animals because the marine environment is so much more uniform than that of the land except for latitudinal differences in climate, and in consequence complex evolution has occurred within some of the more successful groups such as the gulls and terns, cormorants, shearwaters, gadfly petrels or albatrosses on a global scale, with the same general types being represented by at least one race or species in each of the climatic zones of several or all the major oceans in one or both the northern and southern hemispheres. In some groups the situation is then further complicated because individual, often extremely similar, species may undertake long trans-equatorial or east-west movements between the more or less analogous areas of opposite hemispheres or opposites sides of the same ocean, as for example the shearwaters, Common/Arctic group of terns or smaller skuas in the first direction, or the Sooty Tern, which migrates across the tropical Atlantic between breeding stations off Florida and a 'nursery' in the Gulf of Guinea (Robertson 1969) in the other.

In general the seabird communities of the world can be divided into four main groups with an analogous distribution on either side of the equator associated with that of the main belts of planetary winds and ocean currents (Bourne 1963). Thus tropical communities are found associated with the belt of doldrums and monsoons along the equator; subtropical ones with the trade-winds blowing from the east in low latitudes on either side of the equator; temperate, boreal or subantarctic communities (possibly the first term is clearer) in association with the westerlies in higher latitudes, and polar communities in association with the belt of east winds around the poles. These communities have recently been considered in detail by Ashmole (1971), and here it is sufficient to discuss the position in the North Atlantic. This is not entirely typical of the situation in a larger ocean where the direction of wind and water flow tends to become aligned parallel to the equator, with the main vertical air and water circulation occurring along the fronts between winds and currents flowing in opposite directions, since owing to the land-locked configuration of the present North Atlantic the circulation tends to occur in a clockwise direction around a central anticyclone situated near the Azores, but the similarity in conditions to those found in the larger oceans, such as the North Pacific or south of the equator, is great enough to permit useful comparisons.

If we consider the general pattern of water movement outlined in

Map A, therefore, and its ultimate influence on birds, let us start where cool bottom water rich in dissolved nitrates and phosphates wells up where the trade-winds blow the surface water offshore along the west coast of Africa. Phytoplankton multiply in this nutrient solution as soon as it is exposed to sunlight, zooplankton feed on the phytoplankton, small shoaling fish and cephalopods feed on the zooplankton, and larger fish, marine mammals and birds feed on the zooplankton, fish and cephalopods, the marine predators helping to make prey available to the birds by driving it to the surface. A particularly rich shorebird and coastal seabird community including many terns, gulls, cormorants, pelicans and the Brown Booby *Sula leucogaster* has recently been found breeding along this coast (de Naurois 1969), while many northern seabirds such as Gannets, Pomarine Skuas *Stercorarius pomarinus*, Grey Phalaropes *Phalaropus fulicarius* (Stanford 1953) and various terns, but especially the Black Tern, winter here, and more loiter for a while on their way to and from winter quarters further south in the similar area of upwelling off south-west Africa (Liversidge 1959) or in the temperate South Atlantic.

As the upwelling water drifts offshore to join the westward-flowing North Equatorial Current, floating food-organisms seem likely to accumulate where some water sinks again and there is more upwelling at a 'roller-bearing' line of convergence and divergence about 100 km. offshore of the sort reported to occur off south-west Africa by Hart and Currie (1960), which doubtless provides the main feeding-ground for the important community of subtropical petrels breeding on the central Atlantic archipelagoes (Bourne 1955; Bannerman 1963-8). Then the Equatorial Current moves on west, supplemented during the winter by further upwelling along the tropical divergences and in eddies to the lee of the Antilles which provide feeding-places for another community of tropical terns, boobies, the Brown Pelican, Magnificent Frigate-bird *Fregata magnificens* and Audubon's Shearwater *Puffinus (assimilis) lherminieri* (Ingham and Mahnken, 1966; Erdman, 1967) before it eventually turns north-east to leave the Caribbean past Florida as the Gulf Stream, where vast colonies of tropical terns breeding on the Dry Tortugas feed on the young tuna travelling with it (Robertson, 1964; Potthof and Richards 1970). It then flows on past the great devastated seabird station of Bermuda (Bourne 1957b) to divide into two branches as it approaches the Azores. The first of these turns south-east to complete the circuit of the Sargasso Sea as the Canary Current, while the second flows on north-east as the North Atlantic Drift towards Western Europe and the Arctic.

By the time the oceanic water of the North Atlantic Drift approaches our shores it has become very warm and saline as a result of its long passage through the tropics where there is much evaporation, and the

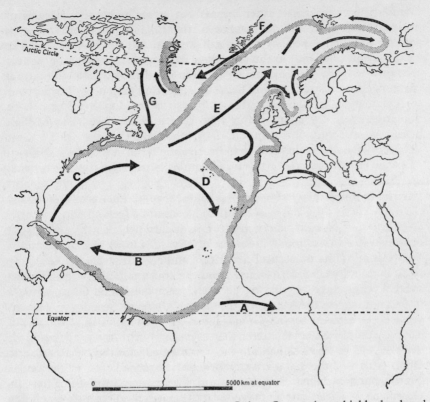

A Water circulation in the North Atlantic. A: Guinea Current (most highly developed late in the year; a branch of the Southern Equatorial Current extends north across the equator in the west in the spring). B: North Equatorial Current. C: Gulf Stream. D: Canary Current. E: North Atlantic Drift (carrying warm oceanic water to western Europe and the Arctic. F, G: East Greenland and Labrador Currents (carrying cold water from the Arctic and Davis Strait south to sink under the North Atlantic Drift). Areas of marked vertical water circulation along boundaries between water masses, diverging currents and lee shores are shaded.

nutrient salts which support plankton growth are becoming exhausted. As it moves in over the continental shelf it then encounters a highly distinct type of coastal water diluted and enriched by the outflow from rivers, which is normally warmer and therefore less dense in summer, when it tends to spread out to sea on the surface, but cooler and denser in the winter, so that it tends to sink to the bottom along the coast. The approximate boundary between the two water masses at different seasons is indicated by the 35 parts per thousand salinity line indicated in Maps 30 and 31. Marked vertical mixing with an associated high marine productivity during the long, calm days of summer is found along the boundary between these water masses out at sea and where streams of oceanic water enter the approaches to the English Channel, Irish Sea and Minch, and especially the north-western North Sea between the Orkneys and Shetland, in the last case carrying oceanic plankton with it as shown in Map 32. The mixing is often intensified where strong tidal currents occur in straits and off headlands, floating food being turned over so that it may become accessible to birds (as in Map B). The pelagic immature stages of many of our food fish feed in these areas of high marine productivity during the summer, where they are exploited by vast numbers of seabirds that gather to breed near by as shown in Maps 1–3.

As the North Atlantic Drift moves on north-east further water-mixing, associated with the development of rich fisheries and large seabird colonies of much the same species, is found around other island groups to the north such as the Faeroes, Westmanns south of Iceland and Lofotens off north-west Norway, and where the boundary between the coastal and oceanic water curves round the north of Norway into the shallow Barents Sea. The most intense vertical circulation and highest marine productivity of all is found where warm water from the south mingles with the west-ward flowing currents carrying pack-ice from the Arctic Ocean along a front running south-west from the central Barents Sea down the east coast of Greenland to the Grand Banks of Newfoundland, where the icebergs dump the solid matter that they carry with them as they melt and the cold water sinks beneath the northern edge of the North Atlantic Drift. Much of the sinking water probably returns south in the ocean depths, but some apparently moves north-west around the south coast of Greenland as a deep current to reappear as a patch of warmer surface water in the eastern Davis Strait, where it rejoins the south-westerly movement of surface water in the Labrador Current. A distinct community of Arctic seabirds including such species as Brünnich's Guillemot *Uria lomvia*, the Little Auk, and the Ivory Gull and Glaucous Gull *Larus hyperboreus* occurs along the polar front, some individuals moving south-west along it into lower latitudes off Greenland and Newfoundland in the winter (Belopol'skii 1961, Salomonsen 1972).

Certain points may be made about this situation. In the first place, owing to the limited size of the North Atlantic and the constricting effect of the continental coasts, the main climatic zones are not symmetrically distributed as in the larger oceans, but the tropical and Arctic habitats with their westward flowing atmospheric and oceanic circulations are better developed and more widely distributed in the west, approaching each other off south-eastern Canada, while the temperate and subtropical habitats with their eastward·flowing air and water circulations are better developed and more widely distributed in the east. Here the best-de-veloped tropical and Arctic communities are found beyond the strict

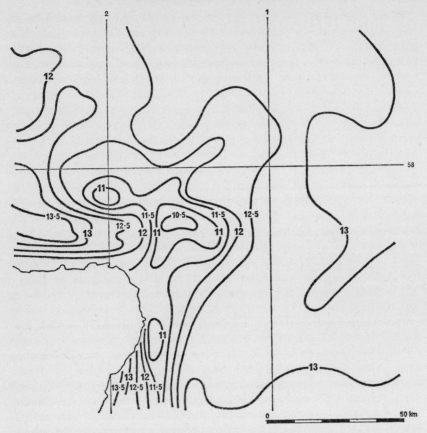

B Surface water temperature in °C off north-eastern Aberdeenshire during 7th-11th July 1952 to show the effect of mixing warm upper and cool deep water in an area with strong currents and tidal streams. Exceptionally large seabird colonies tend to be located in such areas. (Based on information supplied by R. E. Craig; see also Craig, 1959).

limits of the Atlantic Ocean itself in the Gulf of Guinea in one direction and the Barents Sea in the other. In addition, since the continental coasts are irregular in their configuration, the distribution of habitats is often equally irregular, temperate and subtropical elements mixing in the Mediterranean in the south-east and temperate and Arctic ones in the Gulf of St Lawrence to the west, the Davis Strait to the north-west and the Barents Sea to the north-east. For this reason it is often difficult to allocate the affinities of individual species precisely. The situation may be further complicated by migration, especially when birds move between different climatic zones at different seasons or stages of their life-cycle.

Britain and Ireland occur in a strategic position in the centre of the best-developed part of the North Atlantic temperate zone, surrounded by shallow waters teeming with fish in summer and still holding a good many in winter (though some occur at greater depths then) and with an ample supply of isolated island, cliff, and also originally sandbank and inland marsh breeding sites, though the last two have become increasingly disturbed in recent years. They also provide important winter quarters and feeding-grounds on migration for large numbers of birds breeding further north, while immediately to the south the area of cool, upwelling water with its high marine productivity off west Africa also provides winter quarters for their birds and a feeding-ground for those on the way to the South Atlantic. It is therefore hardly surprising that Britain and Ireland furnish breeding places for a high proportion of all temperate North Atlantic seabirds, including a majority of the world population of the Storm Petrel, of the North Atlantic Gannet, Manx Shearwater *Puffinus puffinus puffinus* and Great Skua, of the southern North Atlantic races of the Guillemot *Uria aalge albionis* and Lesser Black-backed Gull *Larus fuscus graellsii*, and most of the European population of about a dozen other species, notably the Fulmar and Roseate Tern *Sterna dougallii*.

During the period of their immaturity and in some cases while they are not breeding as adults (when some, such as the Fulmar and Guillemot, become increasingly sedentary, and tend to return to the breeding stations in fine weather as soon as they have finished the postnuptial moult), British and Irish breeding seabirds may disperse far and wide, throughout the temperate North Atlantic and in some cases more southerly climatic zones. The more migratory young birds in particular may remain away for years in distant 'nursery' areas with a high marine productivity where the species does not breed, for example along the warm side of the polar front off the Grand Banks of Newfoundland, in the Davis Strait, and in the Greenland and Barents Seas, or in the case of the terns and skuas in the subtropical upwelling areas off west and south-west Africa. The Arctic Skua tends to disperse widely in the southern temperate zone, the Manx Shearwater reaches the cool-current area off Argentina and has wandered to Australia (Thomson 1965), and the Arctic Tern visits the Antarctic pack-ice (Salomonsen 1967).

In the late summer when shoaling fish are most abundant what are, apparently, non-breeding populations of several southern shearwaters, including Cory's Shearwater *Calonectris diomedea* and the very distinct western Mediterranean form of the Manx Shearwater, known as the Balearic Shearwater *Puffinus puffinus mauretanicus*, which breed imme-diately to the south, and Great and Sooty Shearwaters *Puffinus gravis* and *P. griseus* breeding in the temperate South Atlantic, also visit north-west European seas, sometimes accompanied by small numbers of other subtropical petrels breeding at the central Atlantic archipelagoes, and Wilson's Storm-petrels which breed in the Antarctic, though their normal range usually stops at the Bay of Biscay (Lockley 1953b; Ash and Rooke 1954; Voous and Wattel 1963; Phillips 1963; Roberts 1940; Bourne and Sharrock in Sharrock 1973). Tropical species may also occur rarely at this time, possibly birds which have gone astray during the passage of hurricanes past the Caribbean and up the east coast of North America and then drifted east across the north Atlantic in the west wind zone.

It is notable that while north-west Europe is visited by vast numbers of temperate seabirds breeding further north in winter, truly Arctic winter visitors are scarce, except during occasional incursions of sick or starving Little Auks and the small-billed Arctic race of the Fulmar *Fulmarus glacialis glacialis* (Sergeant 1952; Pashby and Cudworth 1969). It would appear that if they are not long-distance migrants they tend to travel south-west along the polar front towards Greenland and Newfoundland rather than south-east towards Europe (Salomonsen 1972). With the exception of the Arctic Terns and attendant Arctic Skuas which may linger on autumn passage the long-distance migrants to the south are often also inconspicuous in north-west Europe, presumably because they tend to pass by rapidly either high overhead or far out to sea, though they may also appear in numbers coasting along the shore or wrecked inland from time to time as well, as for example the Grey Phalarope (Sage and King 1959), Pomarine Skua (Oliver and Davenport 1972), and especially Leach's Storm-petrel (Boyd 1954). Sabine's Gull which has only recently been found to winter off South Africa (Mayaud 1961, 1965; Zoutendyk 1968) and the Long-tailed Skua *Stercorarius longicaudus* which apparently, though the full position is not yet known, winters far south off southern South America (Murphy 1936) are both particularly inconspicuous on migration in western Europe, possibly because most come from Arctic North America and fly straight to the upwelling areas off Iberia and West Africa (Bourne 1965).

It is notable that when seabird migrants are on the move they tend to show much the same variation in behaviour as landbirds, many moving on a broad front though some tend to follow 'guiding lines', especially around obstacles in their path and during periods of bad weather. However, with seabirds land-masses tend to serve as the obstacles whereas the landbirds tend to avoid the sea, so that whereas the landbirds tend to skirt the sea or fly high over it, the seabirds skirt the land or fly high over that. Seabirds react to bad weather in much the same way as landbirds, and similarly tend to move north in spring during the periods of fine weather with south winds which tend to occur with the arrival of a high pressure system (Hinde 1951; Pettitt 1972), and south in autumn in the cold north-westerly airstream following an eastward-moving depression (Phillips and Lee 1966; Oliver and Davenport 1972). Birds such as the auks (Pettitt 1972), are also liable to settle when the weather deteriorates, though in this case on the water, and it seems possible that pelagic species may move ahead of advancing low pressure systems (Manikowski 1971), since they are particularly liable to appear in inshore waters and participate in coasting movements as they pass, especially when the visibility is poor (Sharrock 1973). Some of these coasting movements, which have been detected along an increasing number of coasts and especially off projecting headlands in recent years since it has been realised where and when to look for them, may involve migration, others feeding movements by birds dispersing from or returning to breeding colonies, and others perhaps weather movements of birds either blown in from the open sea during bad weather or returning to it afterwards.

CHAPTER 2

The Threats to Seabirds

THE seabirds breeding in Britain and Ireland are, then, of many different kinds, varying in habitats, behaviour and ecology. They also differ widely in numbers, ranging from a few thousands for Leach's Storm-petrel to some half a million pairs in the case of the Guillemot and Puffin. Moreover they are responding very differently to the dangers and opportunities in these rapidly changing islands and their surrounding waters. Some species, indeed the majority, have increased in numbers in the last hundred years or so, benefiting from new opportunities in an increasingly man-dominated environment and from protection from human exploitation, hostility or intolerance. Others do not seem to have undergone any marked changes, whilst a few, notably the Puffin, Razorbill, Guillemot and Little Tern, are declining either locally or over wide areas. The present status of the various species, their changing fortunes and the factors that may be responsible in each case are discussed in the next chapter. Here the varying threats posed by man's growing numbers and activities are outlined and some attempt made to assess their possible significance to our seabirds.

Ever since men first appeared on the earth they have had some influence on bird populations. For countless centuries, the effects must have been limited, for the small and scattered bands of primitive men could kill few with their crude weapons or traps and snares, and the eggs they took for food can rarely have been of more than local importance, especially as they were probably unable to reach many offshore and all oceanic islands. The situation has changed radically, however, in the last few centuries and now man's activities for good or ill are of overriding importance for most bird species over large areas of the world.

Hunting, now mainly for sport rather than food, still affects many birds, especially wildfowl, gamebirds and, indirectly, predators, but currently its impact on the seabirds of Britain and Ireland is probably small. A little over a hundred years ago, gulls and other seabirds were massacred for sport in some places around our coasts, but in 1869 an Act to protect them was passed, the precursor of modern bird protection legislation. It was followed by the Wild Birds Protection Act in 1880, covering a much wider range of species. The slaughter was checked and Hudson (1898) recorded the last gulls being shot in London by 'sportsmen' in the hard winter of 1892–3, when the public first began to feed them. So gulls were able to accept cities as safe winter refuges and gradually

found their modern role as urban scavengers, even nesting in some towns
and cities. Shooting abroad, however, may still affect some of our seabirds, for recoveries of ringed Guillemots and Razorbills suggest that
each autumn many from British and Irish colonies are killed off the coasts
of Norway and France. Seabirds were regularly taken for food on islands
off western Ireland during and after the famines of the 1840s and on St
Kilda until it was evacuated in the 1930s (Bourne 1972), but the practice
is now rare or non-existent, except possibly among some foreign fishermen
offshore.

The taking of birds' eggs is now generally prohibited in Britain except
in the case of five of our breeding gulls (Great Black-backed Gull, Lesser
Black-backed Gull, Herring Gull, Common Gull and Black-headed Gull),
whose eggs can in most areas be taken for human consumption or as food
for poultry. Yet, although numbers still feature each year on the menus of
luxury restaurants to be eaten by the unsuspecting gourmets as 'plovers'
eggs', the trade is too small to affect the thriving gull populations. Perhaps
more surprisingly the law specifically allows the men of Lewis to take
young Gannets from the exposed islet of Sula Sgeir. This is an ancient
and hazardous custom, still permitted as an important social function,
but it has apparently little effect on the numbers of the Gannets, which,
like most gulls, are still increasing.

Man's direct effects on our seabirds, therefore, are now small. The
indirect effects of his activities are, however, considerable and steadily
increasing. In many parts of the world the arrival of human beings on
remote islands meant the reduction and often extinction of endemic
species, partly because sailors took the birds and their eggs for food, but
also because they introduced predators such as cats and rats, or grazing
animals like sheep and goats which rapidly wrecked the vegetation. In
Britain and Ireland the introduction of the Brown Rat *Rattus norvegicus*
is thought to have led to the reduction or extinction of the Manx Shearwater at several island colonies in the last century (Parslow 1967).

Man is also impinging more and more on the food supply of birds.
Modern fishing fleets, able to range widely and equipped with radar and
other devices, are taking an increasing toll, and already some experts are
worried that our fish populations are being seriously reduced in numbers
in the English Channel and the waters between Iceland and Scandinavia,
so unless fishing regulations are made more comprehensive and adequately
enforced, a number of fish species may follow the whales of northern
waters into decline. Other experts decry such gloomy forecasts and it is
not easy to establish population trends for different species of fish over
vast areas of ocean, still less to determine what influence any change may
have on the different seabirds which feed on them. Only now are the first
serious attempts being made to ascertain where the birds which range

away from our coast outside the nesting season are feeding and precisely what food they are taking.

Paradoxically, fishing has so far benefited some seabirds by providing them with a ready supply of offal. Fisher (1952b) argued that offal, first from whaling and later from fishing fleets, was the major factor in the dramatic increase and spread of the Fulmar in the North Atlantic. This has been disputed, but there is little doubt that Fulmars and gulls find a ready food supply from the fish waste of trawlers both at sea and in harbours. In turn, some species, especially gulls, have now increased sufficiently to become a threat in certain areas to other seabirds, by preying on them, robbing them of food, usurping their nesting areas or causing an overgrowth of vegetation which can adversely affect nest sites. Fishing nets, which have long been known to trap diving birds as well as fish, are also becoming a more serious hazard with the use of nylon nets which are almost impossible for the birds to see and avoid in darkness or rough weather. One net was reported to have taken 8,000 guillemots and 7,000 salmon, while the total of Brünnich's Guillemots *Uria lomvia* killed by the salmon fishery for west Greenland is now thought to exceed 500,000 each year (Tull *et al.* 1972). The toll is also serious in north Norway, and some losses occur in Britain and Ireland (Bibby 1972).

A growing threat to seabirds and possibly to many other forms of marine life is man's pollution of the world's oceans. This takes many forms, from gross pollution by oil to more insidious pollution by pesticides, polychlorinated biphenyls (PCBs), heavy metals, sewage waste, etc. Oil is not only the most obvious marine pollutant, but also the oldest and probably still the most serious for seabirds. Indeed the growth and appreciation of the effects of other pollutants is so recent that in their authoritative work on seabirds in 1954 the only kind of pollution discussed by Fisher and Lockley was oil. Oil pollution in British waters has been recognised since 1907 when the schooner *Thomas W. Lawson* was wrecked off the Isles of Scilly, releasing some two million gallons of crude oil. It increased during the 1914–18 war following the destruction of shipping, and by 1921 the RSPB was gathering evidence which helped to lead to the first legal controls. It is not possible here to give full details of the many oiling incidents, due to both accidental and deliberate spillages throughout the waters of the world (see Bourne 1968a for a comprehensive account). Suffice to say that after years of attempts both by legislation and improved methods by the more enlightened oil companies, oil is an ever present and probably increasing threat to many kinds of seabirds.

There are two main sources of oil pollution – deliberate, by cleaning of tanks or by waste disposal at sea or in port, and accidental, whether by wrecks at sea or by human error at oil drilling sites and installations. There has been a concerted drive against deliberate spillage by international legislation while the adoption of the 'Load-on-Top' system by the major oil companies has led to the virtual cessation of pollution from tank-cleaning by their ships. Nevertheless, there are too many tankers, often sailing under flags of convenience, which still use the old methods of tank cleaning, and too many ships of all kinds (including cargo ships for which port facilities are often inadequate) which illegally discharge waste oil, secure in the knowledge that it is virtually impossible to detect most breaches of the law. Nowadays any bird landing on the sea almost anywhere in the world may come into contact with oil, but the greatest dangers are on the main shipping routes. In Britain and Ireland, these cover a very large area of the surrounding seas, being particularly concentrated in the western approaches, the English Channel, the waters off northern Scotland and the north-east. Any species of seabird breeding, wintering or on passage in such areas is at risk, whether gull, auk, petrel, diver, sea-duck or cormorant. Yet certain species, by their behaviour, suffer more than others. Thus Bourne (1968b) has shown that while gulls meeting surface oil usually fly away, thus escaping further contamination, other species, such as auks, react by diving, so often emerging into more oil. During the Beached Birds Survey in March 1971 over 80% of the corpses of divers, Razorbills and Guillemots found were oiled; between 40% and 80% of grebes, Fulmars, Gannets, Cormorants and Shags, and under 40% of the wildfowl, gulls and waders (Bibby and Bourne 1971). The auks are at a further disadvantage as they are the most difficult to clean and rehabilitate successfully; indeed few, if any, of the badly oiled auks are likely to be able to live again at sea and breed successfully after cleaning, though techniques now being developed offer greater hopes. Rather more success has been obtained with some wildfowl and in South Africa with the Jackass Penguins *Spheniscus demersus*.

It is almost impossible to assess fully the number of seabirds killed by oil. Even in a major disaster like the *Torrey Canyon*, total casualties can only be estimated, as complete surveys of all beaches are difficult and, more important, because an unknown and varying proportion of the bodies sink before they reach the shore, as was shown by an experiment carried out in 1969 (Hope Jones *et al.* 1970). For this latter reason species like the Puffin, which winters farther away from these shores than other auks, are likely to be inadequately represented in any sample of bodies on our beaches. Moreover, it is now becoming clear that quite minor spills of oil can do enormous damage in certain circumstances. Thus up to 41,000 birds were killed in February 1969 in the Dutch Waddensee by some 150 tons of residual fuel oil (Swennen and Spaans 1970) while the fuel oil spills which killed 12,856 birds in early 1970 off north-east England and eastern Scotland were apparently so small that few traces could be found (Greenwood *et al.* 1971). The total deaths of seabirds from oil probably at present exceed those from any other single pollutant. Despite safety measures, such as the 'Load-on-Top' system and slowly but steadily improving legal controls, any marked reduction in casualties seems unlikely. The world traffic in oil is increasing rapidly and some accidents are almost inevitable; the growth in the size of tankers may mean fewer disasters, but involve far more serious spills when they do occur. Drilling in offshore waters has led to serious damage in the USA, and the North Sea developments are being undertaken in deeper and stormier waters, where much of the technology is new and untried. Marine oil terminals, where leaks may be hard to contain, are being increasingly developed, while the number of oil installations on our shores grows steadily. Moreover the sea is not the only danger, for a recent United Nations report has suggested that, although some 1½ million tons of oil are discharged each year into the oceans of the world, perhaps twice as much reaches the sea from land-based sources (Schachter and Serwer 1971).

The insidious pollutants affecting seabirds are much more recent phenomena. First of these to arouse concern, and still the best studied, were the persistent pesticides used in agriculture for many years, but it was not until the introduction of synthetic pesticides after 1945 that serious pollution problems occurred. Among the hundreds of different kinds of agricultural chemicals many are harmless to birds (though some of these, such as herbicides, may have indirect effects). Others are lethal but soon lose their toxicity, and only the highly persistent ones, such as the organochlorines and mercury, have caused continuing trouble, even though non-persistent pesticides, especially the organophosphorous compounds, have caused mass deaths of birds at times. The organochlorines, which are insoluble in water but very soluble in fat, pass from one animal in a food chain to the next and tend to become concentrated in the process. They are spread in this way, and by dispersal by wind and water, throughout the global environment. Thus their residues have been found wherever tests have been made, not only in agricultural areas throughout the world, but in places far from any point of application – in lichens in the far north of Canada, in fish and seals from the mid-Pacific and in the penguins of Antarctica.

Their effects on bird life are two-fold. They can kill directly as in the case of many farmland species which ate grain dressed with aldrin and dieldrin in England in 1960 and 1961 (Cramp et al. 1962), or the Sandwich Terns and other seabirds killed in the Waddensee by effluent from a factory producing dieldrin and telodrin on the Lower Rhine (Koeman 1971). Secondly, and even more seriously in the long term, they may reduce the fertility of the survivors by affecting their breeding behaviour, interfering with the deposition of eggshell and poisoning the embryos. These sub-lethal effects on fertility have been found so far in birds at the tops of food chains which tend to concentrate these poisons. Such effects have been particularly marked in bird-eating predators, including Peregrines *Falco peregrinus* and Golden Eagles *Aquila chrysaetos*, and in fish-eating species such as grebes and herons (Prestt and Ratcliffe 1972).

In Britain organochlorine residues have been found in the eggs of all seabird species sampled, with relatively larger amounts in Shags and gulls (Moore and Tatton 1965). Few studies have, however, been made here of the possible effects of organochlorines on breeding success of seabirds, but in a study of the Shags of the Farne Islands Potts (1968) thought it unlikely that embryos or chicks had been poisoned and found no increase in the adult mortality rate, although there was some evidence of lower breeding success among the few females with high residues. In the United States, however, eggshell thinning has been found in a number of families of seabirds, including pelicans, cormorants, gulls, auks and petrels (Risebrough 1971). This pollution is known to be having very serious effects on Brown Pelicans, already extinct along much of the Gulf of Mexico, while, on islands off the coast of California, they are laying eggs so thin that they collapse beneath the sitting birds and no young are reared (Blus 1970; Risebrough 1971). The organochlorines must be regarded as a potential threat to our seabirds, although it is encouraging that, with the increasing restrictions on their use in Britain, there are signs of improved breeding success amongst some of our predatory birds, while the dieldrin residues in the eggs of Shags have started to decline (Coulson *et al.* 1972).

More recently still, it has been discovered that seabirds and other forms of wildlife contain residues of another group of organochlorines, the polychlorinated biphenyls or PCBs which come not from agriculture but from industry. Since the 1930s PCBs have been widely used in transformers, plastics, paints, varnishes, etc., but it was not until 1966 that improved methods of analysis led to the discovery that their residues were present in a wide range of living creatures. Thus in the Netherlands residues have been found in fish, shellfish, terns and Eiders *Somateria mollissima* (Koeman *et al.* 1969); in Sweden in fish, shellfish, birds and seals (Jensen *et al.* 1969) and in the United States in petrels, shearwaters, gulls, auks and terns (Risebrough *et al.* 1968). In Britain Prestt *et al.* (1970) have reported residues in the eggs of Guillemots, Razorbills, Shags, Sandwich and Common Terns; indeed they were present in all species sampled at three widely separated colonies. High concentrations have been found in pelagic-feeding seabirds (especially the Great Skua, Fulmar and Kittiwake) from the eastern North Atlantic far from possible industrial sources of these compounds (Bourne and Bogan 1972).

The possible importance of PCBs in British and Irish waters was illustrated by the Irish Sea disaster in the autumn of 1969 when over 15,000 seabirds were found dead on the beaches on both sides of the Irish Sea and the total kill may well have exceeded 50,000. The vast majority were Guillemots. As very few of the birds were oiled, a wide-ranging inquiry was launched, involving scientists from Governmental organisations and voluntary bodies, as well as many amateur observers. Despite months of careful work no certain cause of this immense disaster was established. Residues of many substances were found in some of the bodies, from organochlorine pesticides to a variety of metals, including unusually high levels of PCBs.

The official report (Holdgate 1971) pointed out that the birds showed signs of starvation, although no evidence was forthcoming of any shortage of the fish on which the birds feed. It concluded that the effects of mal-nutrition were probably compounded by natural causes, including moult-ing and gales, and may have been aggravated by the toxic effects of the metallic and organic residues found in many of the dead seabirds. So PCBs, which are known to have many similar effects to the organochlorine pesticides, remain a possible but unproven threat to some of our seabirds. They tend to be concentrated in estuaries such as the Clyde and Thames where industrial sewage occurs, but relatively high levels have also been found in pelagic seabirds such as Kittiwakes, Fulmars, Great Skuas and petrels, which suggests that they may be widely dispersed by winds or dissolved from ships' paint and picked up by the oceanic plankton. A further complication is that the toxicity of commercial PCB preparations is increased considerably by impurities, which may vary widely in different formulations. In 1971 the leading US manufacturer imposed restrictions on the main uses of PCBs which could lead to environmental contamination.

As the analyses of the Irish Sea corpses showed, residues of various metals now occur commonly in living creatures. Their significance is still little understood and recently research has been intensified in many countries to ascertain how widely these residues are spread and in what amounts, as well as on their toxicity to different organisms. The problem is rendered more intractable because metals, unlike organochlorines, occur naturally and are found at higher levels in estuaries where rivers bring them down dissolved in sediments. However, in the case of one metal, mercury, there is clear evidence that industrial wastes have caused serious damage to man and other living creatures. Thus, in Japan the waste from a chemical factory using mercury as a catalyst poisoned fish in the Minamata River in 1953, causing widespread illness and 43 deaths among human beings feeding on them. In Sweden mercury was widely used both as a seed dressing and as a fungicide in paper mills. This led to considerable decreases in seed-eating birds and contamination of the fish in many rivers and coastal waters, with serious effects on birds such as the White-tailed Eagle *Haliaetus albicilla* which feed on them, as well as on other marine creatures, including seals and shellfish. These uses of mercury were banned completely in 1966 but it is expected that it will be many years before the mercury levels return to normal; meanwhile fish are still banned for human consumption in 80 areas.

Mercury residues have also been found in seabirds and seals in the Netherlands and in birds and fish in Canada, while in the United States fish from many rivers have been banned as human food. In Britain and Ireland analyses have so far given no cause for serious alarm, though Dale *et al.* (1973) found high levels in some coastal and estuarine birds. In general, it appears that, although mercury can be a major local danger, the amounts used in industry are so much smaller than those occurring naturally that it is unlikely to be a major contaminant on a global scale.

Other metals found in birds from the Irish Sea included copper, lead, zinc, cadmium, arsenic and nickel, and in some cases the highest con-centrations were above the level at which poisoning may have occurred. All of these could harm human beings as well as seabirds at sufficiently high levels and, like all persistent contaminants, they may be concen-trated by certain marine animals, including plankton and shellfish. Again the main danger is in rivers, estuaries and other waters where sewage sludge with industrial waste is deposited. Cadmium has led to outbreaks of a painful ailment known as *ouchi-ouchi* in Japan, but perhaps most public concern is being aroused at the moment by lead. As this occurs widely in car exhausts, the pollution of the atmosphere and its possible effects on human beings are attracting most attention and controversy, but high levels have also been found in fish.

In our present state of knowledge, the effects of all these metals on marine life, including seabirds, are largely unknown, and it may well be that, except in local concentrations, they are not serious. What is certain is that the use of the world's oceans as a dumping ground for waste of all kinds is arousing the growing concern of marine ecologists. For besides oil, pesticides, PCBs and heavy metals, the seas are receiving, either directly or from rivers, a wide range of industrial wastes often containing a devil's brew of toxic organochlorines. These include also polychlorinated aliphatic hydrocarbons from plastics manufacture, which have killed plankton in the North Sea. There is further the risk of dangerous cargoes being lost overboard after wrecks or accidents; thus an important oyster industry near Corunna was wiped out when 500 drums of dieldrin and mercury compounds were lost overboard after a ship had run aground. Radioactive wastes which are probably safe under the present stringent safety precautions are likely to become a more serious threat as atomic plants spread to countries with more lax control measures, and nerve gases, explosives and other military refuse present possible risks in some areas.

Finally there is eutrophication caused by the nitrates and phosphates which are becoming steadily more common in all water systems. These are derived from human sewage, the vastly increased use of artificial fertilisers in agricultural areas, the growing volume of slurry from cows, pigs, etc. kept indoors under modern agricultural methods, and from detergents. If they accumulate in excess quantities these nitrates and phosphates lead to algal blooms which use up oxygen, release toxins and eventually kill all other forms of life. The harmful effects of eutrophication have so far been found mainly in inland waters such as Lake Erie, but there are already signs of coastal waters being similarly affected. Thus off the coast of Florida the algal blooms known as 'Red Tides', formerly appearing every 16 years or so, have occurred every year more recently, whilst in Britain a spectacular bloom of dino-flagellates occurred in 1968 off the north-eastern coast of England producing toxins which caused the deaths of many Shags (Coulson *et al.* 1968) as well as 85 cases of illness among humans due to eating contaminated shellfish.

To sum up, the direct impact of human beings on the seabirds of Britain and Ireland by persecution or by taking them and their eggs for food has diminished markedly in recent years, but man's growing numbers and mobility have affected species nesting in vulnerable areas, especially on beaches. The indirect effects are more complex. Pollution, both gross and insidious, is increasing and while many of the effects of this are far from fully understood, there is little doubt that most of the auks are now under threat. Yet other species are thriving on increased food supplies due to man's activities, and their growing numbers, especially those of the larger gulls, may adversely affect other seabirds in a variety of ways. We are still too ignorant of the complex ecology of our seas and the effects of pollutants and other factors to assess fully in most cases how serious these threats are now, or may become in the future. The survey of the seabirds of Britain and Ireland in 1969–70 was an attempt to locate and where possible to count the various species breeding around our coasts in order to provide a base-line to assess future changes. In the next chapter the results of this survey are summarised and related to the often limited historical evidence in an attempt to measure recent trends, and to examine how the different species may have reacted to the threats and opportunities posed by man's increasing influence on the marine environment.

CHAPTER 3

Present Numbers and Changing Fortunes

THE enthusiasts who launched the survey in 1969–70 were well aware of the enormous difficulties of attempting to locate and count all the seabirds nesting on the many miles of coast and the hundreds of islands of Britain and Ireland. It was a unique and formidable undertaking, and it offered, if successful, rich rewards in ornithological knowledge. Moreover, it could provide a base-line to measure future changes in the numbers and distribution whether due to natural causes or to the increasing impact of man upon the environment. The first part of the task – to locate the breeding birds – was, though daunting, almost completely successful. Virtually every suitable seabird nesting place on the coast was visited and the only obvious gap was in the case of the Storm Petrel, Leach's Storm-petrel and the Manx Shearwater, where, because of their nocturnal and hole-nesting habits, breeding could not always be confirmed at remote or difficult sites, especially when observers were unable to stay overnight.

The second part of the task – to count the breeding pairs – was much more formidable. There have been very few accurate counts of breeding animals anywhere in the world, except in the case of species whose total numbers are very small. Birds, with fixed and often visible nests, offer fewer problems than most animal groups, but even here, past attempts at censuses over large areas have been limited to a few conspicuous colonial species, including landbirds such as Grey Heron *Ardea cinerea* and Rook *Corvus frugilegus*, or seabirds such as the Fulmar, Gannet and Kittiwake. Many seabirds are both colonial and conspicuous when breeding, but even so there are considerable problems in addition to the major difficulty (and sometimes risk) of visiting so many miles of cliff and coast and so many scattered and often remote islands. The special problems involved in census work for each species are dealt with in detail in the species accounts which follow, but the limitations they impose must be borne in mind throughout this general survey of the results of the 1969–70 census.

Briefly, it is believed that a fairly high degree of accuracy was obtained for 17 of the 24 coastal nesting seabirds of Britain and Ireland included in the survey. These comprise all six species of gulls, all five terns, both skuas, Cormorant, Shag, Fulmar and Gannet. It seems probable that if a survey of this kind is repeated, as ideally it should be at least every ten years, the figures would be accurate enough to reveal changes of the order of say 10% of the total population for most of these 17 species and almost

certainly variations of 20% for all. Of the remaining seven species where
the numerical results are less accurate, it is unfortunate that four are
members of the auk family, which many suspect are under particular
threat at the present time. The auks can usually be seen and counted from
the land or sea, except in difficult terrain, but their nests or eggs are often
invisible or hard to distinguish and no exact formula has yet been found
to enable the number of breeding pairs to be derived from the number of
birds seen at a colony. The extent of the problem varies with different
species. The figures for the ledge-nesting Guillemot are probably the
most reliable, those for the Razorbill, whose eggs are often hidden, are
less so, while for the hole-nesting Puffin and Black Guillemot there is a
considerable degree of uncertainty. However, the totals estimated in the
1969–70 survey should be accurate enough to reveal really major changes
in the future and this would be assisted by the fact that careful surveys of
the extent of many colonies were made. For the three nocturnal hole-
nesting species, however (Storm Petrel, Leach's Storm-petrel and Manx
Shearwater), even the few elaborate and special surveys made in the past
have produced only an approximate order of size and, as many colonies
were not surveyed and some not visited in 1969–70, it is impossible to say
much about total numbers or possible trends in population.

For 1969–70 it is possible, then, to produce some indication of the
varying abundance of the coastal breeding populations of 21 of our 24
seabirds (Table 1). Seven of these are clearly of Order 6, i.e. their total
population in Britain and Ireland was at least 100,000 but under 1 million
pairs. They include two gulls, three auks, the Fulmar and the Gannet.
The two most numerous were members of the auk family, the Guillemot
and the Puffin, estimated at some 577,000 and 490,000 pairs respectively.
These figures can be taken as no more than rough approximations for the
reasons which are stressed in the respective species accounts later (see
pages 173–78 and 183–89). Not far below these came a gull, but not,
rather surprisingly, the best known of our coastal gulls, the Herring Gull,
whose rapid increase in recent years has caused disquiet both to some civic
authorities and to conservationists, but the smaller Kittiwake, with 470,000
pairs. The Herring Gull, much more widely distributed round the coasts
of Britain and Ireland, came only fourth with some 333,000 pairs. Just
below this was the classic expanding species, the Fulmar, with an estimated
306,000 pairs, showing a very large increase over the total in 1959, due
both to genuine increases and more complete coverage. The sixth was
probably the Razorbill, where the best estimate of the numbers in 1969–70
was about 144,000 pairs, although no accurate figures are available for
two of its major colonies. The seventh and last in this first group was the
Gannet, much less difficult to count, with about 138,000 pairs.

The second category, with between 10,000 and 99,999 pairs breeding

TABLE I.   *Estimate of the numbers of seabirds breeding on the coasts of Britain and Ireland in 1969-70*

		Thousands of Pairs
Order 6	Guillemot *Uria aalge*	(577)
	Puffin *Fratercula arctica*	(490)
	Kittiwake *Rissa tridactyla*	470
	Herring Gull *Larus argentatus*	333*
	Fulmar *Fulmarus glacialis*	306
	Razorbill *Alca torda*	(144)
	Gannet *Sula bassana*	138
Order 5	Black-headed Gull *Larus ridibundus*	74*
	Lesser Black-headed Gull *Larus fuscus*	47*
	Shag *Phalacrocorax aristotelis*	31
	Arctic Tern *Sterna paradisaea*	(31)*
	Great Black-headed Gull *Larus marinus*	22*
	Common Tern *Sterna hirundo*	14*
	Common Gull *Larus canus*	12*
	Sandwich Tern *Sterna sandvicensis*	12
Order 4	Black Guillemot *Cepphus grylle*	8.3
	Cormorant *Phalacrocorax carbo*	8.1
	Great Skua *Stercorarius skua*	3.1
	Roseate Tern *Sterna dougallii*	2.3
	Little Tern *Sterna albifrons*	1.8
	Arctic Skua *Stercorarius parasiticus*	1.1
Numbers unknown	Manx Shearwater *Puffinus puffinus*	Order 6 Over 175,000 pairs
	Storm Petrel *Hydrobates pelagicus*	Order 5 or 6
	Leach's Storm-petrel *Oceanodroma leucorrhoa*	Probably Order 4

Note These estimates must be considered in the light of the varying degrees of accuracy of the census techniques for the species concerned, which are discussed fully later in the species accounts. Where the figures above are shown in brackets, the errors are likely to be very considerable. For species marked * there are, in addition, an unknown number of pairs breeding inland, though probably only with the Common Gull and Black-headed Gull do these represent a large proportion of the population.

on our coasts in 1969–70, comprised eight species – four gulls, three terns and the Shag. The first of these was the Black-headed Gull with some 74,000 pairs in coastal colonies, but this species often nests inland and these were not counted in 1969–70. In an earlier census of the species in

1958 covering all the colonies in England and Wales (Gribble 1962), about one-third of the total population was found breeding in inland colonies, so that if a similar proportion obtained for the whole of Britain and Ireland, and it may well have been higher in Scotland and Ireland, the total population of this species in 1969–70 would have been some 110,000 pairs. There is then a large drop to the next species in this group, the Lesser Black-backed Gull, with 47,000 pairs, though this species also nests inland to an unknown but proportionately small extent. Next came the Shag, breeding only on the coast, and the most numerous of our terns, the Arctic Tern, both with about 31,000 pairs. The fifth in this group was our largest gull, the Great Black-backed Gull, with about 22,000 pairs, followed by the Common Tern with over 14,000 pairs nesting on the coasts. For both these species there are likely to have been others breeding at inland colonies, though their numbers were probably not large. Then came the Common Gull, which, with just over 12,000 breeding pairs, was certainly the least common of the coastal nesting gulls, though here there are likely to be very considerable numbers breeding inland. Finally there was the Sandwich Tern with almost 12,000 nesting pairs; half the West European population, since the catastrophic decline in the Netherlands due to pesticides (Rooth and Jonkers 1972).

The last group contains the six rarest of our coastal seabirds whose numbers can be given with some accuracy. They include the two skuas, two terns, the Black Guillemot and the Cormorant, all with at least 1,000 but less than 10,000 breeding pairs in 1969–70. The Black Guillemot and the Cormorant were almost level with just over 8,000 pairs, although the actual numbers of the hole-nesting Black Guillemot might have been higher. The other four species in this group were much less numerous, ranging from the Great Skua with just over 3,000 pairs to the Roseate and Little Terns, both around 2,000 pairs, and the Arctic Skua with barely more than 1,000 pairs.

Finally there were the three nocturnal species, for which a number of colonies were not surveyed at all in 1969–70, while only at a few of those visited was it possible to hazard more than a tentative estimate of numbers. Despite this, it seems that the Manx Shearwater was the most numerous of the group with almost certainly more than 175,000 breeding pairs in 1969–70 and perhaps more than 300,000 pairs, thus ranking with the seven most numerous coastal breeding seabirds in Britain and Ireland. The Storm Petrel, with many colonies not visited in 1969–70 (and probably with colonies on some islands and coastal cliffs which have never been recorded), is still more difficult to estimate, but the breeding population seems likely to have been over 10,000 pairs and perhaps more than 100,000 pairs. Leach's Storm-petrel, with only four colonies now known and all on remote islands difficult of access, is the least numerous of this group, but there are few reliable indications of its past or present numbers in these islands on the edge of its range.

Writing in 1940, James Fisher, whose work on the population trends in the Gannet and the Fulmar did much to inspire this first comprehensive survey of our coastal breeding seabirds and who coined the name 'Operation Seafarer' for the 1969–70 survey, said 'The numbers of seabirds are extremely large, probably as large in Britain as those of birds inland.' The reality now appears to be far otherwise. There is no exact figure, nor is there likely to be, for the total population of breeding landbirds of Britain and Ireland, but he put forward a tentative estimate of some 60 million pairs of landbirds nesting in Great Britain in May. This was based on a limited amount of census work in particular habitats and not on nest counts, so it must be taken as only a rough approximation. As, however, the total number of breeding seabirds in both Britain and Ireland in 1969–70 was of the order of some 3 million pairs, it seems clear that, whatever the limitations of the estimate of breeding landbirds, they are more numerous than our seabirds. Indeed the most common landbird species may well exceed in number the total of our coastal breeding seabirds, for Summers-Smith (1963), using more detailed habitat figures, thought that the House Sparrow *Passer domesticus* in England and Wales alone might total some 9½ million birds, whilst James Fisher suggested that, in the same two countries, both the Blackbird *Turdus merula* and the Chaffinch *Fringilla coelebs* might reach some 10 million individuals.

Our past knowledge of seabird numbers in Britain and Ireland is limited and this makes any estimate of population trends difficult for most species and sometimes impossible. Indeed the main justification for the 1969–70 survey was to provide an accurate base-line for as many species as possible. However, for two birds, the Gannet and the Fulmar, there are full counts over a number of years with a considerable amount of data for earlier periods, whilst surveys of the Kittiwake and Little Tern in both Britain and Ireland were made in 1959 and 1967 respectively, though in both cases coverage was less than complete in Scotland and Ireland. There have also been counts over considerable areas for species such as the Shag, Cormorant, Great Black-backed Gull, Arctic Skua and Great Skua, whilst for many tern colonies counts extending over a number of years are available. For all other seabirds, any precise assessment of numerical trends is impossible, but in some cases the historical record is adequate to indicate changes in breeding ranges in some areas which may reflect parallel changes in numbers, although this can never be taken for granted.

With these limitations in mind, it is possible to make some overall assessment as to how the seabirds in Britain and Ireland have fared in recent years. In the light of the threats from the increasing pollution of our seas which have been outlined earlier, it is perhaps surprising that for five species (Gannet, Fulmar, Kittiwake, Herring Gull and Great Skua) there have been definite and often marked increases in recent years; for four (Shag, Cormorant, Great Black-backed Gull and Black-headed Gull) there have been increases over considerable parts of their ranges, though sometimes accompanied by decreases elsewhere; and for three species (Sandwich Tern, Common Gull and Lesser Black-backed Gull) there has probably been an overall increase, although the evidence is far from conclusive. Against this there is one species (Little Tern) where total numbers have certainly decreased markedly, and three (Guillemot, Razorbill and Puffin) where many suspect that overall declines have taken place, though in most cases firm evidence is only available for certain parts of their ranges. For two terns, Common and Arctic, marked fluctuations in the numbers may occur at individual colonies and the historical data are deficient for the remoter ones, so that any assessment is hazardous, though some people believe that they may have declined in recent years. The Roseate Tern, after a marked resurgence earlier this century, may have declined somewhat recently. In the case of the Arctic Skua, both increases and declines have been reported, so that any over-all trends are uncertain, while for the remaining four species (Manx Shearwater, Storm Petrel, Leach's Storm-petrel and Black Guillemot) it is impossible to venture even a tentative guess as to the population trends.

A number of explanations have been offered for the rises in population among the increasing species during this century and above all within the last 30 years or so. These explanations fall into two main groups. Firstly, the cessation or reduction of human persecution following protection legislation from 1869 onwards, often accompanied more recently by active conservation measures; and secondly, changes in natural factors such as food supply or habits. These are not, of course, mutually exclusive; indeed it is likely that for most species both sets of factors are relevant. It has been mentioned earlier that the first Act to protect seabirds in Great Britain was passed in 1869 and how this, and changing public opinion, led to the gradual decline of the sport of shooting seabirds, whether from sea cliffs or from bridges over the Thames, towards the end of the century. There seems little doubt that this had an effect on the numbers of Gannets which, after some decline earlier in the century, seem to have begun a slow recovery from about 1885, helped also by the gradual cessation of controlled exploitation by man at some island colonies. The changes in Gannet numbers since then are better known than for any other seabird and, despite the very real difficulties of estimating numbers at large colonies and some gaps in the historical record, it seems undeniable that total numbers in Britain and Ireland increased threefold (from approximately 48,000 to 138,000 pairs) between the earlier years of this century and 1969–70, with the number of its colonies doubling from eight to 16. The relative population increase was 13% from around the turn of the century to 1939, then increased markedly to 17% in the next ten years, and explosively to 120% between 1949 and 1969–70. Although, as Coulson (1963) has shown for the Kittiwake, quite small changes in the adult mortality rate can influence populations markedly, it may be wondered whether this upsurge in Gannet numbers in the last 20 years is not at least partly due to other factors besides the virtual ending of human persecution and exploitation. If so, the nature of these factors is virtually unknown.

The expansion and spread of the Fulmar in Britain and Ireland has been even more striking. It forms part of a wider population explosion involving one relatively small part of this widely dispersed species. The large-billed form of the Fulmar breeding in the warmer waters of the eastern North Atlantic began to spread in Iceland over 200 years ago, moved to the Faeroes about 1839, then to Britain and Ireland in 1878 (other than St Kilda, where it had long maintained an outpost) and in this century to Norway and northern France. This striking phenomenon continues to perplex ornithologists. It has been documented and analysed in great detail by Fisher (1952a, 1966b) who maintained that the basic cause was the new rich food supply made available to the Fulmar by offal, first from whaling and later from fish trawlers. He argued that there was a good correlation in this century between the increase in Britain and Ireland (excluding St Kilda) and the changing amounts of fish landed at our ports. In particular, he linked the marked slowing down in the rate of increase of Fulmars between 1949 and 1959 with the recent decline in the fish offal available to them. However, it now appears that poor coverage in some areas led to an underestimate of the population in 1959 and that, though the rate of expansion has slowed down from c. 420% in the period 1929–49 to c. 280% between 1949 and 1969–70, it is still remarkably high, at almost 7% a year (compound interest).

Earlier Wynne-Edwards (1962) had argued that the correlation between the available fish offal and the Fulmar spread was poor and had suggested that a more likely explanation was that a special genotype had arisen in Iceland, enabling the species to spread into lower latitudes and to accept small straggling colonies instead of the dense rookeries favoured over much of its range. Others (Salomonsen 1965; Brown 1970) have stressed temperature and other oceanographic factors rather than fish offal. Salomonsen in particular pointed out that this large-billed boreal population favours the warmer waters, which have increased in extent following the gradual warming of the eastern North Atlantic in the last 100 years. It is probably fair to conclude that further information is essential, particularly reliable quantitative data on the Fulmar's diet in winter, before an entirely satisfactory explanation will be possible.

For the Kittiwake, the numerical information on population trends is more recent, as the first attempt at a full census in Britain and Ireland was not made until 1959. This showed that about 37,000 pairs nested in England and Wales, while in Scotland and Ireland, where coverage was less complete, it was estimated that there were at least 100,000 and 36,000 pairs respectively, and probably considerably more. The population then appeared to be increasing at probably 3% per annum, and perhaps at a considerably higher rate in some areas (Coulson 1963). In 1969–70 there were some 470,000 breeding pairs, of which the great majority (370,000 pairs) were in Scotland, about 57,000 in England and Wales, nearly 43,000 in Ireland and 12 pairs in the Channel Isles. This represented an increase since 1959 of 49% in areas covered in both years, with indications that the Irish colonies may have increased faster than elsewhere.

Dr J. C. Coulson (see pages 134–41) describes this increase of the Kittiwake as a population explosion comparable to that which has taken place in the Fulmar, which can similarly be traced back to the beginning of this century. He considers, however, that the explanation for this is not, as James Fisher argued for the Fulmar, any change in their food supply, but reduced predation, especially by man. As with the Gannet, the Kittiwake population tended to decrease during the 19th century as a result of human exploitation (for feathers and food, or for sport), facilitated by better weapons and improved transport, which made the colonies more accessible. Following the passing of protective legislation this exploitation was at first reduced, then almost completely abolished; moreover, the Kittiwake has few natural predators in these islands. The expansion of the Kittiwake has occurred also in southern Norway, Denmark, Sweden, Heligoland and Brittany and even on Bear Island in the Barents Sea. It was at first largely overlooked in Britain and Ireland because the Kittiwake tended to expand in existing colonies rather than form new ones. More recently it has begun to spread geographically, to nest on lower cliffs and even on buildings in populated areas. Coulson considers the food is superabundant, and that only predatory fish feeding on the species eaten by the Kittiwake or the human exploitation of sand-eels seems likely to prevent the population increase of the Kittiwake continuing for many years. It has also been pointed out that in addition to catching their own food Kittiwakes follow trawlers a great deal in some areas (W. R. P. Bourne *in litt.*) so possibly its increase may owe something to human fishing activities.

For other gulls, however, the evidence for increases in the total population in Britain and Ireland cannot be assessed numerically as the counts in 1969–70 were the first complete surveys. There have been a number of inquiries covering more limited areas, usually England and Wales only. Thus for the Great Black-backed Gull previous censuses were undertaken for England and Wales in 1930 (Harrisson and Hurrell 1933) and in 1956 (Davis 1958). From these it appears that a substantial decrease occurred between 1849 and 1893, when there were only 20 pairs nesting in six counties. Once again, a recovery began at the turn of the century, so that the numbers rose to between 1,000 and 1,200 breeding pairs in 1930, and to at least 1,600 by 1956. By 1969–70 there were 2,892 pairs in England and Wales and, although there are no previous figures for Scotland and Ireland, there is some evidence of both increases and extension of range there as well.

In the case of the Black-headed Gull, sufficiently accurate population figures for the past are available only for England and Wales. One observer suggested in 1884 that the species was faced with extinction after a decline in the middle of the last century (Gurney 1919). Yet between 1889 and 1938 175 new colonies were founded, whilst only 70 were deserted, and the total population reached some 35,000–40,000 pairs (Hollom 1940; Marchant 1952). A repeat survey in 1958 (Gribble 1962) showed a further increase to 46,000–51,000 pairs in England and Wales. The 1969–70 survey was restricted to coastal colonies, and at this time in England and Wales there were nearly 55,000 pairs nesting on the coast compared with nearly 16,000 pairs in 1938 and over 35,000 pairs in 1958. Thus the coastal population rose by about 120% between 1938 and 1958 and by some 52% between 1958 and 1969–70. It is not known, however, whether the total population in England and Wales increased at this rate, for a considerable proportion, about one-third in 1958, nest inland. The historical data for Scotland and Ireland are inadequate to decide whether similar changes have occurred there.

For the remaining three species of gulls there is even less exact information. The Herring Gull, the second most numerous gull in Britain and Ireland, has been regarded as the classic example of the 'gull explosion', with steady increases in recent years on both the eastern and western sides of the Atlantic. Yet precise evidence of the extent of this increase in Britain and Ireland is surprisingly limited. No one has attempted a complete survey of this numerous and widespread species before, so any assessment must be based on general impressions by local observers, supplemented in a few cases by exact counts which rarely extend back before 1930. Parslow (1967) concluded that it had greatly increased in all parts of its breeding range, especially during the preceding 20 years, and thought that numbers in England and Wales had probably at least doubled in this period. There have been some spectacular increases at certain colonies, e.g. Walney Island and in the Bristol Channel and the Firth of Forth. In general the Herring Gull appears to have increased around developed parts of the mainland wherever nesting conditions are suitable (and is even colonising the low-lying coast between south Yorkshire and south-east Kent) in estuaries and around some ports, though its numbers may have remained stable in more peripheral areas and may even have declined in Shetland. Like the Kittiwake, the Herring Gull has taken to nesting on buildings in populated areas, but on a more extensive scale (at 55 sites involving over 1,250 pairs compared with seven sites and 410 pairs in the Kittiwake), and this presumably also reflects a pressure on normal breeding sites caused by population growth (Cramp 1971).

The third species to adopt the habit of nesting on buildings to an important extent is the Lesser Black-backed Gull (at five sites containing some 60 pairs) but here the evidence on population trends is less certain. Parslow (1967) considered that the population as a whole was probably increasing but, because of a marked decrease in Scotland at and after the end of the last century, he thought it doubtful whether it was more numerous than 60–70 years earlier. Some increases have taken place in England, Wales and southern Scotland (very large at certain colonies, such as Walney Island, Newborough Warren and the Isle of May), but further north in Scotland there have been decreases in Orkney, Shetland and the Outer Hebrides, though apparently small increases on St Kilda and in Aberdeenshire and elsewhere on the east coast. In general, the impression is one of increase except where the Lesser Black-backed Gull has met competition from two larger and increasing species, the Great Black-backed Gull and, in Shetland, the Great Skua.

The last species, the Common Gull, seems to have increased in Shetland and Orkney and to be extending its range inland in southern Scotland, while there are reports of increases and spread in Ireland and of more attempts to nest in England and Wales. All this suggests there may have been an overall increase, but as there was no attempt at a full survey of coastal colonies before 1969–70, and virtually nothing is known about the precise numbers or changes among the many which nest inland in Scotland and Ireland, this cannot be proved.

Among the five *Larus* gulls breeding in Britain and Ireland, then, three seem to have definitely increased (the Herring Gull overall, the Great Black-backed and Black-headed Gull at least over considerable parts of their ranges), whilst the Lesser Black-backed Gull has probably increased and the Common Gull may have done so. Various reasons have been suggested for the increase in these *Larus* gulls, in some cases in other countries as well as Britain and Ireland. These reasons include changes in climate, the increased role of gulls as urban scavengers and reduced persecution, but there have been too few detailed ecological studies to assess fully the relative importance of these different factors. Climatic amelioration might have played a part in the northward expansion of these species in Europe, notably to Iceland (see Voous 1960), but seems unlikely to have been the major factor in the changes in Britain and Ireland. All five species have almost certainly benefited from reduced persecution here and, although they are among the very few species in Britain whose eggs can legally be taken for food (for human beings or poultry), losses from this have almost certainly decreased considerably and must form a diminishing proportion of the eggs laid. Many gulls have been taking increasing advantage of fish refuse discarded around ports and trawlers, while in a number of urban areas their importance as winter scavengers has grown enormously in the last 50 years. They frequent rubbish dumps, both urban and rural, and railway sidings, while they are fed by the public in parks and gardens, and from office windows. All this would not have been possible if the human attitude to gulls had not changed. Moreover they are now able to use reservoirs, often far inland, as safe roosting sites, while feeding on agricultural land by some species has increased greatly in the last 50 years.

The terns present special problems because their colonies may move or fluctuate markedly in numbers from year to year. So, although there is a wealth of information on the numbers breeding at individual colonies in the past, this is difficult to interpret. For any accurate assessment of trends, it is essential to count all the colonies in the same year, and this was not done (except for the Little Tern, which is discussed later) until 1969–70. On the information available it seems that the Sandwich Tern is increasing after a probable decline in the last century, that the Common Tern and the Arctic Tern may be static or declining slightly, while the Roseate Tern, after a marked recovery this century, appears to have decreased somewhat in recent years. The Sandwich Tern has shown a marked overall increase from about 1,000 pairs to nearly 6,400 pairs since the 1920s in south-east Scotland and eastern England where the bulk of the population is found. There is no sign at present of any slowing down, except perhaps in eastern Scotland where it is suffering from disturbance where not protected. For the Common Tern, past information for Scotland and Ireland is too patchy to be of value and it is a very local species in Wales. For England, however, Parslow (1967) suggested that the population in 1964–66 was between 5,500 and 6,000 pairs, which he considered was certainly more than were breeding at the beginning of the century but probably somewhat lower than in the 1930s. By 1969–70 there had been a slight increase to 6,117 pairs.

Our most numerous tern, the Arctic, is a more northerly breeder with large colonies in the north and west of Scotland (especially Orkney and Shetland), where not only are the historical data limited, but it was difficult in some areas to make accurate counts even in 1969–70. The only clear evidence of changes, though they cannot be assessed numerically, is in Ireland, where all reports speak of decreases, especially at inland colonies. The Roseate Tern suffered great decreases in the last century and became almost extinct. It began to recover this century, recolonising Ireland, now its main European headquarters, in 1906, and there were further increases and spread during the 1939–45 war and after. In recent years, however, the somewhat patchy information suggests a decline from the population in the early 1960s, affecting most colonies. These changes might be linked with the climatic amelioration in the first part of this century and its reversal in recent years. Terns are so vulnerable to human disturbance or persecution that, except in remote areas, their future in these overcrowded islands depends almost entirely on protection being given to their colonies. The setting up of reserves by the Nature Conservancy and national and local voluntary societies is the main reason for the recent increase in the Sandwich Tern and the recovery of the Roseate Tern after near extinction. It has ensured some improvement in Common Tern numbers since the early years of the century, and, though the population trends in the Arctic Tern are obscure, it seems certain that without protection its numbers would have fallen considerably by now.

Protection has also been a factor in the fortunes of the Great Skua. This species was first found breeding in these islands in 1774, when there were thought to be only 10 pairs, all in Shetland. Local efforts at protecting the species, then much persecuted, began in 1831 on Unst and during the 1870s on Foula. Since then it has spread and increased greatly in Shetland and colonised Orkney, the Outer Hebrides and Sutherland, with a total population of 3,172 pairs in 1969–70. There has also been a marked increase in the Faeroes since 1897. Contrasting with these increases in the south of its range, Iceland, which in 1954 was thought to hold the bulk of the North Atlantic population, has seen far fewer nesting in recent years and the fall has been attributed to the decline of the fishing industry on the south-east coast there (Gudmundsson 1954). It remains a matter of conjecture as to whether there is any connection between these changes.

The smaller and much less numerous Arctic Skua also has its main headquarters in the north of Scotland, especially Orkney and Shetland. Here the population trends are obscure because there were no full counts before 1969–70, but there appear to have been some decreases in the south of its range (the mainland of Scotland, the Outer Hebrides and possibly the Inner Hebrides), while it has extended its range in Orkney and may have increased in numbers in Shetland. Where the ranges of the Arctic Skua and the Great Skua overlap, it has been suggested that the former may have decreased (Venables and Venables 1955), perhaps because the Great Skua arrives first on the breeding grounds and also preys on the young of the smaller bird. However, this can hardly account for decreases in the Arctic Skua elsewhere.

The Cormorant and Shag are closely related species, both feeding mainly in coastal and estuarine waters and both considered by fishermen, with limited justification, to be direct competitors in many areas. Human persecution has therefore been considerable in the past, with bounties being offered in some places, and it still continues in certain areas. No full counts of either species have been made previously, although there is sufficient information to assess the trends numerically since 1905 in eastern Scotland and north-east England. Both species have increased markedly in these areas, with the total population of the Cormorant in the Firth of Forth and in the Farne Islands growing by about 4% per annum, compared with 11% for the Shag. Elsewhere, in the case of the Cormorant, increases are probable in Yorkshire and north-east Scotland, with declines in north-west Scotland. The more numerous Shag seems to have increased in most areas for which information is available except for south Devon, the Clyde and the northern Inner Hebrides. Parslow (1967), whilst agreeing that the relaxation of human persecution may have played a part in the increases of the Shag, suggested that, though direct evidence was lacking, a more plausible explanation was provided by changes in the distribution or abundance of the species of fish on which Shags feed, perhaps connected with environmental or climatic change. However, Potts (1969) found no clear evidence of any long-term changes in the fish prey of the Shag and thought it unlikely that the small population in eastern Britain in the latter half of the 19th century could have been held down by food shortage. He pointed to the decline in many seabirds during the 18th and 19th centuries, when there was much evidence of excessive human exploitation, and to the parallel increases in the Gannet, Kittiwake and Great Skua, as well as the Shag, which began as soon as protection was afforded, mainly from the period 1880–90.

There are relatively few declining species of seabirds in Great Britain and Ireland. Among these is the Little Tern, probably one of our two rarest regular breeding seabirds (the present population of the uncommon Leach's Storm-petrel being unknown), which is a special case. It is vulnerable because it nests on beaches, which human beings, with increasing living standards and greater mobility, are visiting in ever-growing numbers. So, although there is little direct persecution, its open nests are trodden on, or the parent birds scared away from eggs or young. In recent years more and more conservation bodies have taken steps to protect the relatively small colonies of the Little Tern during the few critical weeks, and, though its population is unlikely ever again to reach its size in earlier centuries when so many miles of our beaches were undisturbed, it may be possible to hold it near the present figure.

The other species whose future is causing concern are the three auks, the Guillemot, Razorbill and Puffin. Here there is uncertainty about both the precise extent of any population declines and the factors which may be responsible. These species rank at present amongst the eight most numerous breeding seabirds in Britain and Ireland and, as the largest numbers nest in the more remote parts on cliffs often difficult of access and they are difficult to count, it is hardly surprising that no full survey was attempted earlier. Although the 1969–70 survey covered all the colonies for the first time, the problem of assessing the numbers of breeding pairs remains far from solved. The figures obtained, therefore, are of limited accuracy, though it should be possible to detect *major* changes in the future. For some years now there have been reports of declines of all three species in the smaller, more southerly colonies. Thus for the Guillemot, despite the limited data and the major difficulties in counting, there seems to have been an undoubted decline, in some cases very marked in southern England and Wales and locally elsewhere. The position is rather similar with the Razorbill, with decreases in the same areas in southern England, in some parts of south Wales and at one colony in Ireland, though at other colonies in Wales and Scotland there is little evidence of any change in numbers and even indications of increases in some cases.

The Puffin too has shown marked decreases, in the last century and since, in south-west England, Wales, Ireland and south-west Scotland, but until recently little was known of changes in numbers in most of the numerically far more important colonies further north. It now seems clear, however, that numbers have declined severely in recent years at the largest colony of all on St Kilda, as well as in the Shiant Islands, in the Outer Hebrides and elsewhere in the north. Indeed, only in the Firth of Forth have there been definite, though relatively small, increases in recent years.

Some of the declines at certain Puffin colonies may be due to local factors, such as rats, erosion, or predation by gulls and skuas, but it seems likely that there are more general reasons which may be adversely affecting all the auks. There has been considerable debate on this. Until recently two main theories held the field. Many blamed oil pollution for, as described in the previous chapter, the behaviour of the auks makes them particularly susceptible to oiling and large numbers of oiled Guillemots and Razorbills are found dead on our beaches. Puffins, however, are found much less frequently on beach surveys, probably because they disperse much farther out to sea after breeding and migrate southwards to a greater extent, so that few remain in our area in winter when oiling is at its worst, and their small bodies, if affected, are unlikely to last long enough to come ashore. Many of the auk colonies which have suffered declines are in areas where tanker and other sea traffic is heavy and where illegal discharges, accidental spills, or disasters such as the *Torrey Canyon* wreck are most frequent. Yet other experts, whilst admitting the impact of oil pollution, considered that the main cause of these declines in the more southerly colonies was some change in food supply. They argued that this was to be expected if the fish on which the auks feed had declined in numbers in the south, whether due to climatic amelioration or over-fishing. As little was known of what was happening among the very much larger auk colonies further north and information was lacking on trends in the populations of the various fish prey species, it was impossible to settle the debate.

More recently, the position has changed in two ways. Firstly, after the Irish Sea disaster in the autumn of 1969, when over 15,000 seabirds, the vast majority being Guillemots, were found dead on the beaches, it was suggested that starvation, probably compounded by natural causes including moulting and gales, may have been further aggravated by the toxic effects of the metallic and organic residues (including PCBs) found in many of the dead birds (see previous chapter). Secondly, there have been the recent indications of major declines in the Puffin in some large northern colonies, as described earlier. So there are indications that the declines, at least in the Puffin, are more serious than was thought previously, while the causes may be more complex.

The relative importance of the factors which may be responsible for a decrease of auks will not easily be ascertained, but detailed research has already begun in a determined attack upon the problem. This research will include more intensive surveys of our beaches to assess the numbers and proportions of oiled birds cast up, analyses of their corpses and other material such as eggs or food to determine the degree of contamination by various pollutants, annual surveys of sample colonies (combined with studies to refine census techniques) to give early warning of any dramatic changes, studies of laying, hatching and fledging success, on the feeding and growth rates of the young, and, most difficult of all, surveys of their distribution at sea, their food and liability to pollution in the long months away from land when they are not breeding.

We cannot attempt to understand the changing fortunes of most of our seabirds unless close links are maintained with scientists studying other aspects of life in our seas. With growing fears that man may be threatening the vast food supplies provided by the world's oceans, whether by recklessly using them as a dump for his manifold wastes or by overfishing, there is now the chance that concern at both national and international levels will lead to a much overdue strengthening of all aspects of research into marine life. The seabirds of Britain and Ireland are one of the most valuable indicators of ecological danger. The Irish Sea disaster showed how quickly the network of amateur observers could give warning of sudden catastrophe, while the background knowledge on numbers and distribution, still incomplete, but enormously strengthened by the 1969–70 census, can provide the base-line to assess more gradual changes. There is much we still need to know and far more we must understand, but in the multi-disciplinary approach to the exciting and complex problems of life in our seas, the ornithologists can make a major contribution.

Species breeding regularly

THE 24 species of seabird which now nest every year in Britain and Ireland are discussed in detail in the sections which follow. Each section contains notes on identification, food and feeding habits, breeding, movements, world distribution and past history. These will, it is hoped, provide the essential background information for the general reader, as well as full references to the great volume of research into seabird problems for those who wish to study particular aspects more fully.

Then the results of the 1969–70 inquiry into distribution and numbers of the coastal breeding seabirds are summarised and changes in their status analysed and discussed. These are supplemented by the maps for each species (pages 193–224) and the fuller numerical information given in the tables in the Appendix (pages 225–64). It is clearly impossible to list every seabird colony around the coast, as the complete results fill many volumes. For the serious student complete copies of the results are being deposited in the libraries of the following organisations: British Trust for Ornithology (Tring), Edward Grey Institute (Oxford), Nature Conservancy Council (London and Edinburgh), Royal Society for the Protection of Birds (Sandy) and the Seabird Group (Aberdeen).

The maps show the precise locations of all seabird colonies wherever practicable. However, for some widespread and numerous species (Fulmar, Cormorant, Shag and all the gulls and auks) it was not possible always to show colonies singly on maps of this scale, so where a series of colonies is found along 15 km. of coast or on islands up to 225 sq. km. in area, these have been merged into a single symbol. Finally, to protect their vulnerable colonies, the totals for all species of tern have been mapped on a vice-county basis.

FULMAR *Fulmarus glacialis*

Identification

Although appearing similar in some ways to gulls, the Fulmar should not
be confused with them. In size it is mid-way between the Common and
Herring Gulls, but its large round head and short thick neck together give
it a well-built, stocky appearance which is increased by its thick, fluffy
plumage. In flight the wings are held straight and stiff; the leading edges
have virtually no angle at the carpal joint, in contrast to those of gulls.
The head, neck and underparts of most Fulmars in Britain are normally
white, sometimes tinged yellow, but very rarely they may be pale silvery-
grey like the back and uppersides of the wings. These darker birds are
commoner out at sea further north and predominate in parts of the Arctic
and North Pacific, where extreme examples are dark brown. The primaries
are slightly darker than the back, and a pale 'watermark' is visible in the
centre of each wing-tip. The legs and feet vary in colour from yellow
through greenish to bluish-flesh. The heavy, hook-tipped beak, with its
prominent tubular nostrils on the upper mandible, also varies a good
deal in colour from olive-green to blue-grey, the tip normally being yellow.
Fulmars have a cackling call best described as 'aark-ag-ag-ag-ag-ag-ag',
used both at sea and at breeding sites; it may be delivered quietly or,
during greeting ceremonies at the nest, may rise to a crescendo of full-
throated chuckling.

Fulmars shuffle awkwardly about on their tarsi, though great mobility
on land is not necessary for a species that normally settles only at or close
to the nest site. At sea they swim buoyantly but may have to beat across
the surface for several yards to take flight in calm conditions. Once in the
air they glide, except for occasional rapid wing-beats to maintain momentum, on stiffly held wings. They are masters of the air, planing effortlessly
over the wave crests or hanging motionless, steering themselves with their
webbed feet, in upcurrents along cliff faces.

Food and feeding habits

Fulmars feed at sea where their natural diet is uncertain, though they are efficient scavengers. The earliest descriptions of their feeding habits are contained in the accounts of the northern whale industry, which commenced during the 17th century. No whale could be flensed without attendant hordes of Fulmars, sometimes numbering several thousand, eagerly searching for scraps of blubber and offal. Trawling operations, which commenced during the mid-19th century, also attract large numbers when offal and unmarketable fish is thrown overboard; the main items eaten seem to be the liver and guts. Live fish are rarely taken, though Fulmars have been observed ripping open the stomachs of dead fish in order to reach the liver. Perhaps because of these noticeable, and at times spectacular, feeding habits, firstly around the whaling fleets and more recently around trawlers, the fact that Fulmars also take more natural foods has often been overlooked and little studied. They take many zooplankton, including jellyfish, ctenophores, copepods, isopods, amphipods and euphausians, and must have relied virtually entirely upon such items before the advent of rich man-made sources about 300 years ago. The relative importance of natural food and that provided by man has yet to be studied in detail, though there has been much discussion in relation to the recent increase in the Fulmar population of the North Atlantic (Bourne 1966; Brown 1970; Fisher 1952a,b, 1966b; Salomonsen 1965).

Breeding

Most Fulmars nest on cliffs abutting or overhanging the sea, generally on the broader ledges, or in embrasures and hollows on steep grassy slopes or in the more broken areas often near the top. They seem as much at home on low cliffs as on precipices such as 900-foot Clo Mor (Sutherland), 1,141-foot St John's Head (Orkney), and 1,397-foot Conachair (St Kilda) where they nest right up to the summit. On some more isolated islands they nest on the ground, often at the base of field walls as on Mousa (Shetland), less frequently among sand dunes as on the Monach Islands (Outer Hebrides). Some pairs nest on the tops of walls and even on ruined dwellings in remote areas. Artificial cliffs which have been prospected by Fulmars include Tantallon Castle (East Lothian), Bamburgh Castle (Northumberland) and Dunrobin Castle (East Sutherland); at the last site, now a school, one of the eight pairs present in 1970 occupied a common-room window-ledge. Inland colonies have been established in a number of counties, most frequently in northern Scotland, Northumberland and north-east Yorkshire. These are mostly on rock faces within a mile or so of the coast, but some Fulmars have nested much further inland, as at Hasty Bank, twelve miles from the sea in north-east Yorkshire. In the Arctic they may nest high on precipices far inland.

Fulmars start to return to their colonies in November and December and the numbers gradually increase as the winter proceeds, though during stormy weather they may temporarily desert the cliffs. The only courtship display that has been noted consists of much gaping accompanied by loud cackling. Birds perform in this way both at the nest ledges and on the sea beneath the colony. They may also engage both singly and in groups in ceremonial bathing, though this was not considered by Fisher (1952b) to be a courtship display; they rear forward and up with their heads dipped and tails spread, while beating the water vigorously with their wings.

Pairs desert the nest site for about a fortnight prior to egg-laying, though as this occurs over a period of several weeks the colony is never completely vacated (Dunnet *et al.* 1963). It has been suggested that this so-called 'honeymoon' period, which has also been noted in some other petrels, enables the birds to establish fat reserves to help them through the breeding season ahead. The eggs are laid directly on bare rock, or where there is vegetation or loose soil in hollows worn by the birds; abandoned nests of other species, such as gulls, are sometimes used. Laying commences in early May and continues into June. Only a single egg, white and with a coarse surface, is produced by each pair, with no replacement should it be lost. Most egg losses occur within a few days of laying and are due mainly to breakage on rock surfaces or to predation by gulls (Dunnet *et al.* 1963). Following laying, the female incubates for a short period, usually less than 24 hours, and then leaves; the male then takes over, remaining at the nest on average for seven days before she returns. The rest of the incubation period is shared approximately equally by both sexes, each sitting for about five days at a time. As hatching approaches these spells become much shorter, generally of less than two days' duration (Williamson 1952). Incubation lasts on average 53 days, with known extremes of 41 and 57 days (Fisher 1952b).

On hatching, the chick is already covered in fine white down and is continuously brooded at first by one or other parent. It is fed by regurgitation, placing its beak deep inside its parent's to receive an oily liquid containing fish offal and plankton. Feeding seems to take place only once or twice a day. Unattended young defend themselves at the nest by squirting an oily, usually amber-coloured liquid with an unpleasant smell, mainly through the mouth. The maximum horizontal range seems to be three to four feet, and there may be several ejections in quick succession. Chicks squirt oil not only at potential predators but also during any disturbance at the colony, and even when the parents return to the nest during their first two or three weeks (Duffey 1951). The adults also squirt oil when alarmed.

The chicks grow fast, and towards the end of their seven weeks or so at the nest site weigh more than the adults (about 700 gm), some reaching just over 1,000 gm. (Fisher 1952b). By then they have moulted their down and resemble the adults, though their plumage is fresher. Feeding ceases a few days before departure, though the parents continue to visit the ledge and may do so even after the young have left. The chicks become very restless at this time, wandering about the ledge, exercising their wings at the very brink or pulling at vegetation. Williamson (1954) found that most young leave between 10.00 and 13.00 hours, their first flight taking them well clear of the cliffs. The last birds leave the colonies during mid-September, so that these are completely vacant for only a month or two before the return starts in November.

Young Fulmars apparently spend three or four years at sea, and when they finally return to the cliffs they visit or 'prospect' nest sites with increasing regularity for several more seasons before commencing to breed in about their seventh year. From then on they breed annually, and the mean expectation of adult life is 16 years (Dunnet et al. 1963). Following observations at St Kilda, Bourne (1966) suggested that some Fulmars may live long enough to become senile and cease to breed, spending their time idling at colonies or wandering at sea. Indeed, as Fisher (1952b) remarked, the potential life span is probably great, perhaps as long as 50 years.

Movements

When away from their breeding colonies, Fulmars wander widely across the North Atlantic Ocean and into northern seas. Except on the Grand Banks, Newfoundland, where some reach 43°N, they do not normally move much farther south than 50°N. They range deep into the Arctic wherever there are leads of open water amongst the pack-ice, even approaching the North Pole. In winter they withdraw south, keeping to the open sea and the edge of the pack-ice. By the end of 1969 17,993 Fulmars had been ringed in Britain and Ireland, of which 206 had been recovered (Spencer 1971). Besides those recovered in home waters, others have crossed the Atlantic to Nova Scotia, Newfoundland, Labrador and the Davis Strait. Several have wandered to northern Spain, and there have been recoveries around the Faeroes, Iceland and Norway, and in the Barents Sea to 71°25′N 42°40′E (Bannerman 1959; Fisher 1952b; Spencer 1959 et seq.).

World distribution

The Fulmar has three races: in the Pacific, *F. g. rodgersi* breeds from the Kurils to Alaska and north to the Bering Sea, dispersing south with cool currents as far as California and northern Japan in winter; and in the Atlantic, the small-billed nominate race breeds in the high Arctic and disperses south in winter, and the larger-billed *F. g. auduboni* breeds around the shores washed by the warmer North Atlantic Drift from Iceland through the Faeroes to Britain and Ireland. A mixed population has been collected in the Greenland–Spitsbergen area and may represent an intermediate stock or a mixture of stray birds of both races. The distribution of these subspecies has been associated with that of zones of the marine environment by Salomonsen (1965), but these tend to break down under the complex hydrographical conditions of the North Atlantic. The small-billed race certainly tends to occur in association with Arctic surface waters, although it reaches Britain in the winter, and the large-billed one – which has increased so spectacularly in western Europe from Norway to Brittany in recent years (Fisher 1952b) – with warmer surface waters.

The Southern Fulmar *F. glacialoides* of the Antarctic is very closely related to *F. glacialis* (Mougin 1967; Voous 1949). It is usually assumed that the latter is derived from the former, but an alternative hypothesis that the genus *Fulmarus* evolved in the north following colonisation by a primitive southern Fulmar stock, *F. glacialoides* resulting from a recolonisation of the south, seems equally possible (Dr W. R. P. Bourne *in litt.*).

Census methods

Although most Fulmars nest on open cliff sites, it is often impossible to obtain an accurate count of the breeding population, as immatures may occupy ledges for several years before actually laying. Late counts, when the large downy chicks are conspicuous, do not take into consideration earlier egg or chick losses. The most satisfactory census method is to count or estimate all *apparently occupied nest sites*. Although this includes both prospecting and breeding pairs, it does provide an index of the population by which comparisons can be made between surveys. The ideal time for a census is late June when breeding birds sit tight and many pairs are together on the ledges. Counts may, however, be made from the end of May until early August. Before this period, pairs may temporarily desert the colony prior to laying, while during August the main exodus takes place.

As in previous Fulmar surveys (Fisher 1966b), any group of birds separated from the next by more than a mile of coast or open sea is considered a separate colony. For administrative convenience, however, the parts of a colony split by a county boundary are treated as separate colonies. With the virtually complete coverage of the British and Irish coasts in 1969–70, many colonies formerly considered separate were found to be continuous, some as a result of recent increases, but others because they were not fully investigated in the past. In previous surveys the total population was estimated by means of a calculation involving the number of colonies of each 'order of abundance' (Order 1 = 1–9 pairs; Order 2 = 10–99 pairs; Order 3 = 100–999 pairs, etc.). Using this method on the 'Operation Seafarer' data the estimated total would be some 305,639 occupied sites, whereas the sum of the actual totals is 309,501, the difference being trivial. So that comparisons can be made with previous surveys, therefore, the estimated totals are used here; a full discussion of this point will be presented elsewhere (Saunders *in prep.*).

Status in Britain and Ireland in 1969–70 and past history

With some 305,000 occupied sites in Britain and Ireland in 1969–70 (Appendix Table 1, Map 4) the Fulmar is one of our most numerous breeding seabirds. It nests wherever there are cliffs of any sort and now breeds on nearly all suitable coasts in Britain and Ireland, except in Sussex where birds are still only prospecting. Most Fulmars are found in the extreme north and north-west of Scotland – Shetland, Orkney, Outer Hebrides (including St Kilda) and the north-west Highlands, with 268,000 occupied sites in 1969–70, or 88% of the total population. Until the present survey St Kilda, once the sole breeding locality for Fulmars in Britain and Ireland, was thought to have the only colony with over 10,000 occupied sites. Now those on Unst (north and west coasts), Foula, Fetlar, Fair Isle (all in Shetland) and Hoy (Orkney) have all reached this level. Elsewhere many Fulmars breed on the Atlantic coasts of Ireland, the more exposed parts of the Inner Hebrides, Northern Ireland, and in eastern Scotland. Smaller numbers breed on the Irish Sea coasts, while eastern and south-west England and south-west Wales are thinly populated with only 3,542 occupied sites in 1969–70 (just over 1% of the total population).

The Fulmar population in Britain and Ireland has been the subject of previous surveys by Harvie-Brown (1912), Fisher and Waterston (1941) and Fisher (1952a, 1952b, 1966b). A pattern of inquiries at ten-year intervals, with partial surveys in 1954 and 1964, has evolved since the 1930s and the Operation Seafarer survey of 1969–70 was a continuation of these.

St Kilda is our oldest Fulmar colony. Linguistic and archaeological evidence indicates that the birds have been present for at least eight or nine hundred years (Fisher 1966b; Lockwood 1954). The first census, however, was not carried out until 1939 and the difficulties of making accurate counts are so great on most of the islands in the group that only in 1949 were all of them surveyed. For other years estimates have been made based on extrapolations from the main colony on Hirta (Table 2). On this basis, the estimated total for the group has fluctuated between about 37,000 and 43,000 occupied sites in recent years. There is, however, no evidence of the increases found everywhere else between 1959 and 1969; indeed the figures suggest that the population here has reached its ceiling. As four areas have not been counted since 1949, it is impossible, however, to make any accurate assessment of population trends in the St Kilda group.

TABLE 2. *Number of occupied Fulmar sites at St Kilda*

	1939	1949	1956	1961	1968	1969
Hirta	11,770	19,943	19,415	19,716	22,940	19,047
Dun	1,610	3,600	(c3,360)	(c2,450)	2,307	2,417
Soay and Stacs	4,500	7,550				
Boreray	2,500	5,600				
Stac Lee	Not counted	35	Not counted			
Stac an Armin	400	1,450				
Totals	20,780*	38,178	(c37,000)	(c38,000)	(c42,720)	(c36,600)

Bracketed totals are estimated from partial counts.
* Count excluding Stac Lee.
1968 counts from A. A. Anderson and Gordon Birnie (Aberdeen University).

Elsewhere in Britain and Ireland no Fulmars nested until some 12 pairs were discovered on Foula (Shetland) in 1878, beginning the fantastic expansion in range and numbers of this species in Britain and Ireland. The Shetlands have now become virtually one giant colony, with nests all round the coast except on low shores in the deeper voes. The enormous estimated increase in the population there by 81,000 (some 226%) since 1959 is at least partly due to the fact that more complete cover was obtained in 1969–70 than had been possible in any previous survey, indeed some colonies had not been counted since the 1930s. Many formerly considered to be discrete units had merged. There were, however, genuine increases at some colonies which had been visited recently, for example Fair Isle which rose from 5,000 occupied sites in 1959 to 17,264 in 1969–70, Hermaness from 5,880 in 1965 (Dott 1967) to 9,463 and Saxa Vord from 1,635 to 3,211, but little change at others, including Noss and Papa Stour.

The largest recorded increase of Fulmars between 1959 and 1969–70 in any part of Britain and Ireland was in Orkney where the population apparently leapt from 13,917 occupied sites to 47,304 (some 240%).

However, many colonies were not counted in 1959 and this probably explains the tiny increase of 360 occupied sites between 1949 and 1959 and the huge increase since. By contrast, the rate of increase in the Outer Hebrides between 1959 and 1969 was 27%, the lowest recorded anywhere in Britain and Ireland. Although many small colonies have been visited infrequently, the major ones there, such as North Rona, the Shiants and Flannan Isles, Mingulay and Berneray were all covered at least once in the late 1950s or early 1960s, so that the increase in this region between 1959 and 1969 may be regarded as largely genuine, suggesting that the population in this area may be reaching its limit.

Fulmars first nested in the North Highlands in 1903 on Handa, in West Sutherland, and this county and Caithness together now hold the bulk of the population in this region. Once again the improved coverage in 1969 compared to previous surveys accounts partly for the increase, but two of the largest colonies were counted in 1959 showing increases on Handa from 1,400 occupied sites in 1949 to 1,600 in 1959 and 2,406 in 1970 while Clo Mor on the north coasts of Sutherland had 4,800 in 1959 and 4,963 in 1969. In eastern Scotland, where Fulmars first nested in 1916, the colonies appear to have been fully surveyed in 1959 so the trends shown are probably genuine.

In the Inner West region Fulmars have steadily expanded their range since 1921, when Rathlin Island off the coast of Northern Ireland was colonised. The population, however, remains small considering the large area involved, with only 10,488 occupied sites in 1969–70 of which more than half, 6,376, were in two areas – the northern Inner Hebrides from Mull to Skye, and Co. Antrim, which holds most of the Fulmar population in Northern Ireland. In 1942 the Northern Ireland colonies contained about 1,000 birds (Rankin and Rankin 1943) whilst 20 years later there were estimated to be a minimum of 1,600 pairs (Rogers 1965) and in 1969–70 there were 2,269 occupied sites. On the Atlantic coasts of Ireland from Donegal to Wexford, first colonised during the early years of this century, the fuller surveys in 1969–70 must be responsible in part for the enormous apparent increase of 23% recorded in the last ten years.

In eastern England, south-west England and south-west Wales Fulmar colonies are generally small and there has been good coverage of most colonies in the past so that increases here, such as 674 to 1,852 occupied sites along the coasts between Cardigan and Sussex, are genuine. Between Northumberland and Kent the population increased from 945 occupied sites in 1959 to 1,690 in 1969, although a decrease was noted at one colony – Marsden (Co. Durham) where there were 193 occupied sites in 1959 and only 123 in 1969–70.

The dramatic increase in numbers and spread of the large-billed Fulmar of the warmer and more southerly parts of its range in the North Atlantic was first noticed in Iceland in 1753. Since then it has affected the Faeroes (since about 1839), Norway (since about 1920) and northern France (first breeding 1960), while in Britain and Ireland, where the species was once confined to St Kilda, it now nests on almost all suitable coasts. The remarkable expansion in our islands since 1878, when a cliff on Foula (Shetland) was first occupied, has been described in detail by Fisher (1952a,b, 1966b). He showed that the mean annual (compound interest) increase in the half-decades from 1904 to 1949 for all colonies except St Kilda varied between 6.4% and 16.5% and then fell to little more than 3% between 1949 and 1959. Between the ten-yearly censuses the relative increase fell from about 160% between 1929 and 1939 to 100% between 1939 and 1949 and then to only 38% from 1949 to 1959.

The census in 1969–70 indicated, however, an apparent abrupt reversal of this trend outside the Outer Hebrides, with an increase rising sharply to 177% or the highest since the 1929–39 decade. However, a careful examination of the results makes it clear, as has already been described, that some of the more remote areas were not fully covered in the 1959 survey, so that the increases based on the 1959 counts are misleading. It is probably more meaningful to compare the totals for 1949 and 1969–70, which show a total increase of 280% in 20 years, whereas in the previous 20 years the total increase was about 420%. This suggests that the Fulmar population of Britain and Ireland, excluding St Kilda, is still growing at the remarkable rate of almost 7% a year compound, though less quickly than between 1929 and 1949.

There has been considerable speculation over the reasons for the dramatic increase and spread in the last 200 years of this population of Fulmars in the more southerly areas of the eastern North Atlantic, especially as there has been no detectable population increase or expansion in any other part of the extensive range of the species (Wynne-Edwards 1962). It was argued strongly by Fisher (1952a) that the spread was correlated with the provision of highly suitable food from offal, originally from Arctic whaling and subsequently from trawlers. This was challenged by Wynne-Edwards (1962) who thought that any correlation was poor and suggested that a special genotype may have arisen in Iceland which was able to strike out into lower latitudes and be satisfied with small straggling colonies. He proffered an alternative, though probably less likely explanation, that an unorthodox turn in general behaviour originated and spread purely by imitation. In either case he concluded that it was a wholly natural evolutionary phenomenon, quite unconnected with the activities of man. Fisher (1966b), however, maintained his position and linked the apparent slowing down in the rate of increase between 1949 and 1959 to a decline in the available trawler offal in this period, while Bourne (1966) suggested that the critical period when offal was important might occur in the winter, when little evidence is available anyway.

Salomonsen (1965) laid stress on oceanographic factors. He argued that the expansion and increase had involved only the relatively small population of Fulmars breeding in boreal waters with a mean temperature of 5°–10°C and that much of this expansion coincided with the gradual warming up of the eastern North Atlantic within the last 100 years, which in turn caused an increase in the total area of these warm waters. He thought that the original boreal population of Fulmars had exploited this new opportunity, perhaps helped by a mutation. Brown (1970) found that in the western North Atlantic, where the species does not breed south of the Arctic, though many European birds occur as non-breeding visitors, its distribution appeared to be more closely linked with cool water than the supply of fish offal. However, in the absence of reliable quantitative data on the diet of the Fulmar, he considered it impossible to explain the differences in ecology between the birds of the eastern and western North Atlantic, either in oceanographic terms or by the availability of fish offal. It will be interesting to see what happens in this area in the west if the birds now reported to be visiting rocks off Newfoundland (R. G. B. Brown *in litt.*) found a colony there too.

MANX SHEARWATER *Puffinus puffinus*

Identification

The Manx Shearwater is some 14 inches in length, of slender build with
long, narrow wings and a short tail. With its contrasting sooty-black
upperparts and pure white underparts, it cannot be confused with any
other species in British waters save for the much smaller and very rare
Little Shearwater *P. assimilis*. Its bill is black, slender and hooked at the
tip, with tubular nostrils; its legs and feet are flesh-coloured with dark grey-
blue margins. At the breeding colonies its voice is a weird mixture of
screams, gurgles and cackles delivered in a most exuberant manner, most
frequently at night, though bursts of excited calling may occasionally be
heard from nest burrows during the daytime. With its long wings the Manx
Shearwater takes advantage of air currents created by wave troughs and
crests, gliding along just above the surface in a most distinctive manner,
with only occasional wing-beats, one minute showing its white underparts,
then suddenly twisting to reveal the dark upperparts. In calm conditions a
more flapping flight with short, shallow glides is adopted.

On land the Manx Shearwater is seen only at night, since it spends the
day in the nest burrow or at sea. It shuffles along awkwardly on its belly,
at best making stumbling runs before falling forward again. On calm
nights it requires a slope or other prominent feature on which to climb
before taking off, and because of its clumsiness ashore often falls easy
prey to Great Black-backed Gulls in the open at dawn or on moonlit
nights. Nocturnal activity at the colonies, both audible and visible, varies
greatly with weather conditions: on bright nights there is relatively little
calling and few birds linger outside the burrows.

Food and feeding habits

Manx Shearwaters feed mainly on small fish – young Pilchards, Herrings
and Sprats – which they catch while hovering briefly, with feet paddling

the surface, or during shallow dives. They range some distance from the colonies in search of food. Lockley (1953b) considered that many from Skokholm Island (Pembrokeshire) travelled regularly to the Bay of Biscay throughout the breeding season, a round journey of between 600 and 1,200 miles, but only one bird known to be feeding a chick on Skokholm has been recovered in the Bay of Biscay and the numerous other summer records there may well have involved pre- or failed breeders. Harris (1966a) found that breeding adults on Skokholm returned to feed their chicks too frequently for really long journeys to have been made and suggested that a 200-mile range was much more likely; this would still include fishing grounds in the Irish Sea, Bristol Channel and St George's Channel, and off south-west Ireland.

Breeding

Manx Shearwaters nest in colonies, usually on small islands, from just above high water mark to a considerable altitude and sometimes far inland. On Rhum (Inverness-shire), for example, they breed up to two miles inland and at over 2,000 feet. Nests are always situated below ground in burrows or rock crevices, and where the soil is soft the birds easily excavate their own burrows.

The Manx Shearwater has a prolonged breeding season, adults first coming to land as early as February and remaining until September or even October; there is even a record of a downy chick in late November on Bardsey (Caernarvonshire) (Walker 1961). On Rhum the birds often have to clear snow away from their burrows during the early part of the season. In the first weeks they spend about a quarter of their time in the burrows, but they leave the colony altogether for ten days or so just before egg-laying, probably to establish fat reserves prior to the rigours of incubation and feeding the chick. On Skokholm the single large white egg is laid from the third week of April, the peak date being in the first half of May; the laying period is more prolonged than in some other migrant shearwaters. Both parents take turns at incubation, each sitting continuously for about six days on average (though this may vary from one to at least 26 days); the mean incubation period is 51 days. The chicks are covered in pale grey down at first and are brooded for about a week. They are fed by regurgitation on about two nights out of three, eventually reaching nearly twice the weight of their parents when some seven or eight weeks old. Feeding gradually ceases, and the chick then lives on its accumulated fat, looking much like its parents save for tufts of down; each night it emerges to sit near the burrow entrance and exercise its wings. Deserted, it remains at the colony for another week or so before finally departing to the sea at about ten weeks of age (Harris 1966a). In the absence of prominent features from which to launch themselves, chicks from inland colonies may have to struggle many hundreds of yards before they can take flight. On Skokholm and nearby Skomer, young Manx Shearwaters about to leave colonies situated among dense vegetation, mainly bracken, are affected annually to varying degrees by epizootics of a virus disease – puffinosis. The virus is thought to overwinter in an invertebrate carrier. In 1964 about 4% of the chicks reared on Skokholm died from this infection (Harris 1965a).

Movements

Manx Shearwaters speedily leave their colonies during September. Perhaps food declines rapidly, since Perrins (1966) found that young which had fledged early had a higher survival rate than late birds. Young shearwaters from the Pembrokeshire colonies are sometimes blown well inland by storms in early September, and when the weather is exceptionally severe, as in 1967, they may be carried far into England, a few even reaching the North Sea coast. In calmer conditions they travel quickly, aided by trade winds, to their main wintering area off the east coast of southern South America; two Skokholm-ringed birds made the 5,000-mile journey in as little as 18 days. Another Skokholm-ringed bird was found dead on a beach in South Australia in the autumn of 1961 (Spencer 1962), presumably having been carried east from the South Atlantic by the strong prevailing winds. British Manx Shearwaters have also been recovered in West Africa in autumn, in the West Indies and along the east coast of North America in the spring and summer (Thomson 1965; Post 1967). They do not return to European waters until their second year, when they begin to visit colonies in June and July, and most do not breed until five years old (Harris 1966b).

Experiments by Lockley (1942) and Matthews (1955) have shown that the Manx Shearwater has remarkable homing abilities, displaced birds returning rapidly from areas not normally visited, such as the Adriatic. Breeding birds from Skokholm were transported to release points where, in sunny conditions, they quickly orientated themselves, 62% setting off within two compass points of the direction of Skokholm. In cloudy weather such direction-finding was not observed, the birds scattering at random or drifting downwind. The most distant return was from Boston, USA, taking $12\frac{1}{2}$ days for the 3,000-mile flight (Matthews 1953, 1955).

World distribution

There are eight races or closely related species of the Manx Shearwater occurring in the North and South Pacific, North Atlantic and Mediterranean. The one found in Britain and Ireland breeds only in the eastern

North Atlantic (though it nested in the past in Bermuda), from the Westmann Islands through the Faeroes, Britain, Ireland and Brittany to the Atlantic islands of the Azores and Madeiras (Bourne, in Palmer 1962).

Census methods

Manx Shearwaters are difficult to census owing to their nocturnal habits on land and to their burrow-nesting. Rough estimates of numbers can be made when they gather in flocks or rafts off their colonies during the evening prior to coming ashore. Several such counts are required, since numbers fluctuate from evening to evening depending on weather conditions. Counts at the colonies after dark are difficult and subject to much variation. From midsummer onwards the arrival of non-breeding birds at colonies makes both these methods inapplicable. Colonies should be mapped where possible, occupied burrows being recognised by their worn entrances and droppings. At Skokholm the population was estimated as 30,000–40,000 pairs using two different ringing techniques (Harris 1966a, Perrins 1967). Wormell (in litt.) estimated the numbers on Rhum by measuring the areas where nutrients from the birds' guano caused green vegetation to grow on an otherwise barren terrain; with sample counts of burrows at selected sites, he was able to estimate the total population as about 70,000 pairs. Without special surveys of this type, it is rarely possible to obtain any accurate idea of numbers; indeed, breeding may not even be confirmed at some smaller colonies unless nocturnal visits are made to locate occupied burrows, or at the end of the season to find young birds above ground, whilst at cliff colonies it may be impossible to prove breeding.

Status in Britain and Ireland in 1969–70 and past history

The survey in 1969–70 was able to produce only limited data on some of the Manx Shearwater colonies in Britain and Ireland, as in such a wide-ranging census observers had limited time to spend on detailed counts and were often restricted to daytime visits, while some of the colonies are virtually inaccessible (Appendix Table 2). Sites where the species has been known to breed in the past, or has been suspected of breeding, which could not be checked in 1969–70 are given in Appendix Table 3.

From the limited information available, it seems that the total population of Manx Shearwaters in 1969–70 was almost certainly over 175,000 pairs and may well have been over 300,000 pairs, so that the species must rank amongst the eight most numerous breeding seabirds of Britain and Ireland. The bulk of the population breeds in three separate areas: the Inner Hebrides (mainly on the island of Rhum), the islands of Skomer and Skokholm, Pembrokeshire and the Blaskets, and Skelligs

Puffin Island, Co. Kerry (Map 5). The last review of distribution of Manx Shearwater colonies was made by Lockley (1953a), but he had little information on the remoter Scottish and Irish colonies. From this and other historical data given in the Tables, it seems that declines have occurred on Foula, some of the Hebrides (including Eigg, Berneray and Pabbay) and possibly on the Isles of Scilly, whilst it is likely that some increase has taken place at the large colony on Skokholm in south Wales. Elaborate and difficult surveys would be needed to obtain any reliable estimate of the total numbers of Manx Shearwaters in Britain and Ireland, and the assessment of any population trends would be a still more formidable undertaking.

STORM PETREL *Hydrobates pelagicus*

Identification

The Storm Petrel is our smallest seabird, only about six inches long and weighing hardly an ounce. From above it is reminiscent of a House Martin *Delichon urbica*, with sooty-black upperparts contrasting with a white rump above a square black tail; it is dark brown below, with some white under the wing, and in fresh plumage it has a narrow white wing-bar. The legs, feet and bill are black, the bill having elongated tubular nostrils with a single opening, and a hooked tip. Storm Petrels are normally silent on the wing, except during courtship chases when snatches of churring and a loud 'terr-chick' call may be heard. The latter is also uttered at the nest where the main call or song is a long, uneven purring ending in a hiccough. The song is comparatively seldom heard from a hole where two birds are present, or after incubation has started. Non-breeding birds sing regularly and it appears that the song is used to attract a mate and proclaim ownership of the territory (Davis 1957).

When ashore these petrels rest on the full length of the tarsi, and in this position shuffle in and out of the nest site, but over open ground they move by fluttering their wings while walking on their toes. During the breeding season they spend the daylight hours either at sea or in their nest chambers. Nocturnal activity lasts from about 1½ hours after sunset to an hour before sunrise (Davis 1957). Unlike the Manx Shearwater (see pages 68–72), the Storm Petrel is not inhibited by moonlit nights; although some head straight for the burrow or, on departure, fly directly to sea on such nights, many others engage in display flights above the colony.

Food and feeding habits

The flight of these small seabirds over water is fluttering, interspersed with short glides, and has been described as bat-like. They feed by hovering briefly, feet pattering the surface, and picking up items with the bill. Their main food seems to be zooplankton and small fish for which they sometimes search in the disturbed wake of ships, though less frequently than some other petrels; they also take small pieces of offal discarded by fishing fleets.

Breeding

Storm Petrels usually nest on small and often isolated islands. Few mainland sites are known in Britain and Ireland, though potential localities are likely to be inaccessible and therefore unexplored. The nest is always hidden, though generally at no great depth. Favoured spots are crevices among rocks on storm beaches, in cliff faces and rock outcrops, and the walls of ruined field systems and dwellings which are such a familiar feature of many small and now uninhabited islands. On Mousa (Shetland) the honeycomb of drystone walling in the great broch is the site of a large colony, as are the oratory and monks' beehive cells on Great Skellig (Co. Kerry), while on Skokholm (Pembrokeshire) a pair occupies a long-established site in the wall of the bird observatory. Where the soil is soft the birds excavate their own burrows, or make small side passages in holes occupied by Manx Shearwaters, Puffins and Rabbits, or use the main compartment of such holes if deserted by their former occupants. They sometimes nest under long vegetation or turfs. A shallow depression on the floor of the chamber suffices for a nest, sometimes lined with a few small stones or short pieces of vegetation. Major R. F. Ruttledge (*in litt.*) has noted such material only in earth burrows, where tangled wool and feathers may form a mat up to 3½ inches across and half an inch thick, and not in nests in rock crevices or under stones.

Most studies of the breeding biology of the Storm Petrel have been made on Skokholm. Although some birds return to the island during the second half of April, the main arrival is not until mid-May. A single egg, white with a few red speckles, is normally laid during the second half of June, though extreme dates of 28th May to 20th August have been recorded. Incubation usually lasts between 38 and 42 days; one egg which had undergone chilling for a total of eleven days hatched after 50 days. Both sexes incubate in turn, sitting for short spells, usually of two or three days' duration. The newly-hatched chick is covered with silvery-grey down and is brooded continuously for about the first week, after which it spends the day alone in the nest chamber. It is fed almost nightly for the first seven weeks, until it weighs nearly twice as much as its parents. Meals then become irregular, with gaps of up to five days, though feeding continues until a few days before the departure of the young bird from the nest 56 to 73 days after hatching, by which time most of its down will have been shed. Several nights of wing-exercising near the burrow entrance precede the final departure which is made alone, after further wing-exercising, from some nearby rock or other eminence providing an uninterrupted take-off for the first flight to the sea (Davis 1957).

Movements

Ringing recoveries show some movement between colonies, though whether this is casual wandering or interchange by breeding birds has yet to be thoroughly investigated. Examples of such recoveries are as follows: from Skokholm to Bardsey (Caernarvonshire) and Inishtearaght (Co. Kerry); from Foula (Shetland) to St Kilda, Inishglora (Co. Mayo) and the Faeroes; from the Faeroes to Fair Isle; and from both the Channel Islands and Brittany to Skokholm, including one ringed as a nesting adult on an island off Finistère in 1966 and recovered on Skokholm in 1969 (Hudson 1971). Most of the few distant recoveries are from the Bay of Biscay, though two are from Africa – one off Mauritania and the other in False Bay, South Africa, which from specimens and observations of birds at sea seems to be the main wintering area (Dr W. R. P. Bourne *in litt.*).

World distribution

The Storm Petrel is restricted to the eastern North Atlantic and Mediterranean for breeding. In the Atlantic it is found in the Westmann Islands, Faeroes, Britain, Ireland, Channel Islands, Brittany, Iberia, the Canaries (infrequently) and doubtfully Madeira. In the Mediterranean it breeds off the Tunisian coast and is known to nest as far east as Malta and Sicily (Vaurie 1965; Voous 1960). Birds with brood-patches and others which laid eggs on capture have now been caught during August in the Lofoten Islands, Norway (Myrberget *et al.* 1969; E. Brun, pers. comm.).

Census methods

This is one of the most difficult of all seabirds to census. Even at small colonies the location of singing birds is not an easy matter, for the sound does not carry far, particularly on windy nights or when a swell is running. Nest sites may also be located by the persistent musky smell that pervades them. For large and scattered colonies there is at present no method whereby numbers may be reliably counted, or even estimated. Attempts were made during the early 1960s to catch large numbers in mist-nets and to estimate the total population using recapture techniques, but the issue is apparently complicated by a large non-breeding population and a good deal of visiting between colonies.

Status in Britain and Ireland in 1969–70 and past history

There has been no previous full survey of the Storm Petrel in Britain and Ireland, and very little new information was gained during the course of Operation Seafarer. Without doubt there are unrecorded colonies on some islands and possibly on mainland coasts, but to locate these and to provide some assessment of the total population would require a mammoth effort devoted solely to these ends. Colonies, many apparently small, are scattered along the west coast from Shetland south to the Isles of Scilly and Channel Islands. The largest concentration seems to be on islands off Co. Kerry where two – Inishvickillaun and Inishtearaght – are classed as Order 5 (at least 10,000 pairs). (See Appendix Tables 4 and 5; Map 6.)

There are few indications of trends in the population, though Baxter and Rintoul (1953) mentioned decreases in Scotland, and Parslow (1965) recorded a marked decrease at the main colony in the Isles of Scilly towards the end of the last century, while more recently it is reported to have decreased in Cornwall (Ryves and Quick 1946) and to have disappeared from three islands off Ireland (Ruttledge 1966).

LEACH'S STORM-PETREL *Oceanodroma leucorhoa*

Identification

Leach's Storm-petrel is larger than the Storm Petrel, about eight inches in length and weighing up to two ounces (40–55 gm.). Generally sooty-brown in colour, somewhat paler beneath, it has a pale band on the wing-coverts and a white rump. The forked tail is difficult to see in flight and the greyish shafts to the central feathers of the rump may be observed only under the most favourable conditions. Its bill (with prominent tubed nostril), legs and feet are black. It has long wings like a tern, and its conspicuously buoyant, erratic flight, constantly changing speed and direction, is its best recognition character. It has a more varied vocabulary than the Storm Petrel. On the wing at the remote island breeding colonies it utters a harsh, staccato laugh, varying from guttural to high-pitched, while from the burrows a crooning 'churrrrrrrrrrrrrrrrrroee-churrrrrr . . .' is continually heard, interspersed with muffled screams and a call similar to the flight-call. Leach's Storm-petrels are not seen above ground at their breeding colonies during the day; at St Kilda, Waters (1964) found that most birds returning to the colony arrived 84 to 164 minutes after sunset, leaving 49 to 122 minutes before sunrise.

Food and feeding habits

These small birds of the open ocean feed on surface-dwelling zooplankton, including small squid and fish picked up as they hover just above the surface; unlike some other petrels, they rarely follow ships. It seems likely that they feed largely at night (Dr W. R. P. Bourne *in litt.*).

Breeding

Leach's Storm-petrels tend to nest in earthier sites than Storm Petrels, in burrows dug by the birds themselves where the soil permits, or otherwise in crevices among rocks or in cliff faces. At some North American colonies on forested islands they occupy holes among tree roots. They perform aerial displays over their breeding grounds, pairs or small parties chasing each other in twisting, turning flights; sometimes two birds appear to collide and fall to the ground, and Williamson (1948) observed that when this occurred they often entered a burrow. The nest may be lined with sheep's wool or dry vegetation. A single dull white egg is laid, usually before the end of May; both parents take turns at incubation, which lasts about seven weeks. The chicks remain in the nest, uttering a loud peeping call at night, for a further nine weeks or so, finally fledging during September and October. (See also summary by Palmer 1962).

Movements

There are very few recoveries of British-ringed Leach's Storm-petrels and none at all away from their breeding colonies. Sight records suggest a slow southward autumn dispersal to winter in the tropics, some exceptionally reaching South African waters. From time to time 'wrecks' of these petrels occur in the North Atlantic when many birds on autumn passage are driven ashore by strong winds and even carried some distance inland. The last major incident was in October and November 1952 when there were at least 6,700 known casualties, though many more must have been eaten by foxes or cats, or remained undiscovered. About a third of the victims came ashore in the Bridgwater Bay area (Somerset), though nearly every county in Great Britain and Ireland was affected and small numbers were found in France, Belgium, the Netherlands, Switzerland and Germany. The whole North Atlantic population seems to have been involved in the disaster, which may have been due to a persistent belt of strong westerly winds preventing the birds from feeding properly so that they drifted steadily downwind, and eventually inland, in an emaciated condition (Boyd 1954). During the autumn Leach's Storm-petrels linger in high latitudes where they are likely to encounter inclement weather, but there may be some other cause for the 'wrecks', possibly an epidemic disease, as they have not occurred during periods of similar weather in other years (Dr W. R. P. Bourne in litt.).

World distribution

In the North Pacific Leach's Storm-petrels nest from western Alaska through the island chain to Hokkaido, Japan, and along the western seaboard of Canada and the United States to Lower California. In the Atlantic the main population is found from southern Labrador to Massachusetts, with outlying colonies on the Westmann Islands, the Faeroes (where breeding was not proved until 1934) and in northern Scotland, while there are past records from western Ireland (Vaurie 1965, Voous 1960). Birds with brood-patches have been caught in the Lofoten Islands, Norway, but breeding has not been confirmed there (Myrberget *et al.* 1969).

Census methods

Like the Manx Shearwater and Storm Petrel, the nocturnal habits of Leach's Storm-petrel at its breeding colonies make accurate census work almost impossible, and moreover the colonies are remote and difficult of access. Nests may be located by listening for calling birds, but this has only a limited application, and while some indication of the size of a colony may be obtained through large-scale ringing throughout a season, this is normally even less practical. Leach's Storm-petrels are occasionally found visiting places where they are not known to breed: although there may be small colonies as yet undiscovered, such occurrences must be assumed at present to denote casual wandering.

Status in Britain and Ireland in 1969–70 and past history

With only four certain colonies known at the present time – at St Kilda, the Flannan Islands, North Rona and Sula Sgeir, all in the extreme north-west of Scotland – Leach's Storm-petrel has, with some justification, been described as just brushing the British Isles with its wing-tip (Map 7). All were visited during the course of Operation Seafarer, though landings were not possible at some sites at St Kilda and in the Flannan Islands, while brief landings on Sula Sgeir in 1969 and 1971 produced no information on this species. Birds were breeding on Eilean Mor in the Flannan Islands and North Rona and present on Hirta and Dun at St Kilda. Unfortunately, however, no surveys of any colonies were made, due to the problems mentioned above.

The first British specimen of Leach's Storm-petrel was obtained on St Kilda in 1818, since when it has been found breeding on all five islands of the group. In 1931 Harrison estimated the population to be at least 1,000 pairs, while Atkinson and Ainslie (1940) considered this colony to be the most populous in Scotland. The Flannan Islands, 20 miles west of Lewis in the Outer Hebrides, have been known as the site of a Leach's Storm-petrel colony since at least 1904, when W. Eagle Clarke found them nesting on Eilean Mor. This colony was mapped in 1937 by Atkinson and Ainslie, and apparently it changed little between that year and 1959 (Anderson *et al.* 1961), when breeding was confirmed on five islands in the Flannan group, but there has been no more recent survey. In 1883 Swinburne (1884) dug out both birds and eggs from the deserted village on North Rona: there is little firm evidence whether the village colony has altered since that time, while its status elsewhere on North Rona is unknown (Robson 1968). On nearby Sula Sgeir Atkinson and Ainslie discovered Leach's Storm-petrels nesting in 1939 and estimated that 400 pairs were present; Bagenal and Baird (1959), who spent a night ashore in 1958, considered the colony to be small by North Rona standards.

Elsewhere in Scotland there have been casual records of Leach's Storm-petrels from several islands. There may still be colonies awaiting discovery and some islands would certainly repay careful attention. On Foula (Shetland) small numbers, some in breeding condition, are caught and ringed annually and there is an old record of one said to have been found in a hole with an egg (Wilson 1958). In other parts of Shetland two were killed by a cat on Whalsay in 1951 (Bruce 1952), a bird was heard on Colsay in the early 1950s (Wilson 1958) and an egg was taken in the parish of Northmavine, Mainland, about 1907 (D. R. Wilson *in litt.*). In 1933 one was found nesting on Sule Skerry, between Orkney and North Rona (Robinson 1934), and in 1967 another was caught there (Stark 1967). Two were discovered in burrows on Bearasay, Lewis, in 1955 (Atkinson and Roberts 1955), while in 1962 Robson and Wills (1963) heard birds calling there but failed to locate a colony. A single Leach's Storm-petrel was found in a hole on Haskeir, off North Uist, in 1939 (Freeman 1940), while Gray (1871) was told that a few nested on Mingulay at the south end of the Outer Hebrides and on Rhum (west Inverness), but there are no subsequent records from these sites.

There are several old breeding records from Ireland, eggs having been taken from Inishtearaght and Inishnabro in the Blaskets (Co. Kerry) in 1886 and 1889, from Blackrock (Co. Mayo) in 1889 and from Duvillaun Beg in the same county in 1908 (Kennedy *et al.* 1954). Since these early occurrences, most of the islands off the west coast of Ireland have been searched at one time or another for breeding Leach's Storm-petrels, but the only reports have been of birds seen and heard on the precipitous and virtually inaccessible slopes of the Stags of Broadhaven off the north coast of Co. Mayo in 1946 and 1947, and on the Great Skellig off Co. Kerry in 1965 (Ruttledge 1966).

GANNET *Sula bassana*

Identification

The Gannet, with a six-foot wing-span and a distinctive cigar-shaped body, is the largest seabird breeding in Britain and Ireland. Adults are easily recognisable by their gleaming white plumage and contrasting black wing-tips, while at closer range the orange-buff head and large dagger-like bill may be seen. The bill is pale blue-grey, marked with black horizontal lines; black lines also surround its base and extend back from the gape, over the yellow eye, and down the upper throat. The legs and feet are greyish-black, with greenish lines on the toes, somewhat more turquoise on the female and yellower on the male – a character by which, at least at the nest, the sexes may often be separated (Nelson 1964a). Juveniles are mottled brown-black, gradually attaining full adult plumage after about four years. Gannets are noisy birds at their colonies, their main call being simply a loud 'urrah-rah-rah-rah-rah-rah-rah-rah-rah'. Their flight is direct and powerful with regular wing-beats, but in windy conditions they glide in long shallow swoops low over the waves. They waddle awkwardly on land.

There are two similar and closely related southern forms – the Cape Gannet *S. capensis* of South Africa and the Australasian Gannet *S. serrator* of Australasia – which some regard as subspecies of *S. bassana*. These southern forms, particularly the Australasian, are slightly smaller and both, especially the Cape Gannet, have some black on the secondaries and tail.

Food and feeding habits

Gannets feed primarily on surface-dwelling fish which they catch by plunge-diving from heights of up to about 140 feet. When hunting they scan the sea below, and on locating prey plummet down with wings half open, to control their direction, before entering the water head-first with considerable force. Just before impact their wings are closed or trailed behind them; their skulls are strengthened and the shock is also absorbed by a system of air sacs, while the location of the nostrils inside the bill prevents the entry of water. The prey is not speared, but grasped in the bill during the few seconds' submersion and swallowed whole as the bird surfaces. Large numbers congregate to feed over fish shoals or at favoured places, such as tidal streams off headlands, so that the air is full of circling and diving birds – a most spectacular sight. Collinge (1924–27) found from an examination of 18 stomachs that fish (including Coalfish, Pollack, Haddock, Whiting, Herring, Sprat, Mackerel and Garfish) formed 84% of the diet, Mollusca 2% and miscellaneous animal matter 14%, the last probably from fish stomachs. In some areas offal and stray fish left by trawlers are also taken (Dr W. R. P. Bourne *in litt.*).

Breeding

Most Gannets nest on steep cliff slopes or the tops of islands. In Britain and Ireland most colonies are on small, usually isolated islands, notable exceptions being found on Noss and Unst (Shetland) and at Bempton Cliffs (Yorkshire). Nelson (1965, 1967) argued that the Gannet shows many adaptations for nesting on cliffs and that the occupation of more level sites may possibly be a recent development due, at least partly, to a cessation of persecution by man and natural predators, but it seems likely that Gannets nested on level sites in inaccessible areas before man arrived. They are highly colonial, nesting no more than three feet apart where the terrain permits. Some colonies have long histories, though the two in Shetland were established as recently as 1914 and 1917 and a number of new ones have been founded during the last 40 years in the Channel Islands, Brittany, Newfoundland, Iceland and Norway. Gannets are completely absent from the colonies for only a short period in early winter. The first birds return by January, but numbers fluctuate greatly until the first eggs are laid in April.

Pair formation takes place only at the nest site. Males 'advertise' by facing females and shaking their heads from side to side, sometimes leaning backwards while resting on their tarsi, with the neck extended upwards and the bill pointing down. Females fly over the colony before landing, and approach an advertising male cautiously, for Gannets are extremely aggressive. Breeding begins at five or six years of age and once a pair has formed they occupy the same nest site for some years. Immatures usually attempt to establish a site in that part of the colony in which they were reared (Nelson 1965).

The nest is large, between one and two feet high, rather volcano-shaped and made from a mixture of vegetation, seaweed, feathers, flotsam and earth gathered from just outside the rim; the cup is lined with grass and feathers. Man-made material, such as discarded fishing net or lines, is also incorporated and may ensnare adults or chicks. Gannets try continually to steal material from other nests right until the end of the breeding season. Excreta directed on to the nest sides cement the structure, a factor of considerable importance at cliff-ledge sites (Nelson 1964a). The nest of the Cape Gannet is entirely composed of guano which is collected annually for use as fertiliser.

A single egg is laid, pale blue at first but rapidly turning chalky white. It may be replaced if lost within the first two or three weeks. The sexes take roughly equal shares in incubation, which lasts on average about 44 days. The egg is kept warm beneath the webbed feet, as Gannets lack brood patches; when it begins to chip, it is kept on top of the feet to minimise the danger from crushing. At first chicks have only a sparse covering of greyish-white down and are brooded beneath the body or between the feet of one of the parents for the first two weeks or so. One or other parent is in attendance right through the 90-day fledging period, probably as a protection against attack by neighbouring adults or by non-breeders seeking to establish a nest site for future years (Nelson 1966).

Chicks are fed several times a day on regurgitated fish which they obtain by thrusting their bills deep into the parents' gapes. Their weight increases from about 60 gm. on hatching to about 4,000 gm. on leaving the nest; adults weigh about 3,400 gm. The fat reserves thus established by this constant feeding are of considerable importance to the young birds during their first weeks at sea. When they are ready to leave, chicks at cliff-ledge sites simply jump off their nests, but those from more inland sections of the colony have to make their way between ranks of adults which attack them unmercifully. The first flight is short and straight to the sea, from which they are unable to take off due to their weight, and from then on they are quite independent (Nelson 1964b).

Movements

Gannets migrate most strongly in their first year, reaching winter quarters off West Africa as far south as Senegal with some entering the Mediterranean; some remain in these waters during the following summer, though as they age they move north to an increasing extent and winter in the Bay of Biscay and off Iberia. Most adults merely disperse through home waters during the winter months (Bannerman 1959, Thomson 1939).

World distribution

Gannets breed only in the North Atlantic, particularly in Britain and Ireland, with smaller numbers in Iceland, the Faeroes, Norway and Brittany. A much smaller population is found on the western side, breeding in Newfoundland and the Gulf of St Lawrence (Fisher and Vevers 1951; Vaurie 1965). The colonies in Britain and Ireland hold nearly three-quarters of the total population of nearly 200,000 pairs (Table 2). By comparison the Australasian Gannet of the Bass Strait, Tasmania and New Zealand has a population of about 35,000 pairs (C. J. R. Robertson and D. L. Serventy *in litt.*); and in 1956 the Cape Gannet totalled some 176,000 pairs, though its numbers are apparently declining with the development of the fishing industry (Jarvis 1970; M. K. Rowan *in litt.*).

Census methods

Small colonies, or large ones divided by natural features into small sections, may be counted by observers on the ground. In most cases, however, the large size of the colony and the difficult terrain do not allow this. Although direct estimates of even the largest have been made from both land and sea, it is more satisfactory to use photographs in the way pioneered by Acland and Salmon (1924) on Grassholm (Pembrokeshire). With the aid of grids, and using a strong lens or binocular microscope, it is possible to count the occupied nests (Barrett and Harris 1965), or to count individuals and then apply a conversion factor, obtained from sample counts, to calculate the population in pairs (Boyd 1961). (The proportion of nests occupied by *both* adults tends to vary with the season,

Plate 1

A Manx Shearwater (*from above and below*)

B Fulmar

C Storm Petrel

D Leach's Storm-petrel

E Guillemot (*winter and*, below, *summer*)

F Razorbill (*winter and*, below, *summer*)

G Black Guillemot (*winter and*, below, *summer*)

H Puffin (*winter and*, below, *summer*)

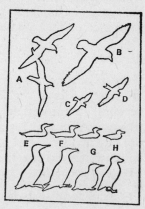

and possibly weather.) There are usually some non-breeders actually occupying nests, but it is generally not possible to distinguish these from breeding pairs except during ground counts and then only at easily accessible parts of the colony; thus the counts in 1969–70 cover all pairs occupying nests. At all colonies there are groups of non-breeding and off-duty birds around the edge of the main body, or at a little distance from it, but these can usually be identified without difficulty on photographs by their variable density compared with the remarkably regular density of birds on nests, and by a comparative lack of guano.

Status in Britain and Ireland in 1969–70 and past history

In 1969–70 there were 16 Gannet colonies in Britain and Ireland with an estimated population of some 138,000 pairs (Appendix Table 6, Map 8). The vast majority of colonies are on the western and northern coasts, with two in the east on the Bass Rock and Bempton Cliffs and two comparatively recently founded colonies well to the south in the Channel Isles. The largest colony of all is in the St Kilda group on Boreray and its satellites Stac Lee and Stac An Armin, where the best estimate is that some 52,000 pairs were nesting in 1969, but, because of incomplete coverage by air photographs, this figure must be regarded as approximate (Dixon, 1973). The smallest and most recent was on Roareim, one of the westernmost rocks of the Flannan Islands (Outer Hebrides), where 16 pairs were found nesting in 1969 during this survey.

Over sixty years ago Gurney (1913) realised that it would be possible to make a full census of the world population of the Gannet, a conspicuous bird, with only 14 colonies known at that time throughout its north Atlantic range. He estimated from surveys made mainly during the early years of the century that the eight colonies in Britain and Ireland held about 75,000 birds. Later, with more information at their disposal, Fisher

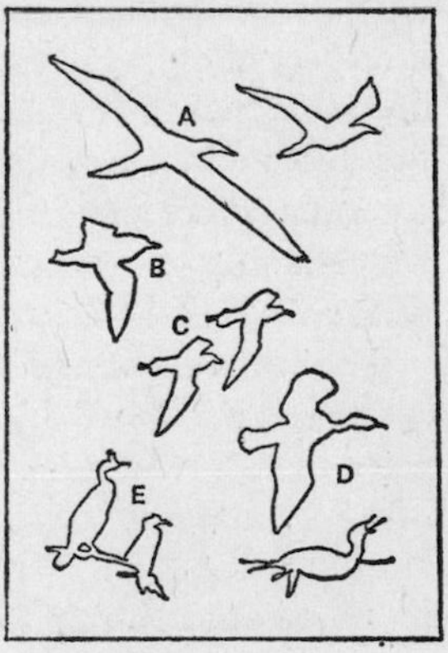

Plate 2

A   Gannet (*adult and*, right, *immature*)

B   Great Skua

C   Arctic Skua (*light and*, lower, *dark phase*)

D   Cormorant (*adult and*, below, *immature*)

E   Shag (*adult and*, right, *immature*)

and Vevers (1943) considered his estimate to be on the low side and suggested that the true figure for these years was about 48,075 pairs. In 1936, from information collected mainly during the early 1930s, it was estimated that the eleven colonies then occupied in Britain and Ireland contained about 53,500 pairs (Wynne-Edwards *et al.* 1936). Further surveys were carried out in 1939 and 1949 (Fisher and Vevers 1951) and the estimated totals were 54,552 and 64,136 pairs respectively. No full survey was made in 1959, but all the known colonies except Noss were counted between 1955 and 1966, with a total of some 107,000 pairs in the 14 colonies surveyed, suggesting that the Gannet population of Britain and Ireland at this period was about 110,000 pairs.

There has thus been a most remarkable increase in recent years in the Gannet population of Britain and Ireland. This must be considered against what is known of the previous history of the species, fully summarised up to 1939 by Fisher and Vevers (1943). They showed that declines had occurred at a number of colonies in the last century. Thus the very old colony on the Gannet Stone, Lundy (Devon), was said to be decreasing in 1871 and, after several years of unsuccessful attempts at nesting, it became extinct in 1909. At Little Skellig in Ireland 500 pairs were present in 1850 but only 30 by 1880, while in Scotland estimates for the Bass Rock give some 10,000 pairs in 1831, about 5,000 pairs in 1847 or 1848 and about 3,400 pairs in 1850, and at Ailsa Craig, where eggs were taken and feathers collected, the 7,500 breeding pairs in 1868 had declined to possibly 3,250 pairs by 1905. However, the extent of any overall decline in Gannet numbers during this period is far from certain. Fisher and Vevers constructed an ingenious table giving estimates of Gannet populations at all the colonies at 5-year intervals from 1819 to 1939 and from these figures there appears to have been a fairly steady, but relatively small decline of under 20% in Britain and Ireland from 1819 to 1889, after which a recovery began. There are, however, so few reliable census figures, particularly for the larger colonies, that it would be unwise to interpret these tentative estimates too precisely. Nevertheless, it seems probable that the destruction of Gannets by man, to which they attributed the decline in the world population of the species in the last century, had its main effect not in Britain and Ireland but on the colonies on the western side of the Atlantic, above all at the largest colony on Bird Rocks in the Gulf of St Lawrence (see below).

The recovery in the numbers of the Gannet in Britain and Ireland since is shown in Table 6 (Appendix). Briefly, they increased from some 48,000 pairs in eight colonies in the early years of this century to over 54,000 in 12 colonies in 1939, then to some 64,000 in 15 colonies in 1949, to around 110,000 in 15 colonies in the period 1955–66 and to over 138,000 in 16 colonies in 1968–70. Many of the figures for individual colonies,

especially the earlier ones, are estimates, and even where counts have been
made using the techniques described earlier there remains some margin
of error at the larger colonies. (See especially Boyd 1961 for a full discussion of the problems involved in counting the St Kilda group.) Even so
the general picture is clear – a slow increase from the early years of the
century to 1939 (just over 13%), a further increase of over 17% in the
ten years to 1949 and an even more explosive increase of over 115%
between 1949 and 1969–70. These latest increases involved all colonies in
differing degrees.

The Gannet colonies of Britain and Ireland cannot be considered in
isolation. The latest figures for all known colonies of the species throughout its north Atlantic range are shown in Appendix Table 7. The total
population is now some 194,000 breeding pairs, of which 163,000 or
nearly five-sixths are found in the eastern Atlantic. This compares with
the 1834 position when it was estimated that there were nearly 167,000
pairs in all, of which less than one-third were found in the eastern colonies.
The 1834 total, however, depends largely on the tentative estimate made by
Fisher and Vevers (1944) of the population on Bird Rocks at this date of
some 110,000 pairs. This was based on limited historical data and involved various assumptions of the possible area of the colony occupied
and density of the nesting birds.

There has also been an extension of range as well as an increase in
numbers elsewhere in the eastern Atlantic in recent years. France was
colonised in 1939 when the most southerly colony of the species was
established on Rouzic, off Brittany, and by 1967 held 2,500 pairs
(Monnat 1969). Then in 1946 the first Norwegian colony was discovered,
probably founded by birds from Britain, since most recoveries of ringed
Gannets in Norwegian waters are of birds from the Bass Rock (Brun
1972), and three more colonies have been established in Norway since
then, giving a total Norwegian population of 569 pairs in 1971 (Brun
1972). In Iceland too there has been an expansion: 20,826 pairs in 1959–62
compared with 13,732 pairs in 1939, with four new, though still small,
colonies established since then. The only decline in the eastern Atlantic
in recent years is in the Faeroes, where the young are still taken. Here
there are no new colonies and the population at the ancient site of Mykines-
holm fell from 1,473 pairs in 1939 to 1,081 pairs in 1966. On the western
Atlantic seaboard there have been no reports of new colonies since 1939,
but all the six existing ones have shown some increase with the total
population growing from some 13,000 pairs in 1939 to over 31,000 pairs in
recent years.

Thus while the Gannets of Britain and Ireland may have declined
somewhat in the last century, there has been an increase from about 1889,
slow at first, greatly gathering momentum from 1939 and becoming

extremely rapid within the last twenty years. Since the early years of this century, the number of colonies has doubled, whilst within the last thirty years new colonies have been established in Iceland and the species has colonised both France and Norway. In the western Atlantic human persecution caused a catastrophic decline in the last century, mainly at the Bird Rocks colony, with a fall from an estimated 110,000 pairs in 1834 to 860 in 1889, with three other smaller colonies becoming extinct, but there too a recovery appears to have begun towards the end of the last century and in the same way has greatly accelerated in recent years. Fisher and Vevers (1944) pointed out that the reduction in the total world population was primarily due to the activities of man, mainly in the western Atlantic. In the east only one small colony became extinct in this period, although others probably suffered some reduction in numbers. They also pointed out that in certain colonies in the eastern Atlantic man had continuously harvested Gannets for his own use, apparently without endangering their numbers. This harvesting ceased at Ailsa Craig about 1880, at the Bass Rock after 1885, at St Kilda after 1910, at Sule Stack after 1932 and at Eldey (Iceland) after 1940.

It therefore seems certain that human persecution caused a major fall in the numbers of Gannets in the last century in the western Atlantic and probably that the same factor led to some decline in the then much smaller numbers to be found on the eastern side. The cessation of mass slaughter led to a slow recovery from the end of the 19th century until 1939 on both sides of the Atlantic, perhaps helped in the east by the gradual ending of more controlled exploitation at a number of sites. Since 1939, and especially since 1949, the numbers on both sides of the Atlantic have increased very markedly, with the world population now nearly 16% higher than the tentative figure in 1834 and three times larger than when the population was thought to be at its lowest in 1894. There is now virtually no human persecution of the Gannet and only limited controlled harvesting, but whether these are the only factors behind the recent explosive increases must remain a matter of conjecture.

CORMORANT *Phalacrocorax carbo*

Identification

The Cormorant, one of our largest seabirds, is easily recognisable by its brown-black plumage, white face and white chin. During the breeding season its white thigh patches are particularly conspicuous in flight, and long greyish-white hair-like plumes give the head a somewhat angular appearance. The bill is pale yellowish-horn, greyer on the upper mandible; the legs and feet are black. Juveniles are brown above and white beneath. Cormorants stand upright on land, often holding their wings out to dry – a familiar sight on harbour buoys, breakwaters and low offshore rocks. They are usually silent but at breeding colonies utter various deep guttural calls, 'karrk' and 'kwarrk'.

Food and feeding habits

The fish-eating habits of Cormorants have long brought them into con- flict with fishermen. In the past this has led to large-scale persecution following the introduction by some river authorities of bounty schemes. In Cornwall, Steven (1933) found that nearly half the fish eaten were of marketable value, mainly flatfish of various species. Lack (1945) stated that eels are a favourite food of Cormorants when fishing in fresh water. Mills (1965) found that on some Scottish freshwater lochs Cormorants were not serious predators on young Salmon, but where their numbers were high they could be detrimental to trout stocks, 42% of the fish taken being Brown Trout. Since the latter are known predators on young Salmon, their removal by Cormorants may assist Salmon stocks in rivers and possibly lochs (Mills 1964; Piggins 1959). On Windermere (West- morland) the taking of Perch by Cormorants was considered beneficial to other fish stocks (Macan and Worthington 1951). Investigations at the Cormorant colonies at the Ord of Caithness and at The Lamb (East Lothian) showed that the diet included many flatfish, particularly Dabs, and while it seems unlikely that fishing by Cormorants would affect fish stocks in the open sea it might do so in the more enclosed sea lochs and in places where fish farming is practised (Mills 1969b). In coastal and estuarine waters on the east coast of Scotland, flatfish again predominate in the Cormorant's diet, only a few individuals taking salmonid fishes (Rae 1969).

Breeding

In Great Britain and Ireland Cormorants normally nest on open sites on the coast, whether on sea stacks, small islands or broad cliff ledges, but abroad they often nest inland in trees and marshes. Some colonies on low islands are almost at sea-level and most are below 150 feet, but that at Berriedale Ness (Caithness) is about 450 feet above sea-level. There are two exceptional colonies on the remains of experimental 'Mulberry' harbour constructions built in Wigtownshire during the 1939–45 war (Smith 1969). A few colonies in trees still exist in Ireland (Ruttledge 1966) but tree-nesting has long died out in Scotland (Baxter and Rintoul 1953) and Norfolk (Seago 1967). An attempt was made by Cormorants to nest in trees at a flooded inland marsh in Kent in 1947, but unfortunately when the floodwaters receded the site was raided and the nests and eggs were destroyed (Gregory 1948). Bones recovered from the peat of the East Anglian fens suggest that Cormorants once nested in the marshes there. Two colonies on freshwater lochs are known in Scotland, both within three miles of the sea: one on low islands in the loch at Mochrum (Wigtownshire), which has existed since at least 1663 (Stuart 1948), and the other on an inland cliff at Loch an Tomain, North Uist. In Wales there has been a colony for many years on an inland cliff five miles from the sea near Towyn (Merioneth).

Cormorants build bulky nests of locally gathered material – seaweed, heather, tree mallow and bracken stems – with finer items as a lining. They perform spectacular displays at the nest, including an elaborate neck-writhing and a ceremony in which the tail is held erect, the head stretched forward and the bill opened wide to expose the yellow gape. Normally three or four chalky white eggs are laid; these are incubated by both parents in turn for just over four weeks. The chicks are naked and blind when newly hatched, their eyes not opening for five days. They quickly grow a coat of black down which is replaced by their brown and white juvenile plumage. Although they can fly when about seven weeks old, they stay near the colony for a further five weeks before finally departing.

Movements

The Cormorant population of Great Britain and Ireland is not truly migratory but there is an extensive dispersal, chiefly southwards, from the colonies. The longest known movements occur in the autumn when part of the Irish population moves to south-west England, some crossing the English Channel to north-west France and thence even to Iberia. On the other hand, hardly any North Sea crossings have been recorded, while even the Irish Sea restricts movements. The birds in each colony seem to have their own dispersal pattern and tend to return to the same colony to nest: this would tend to increase inbreeding and population isolation (Coulson and Brazendale 1968).

World distribution

The Cormorant is one of the most widely distributed of our seabirds. It has a discontinuous range across Europe and Asia, extending south from Iceland and the Murmansk coast of Russia to Brittany, the eastern Mediterranean and the Black Sea. It breeds on many rivers and lakes across Asia, south to India and Ceylon and east to China and Japan, and in Australasia in southern New Guinea, Australia and New Zealand. In North America the Cormorant is restricted to the Gulf of St Lawrence, Newfoundland, northern Nova Scotia and west Greenland (Vaurie 1965; Voous 1960). In Africa it occurs widely in suitable areas, both on the coasts and inland, though the race *P. c. lucidus* is sometimes treated as a distinct species (Williams 1966).

Census methods

Because of their limited numbers and large nests, Cormorants are among the easiest of seabirds to count accurately. Most nest in colonies which are made conspicuous from a distance by a liberal coating of guano, though care must be taken not to confuse them with roosting sites. Instances of single nests were reported during the survey, however, some at a considerable distance from other Cormorants. Where it is not possible to view the colony from afar and a closer approach is necessary, disturbance must be minimised at all times, as gulls may take eggs or small young, and larger young are liable to leave the nests and take to the sea prematurely. The tendency for the young to leave the nests makes counts late in the season difficult, but the nests are usually still recognisable.

Status in Britain and Ireland in 1969–70 and past history

The number of Cormorants nesting in Britain and Ireland in 1969–70 was just over 8,100 pairs. In Scotland, where about 3,670 pairs nest, there is a large concentration in the north-east from east Ross to Shetland, but very few on the west coast south from north Skye to the Mull of Kintyre and none at all on the east coast from the Moray Firth to the Firth of Forth. In England the main colonies are found in Northumberland and from the Isle of Wight and Dorset to the Isles of Scilly. In Wales the strongholds are Anglesey, Caernarvonshire and Pembrokeshire, with small numbers in Cardigan Bay but virtually none on the coast of the Bristol Channel. In Ireland Cormorants breed on all coasts, with the highest numbers in Co. Dublin and Co. Wexford. The small Channel Islands population is found mainly in Jersey. (Appendix Table 8; Map 9.)

There had been no previous complete survey of Cormorants in Britain and Ireland. In Scotland Smith (1969) summarised their status and the history of the colonies, nearly all of which were counted at least once during 1964–8; they then totalled some 3,000 pairs, with signs of increase in the north-east and declines in the north-west. Parslow (1967) considered that current trends in the population as a whole were obscure, though a marked increase had taken place in south-east Scotland and Northumberland. There are too few past counts available for any accurate assessment of population trends, a surprising state of affairs for a large and conspicuous bird nesting in relatively few colonies around the coast, especially in view of the attention it has received from fishermen and river boards. The situation is further confused by the fact that Cormorants may shift their nest sites from year to year (Balfour *et al.* 1967; Darling 1940); usually this is only from one part of the colony to another or to an adjacent island, but the possibility of movement over longer distances must be borne in mind when only scattered counts are available.

There is, however, a full set of data for the Cormorants in the Firth of Forth. They were first recorded nesting there as recently as 1957 when there were five pairs on The Lamb, and by 1968 this colony had increased to 240 pairs; nearby Craigleith had also been occupied in some of the intervening years (Smith 1969). Only 150 nests were counted on The Lamb in 1969, probably due to disturbance earlier in the season by yachtsmen, but there were 220 in 1970. This increase can possibly be linked

Plate 3

A   Great Black-backed Gull

B   Lesser Black-backed Gull

C   Herring Gull (*adult and,* right, *immature*)

D   Black-headed Gull (*summer and,* below, *winter*)

E   Kittiwake (*adult summer and,* below, *immature*)

F   Common Gull (*adult summer and,* below, *immature*)

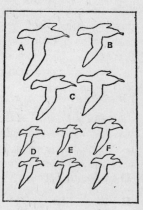

with the fortunes of the long-established colony in the Farne Islands (Northumberland), 50 miles down the coast, where numbers increased from 40–50 pairs in 1885 to 200–300 in 1949 (Watt 1951) and to 300 by 1957 (*Farne Islands Reports*). A decrease occurred when the Firth of Forth colony became established, numbers dropping to 130 pairs in 1962, though about 200 pairs have nested in most years since then (*Farne Islands Reports*) and there were 214 in 1969. Taking the Forth–Farnes populations together, the increase has been about 4% per annum since 1905, compared with about 11% for the Shag (Potts 1969).

In Yorkshire before the 1940s, persecution had driven Cormorants away from some of their old breeding haunts, though they eventually returned to Huntcliff where 35 pairs nested in 1949. Other colonies included Boulby with 30–40 pairs in 1948 and 1952, Ravenscar with 24 pairs in 1949 and Gristhorpe with 24 in 1946 (Chislett 1952). In 1969 there were 18 pairs at Huntcliff, 31 at Ravenscar and 14 at Gristhorpe. Counts made by Clarke and Rodd (1906) in the Isles of Scilly totalled about 100 pairs; in 1945 about 60 pairs nested there (Ryves and Quick 1946), in the mid-1960s 100 pairs (Penhallurick 1969) but in 1969 only 50 pairs, so that despite persecution by fishermen there seems to have been little change. Off Pembrokeshire the largest colony, on St Margarets Island, expanded from 88 pairs in 1949 (Fursdon 1950) to 108 in 1962 (Sutcliffe 1963) and to 262 in 1969. There are few counts from the smaller colonies in that area, however, and population trends there are generally unknown.

Information on the location and past status of Cormorant colonies in Ireland is also limited. On Lambay (Co. Dublin) 300 pairs were noted breeding by Kennedy *et al.* (1954); Ruttledge (1966) recorded a decrease to 100 pairs but there were 320 pairs in 1970. Cormorants once nested on Great Saltee (Co. Wexford) where there were 12 pairs in 1943, but by 1949 all had moved to Little Saltee where 200 pairs nested in that year (Kennedy *et al.* 1954) and 300 in 1969.

Plate 4

A Sandwich Tern

B Common Tern

C Arctic Tern (*adult and*, left, *immature*)

D Roseate Tern

E Little Tern

SHAG *Phalacrocorax aristotelis*

Identification

The Shag is considerably smaller and more slender than the Cormorant, though the two may be confused at a distance. Seen at close range adult Shags have dark glossy green plumage which, depending on distance and light conditions, may look black, whereas Cormorants are brown-black. The gape and mouth parts of adult Shags are bright chrome-yellow; the slender, hooked bill is black, as are the legs and feet. For a short period early in the breeding season, both sexes sport a handsome recurved crest. Immatures on leaving the nest are brown-buff, somewhat paler below, but by the end of their first year this has been replaced by a dark brown plumage. They attain full adult plumage towards the end of their second year, though two-year-old birds commonly breed before it is complete. The Shag is one of the more silent seabirds, the male uttering an 'ark ark ark ark' call at and when approaching the nest site and the female making only hissing and clicking noises during display.

Food and feeding habits

Several studies of the food of the Shag have been carried out in Great Britain and Ireland, mostly to investigate whether or not it takes fish of economic importance. In Cornwall Steven (1933) found that sand-eels were an important element in the diet, 69 out of 188 stomachs examined containing nothing but the remains of these fish. Sprats were also taken, particularly in winter, but the proportion of flatfish and other species of economic value was negligible. In the Firth of Clyde Lumsden and Haddow (1946) found both sand-eels and Sprats prominent in the diet, as well as young Saithe and Pollack. Although most of these fish were not then of economic importance, the current shortage of more desirable food fish and the recent development of industrial fisheries render them increasingly valuable to man (Rae 1969). In Loch Ewe (west Ross) only 32% of the fish taken from the stomachs of 62 Shags were considered to be of economic value, and half of these were Herrings; Mills (1969a) concluded that the birds did not endanger Plaice stocks or fisheries in the loch. On the east coast of Scotland Rae (1969) found that predation on young Salmon was low; in estuaries most Shags ate gadoids and shore fish rather than flatfish, while in open water sand-eels were the main prey. Again, in the Farne Islands area of Northumberland, 80% of the fish taken during the breeding season were sand-eels (Pearson 1968).

Breeding

Shags may breed in large colonies, in small, scattered groups or singly. Nest sites include exposed ledges on sea stacks or high in the roofs of caverns, and more sheltered crevices on the walls of narrow gullies or among boulders on cliff slopes. On Lundy (Devon) Snow (1960) found that in exposed positions the main requirement was that the nest should be clear of heavy spray which might chill unattended chicks. Although most Shags on the Farne Islands nest in the open there is a good deal of competition among the males for the best protected sites. Older birds generally hold these, while those breeding for the first or second time often have their nests washed away (G. R. Potts *in litt.*). Nest material is collected from near the site by the male and consists of plants such as sea beet, bracken and seaweeds; the heavier stalks are used for the base and finer matter for the lining. Although the male may begin gathering material before he has a mate, most activity follows mating and may actually be stimulated by it, the female building his offerings into the nest. Fresh items are added throughout the incubation and fledging periods, while on occasions nests may be rebuilt after the young have departed, usually by another pair (Snow 1960, 1963).

The start of the breeding season is variable. Witherby *et al.* (1940–41) attributed this to the effect of weather at the exposed nest sites; their earliest date for egg-laying was 24th February. Snow (1960) wrote that on Lundy most clutches were completed within three to four weeks, the first eggs having been laid in early April, and she suggested that the breeding season was timed for the chicks to be in the nest at the period of greatest availability of sand-eels in May and June. On Llanddwyn Island (Anglesey) winter breeding has been recorded, eggs having been laid as early as 20th November (Potts 1967; Tong 1967). Early breeding may also occur on the Caernarvonshire coast where fledged young have been observed in May and material has been taken from the used nests of Shags by other species; at one site there a Fulmar occupied the nest after the young Shags had left (E. I. S. Rees pers. comm.).

The eggs are chalky white and the normal clutch is three, though up to six have been recorded, probably involving more than one female. They are incubated by both parents who position them on top of their broad webbed feet which are very warm to the touch. On arriving at the nest the incubating bird slowly shuffles its feet beneath the eggs. The feet are withdrawn just as slowly when it leaves, though if it is suddenly disturbed the eggs may be knocked aside. Incubation lasts from 30 to 35 days. Newly hatched chicks are dark grey, blind and naked, and are fed by both parents by regurgitation. Observations on the Farne Islands suggest that the maximum feeding range during the breeding season is about twelve miles (Pearson 1968). The young fledge when 48 to 58 days old (53 days on average), after which they frequently gather in groups on low rocks near the nest sites, being fed by their parents for a further month and occasionally longer (Snow 1960); Potts (1969) estimated that 55 ± 1 days are spent in the nest, but the young are not independent until 76 days.

Movements

Young Shags disperse in their first winter through British waters; subsequently they tend to return to their natal areas and become much more sedentary. Juveniles from the Farne Islands move south as far as the Straits of Dover, and sometimes west at least to Hampshire; there have also been a few recoveries in northern France, Belgium, the Netherlands, West Germany and Norway (Coulson 1961). Shags ringed on Canna (west Inverness) disperse through the Hebrides and one has been recovered in Co. Down (Evans and Flower 1967), while those from Lundy winter in Devon, Cornwall and north-west France (Snow 1960). Movements further south in France are unusual, though there is a remarkable record of a bird ringed as a nestling on Grassholm (Pembrokeshire) being recovered in Valencia, Spain, when three years old (Spencer 1967). Potts (1969) showed that the dispersive movements of Shags are irregular; in adverse weather, when disturbed seas affect feeding, eruptive movements or 'wrecks' may occur, some birds wandering far inland.

World distribution

The Shag is mainly a European breeding species with outposts on the coasts of Morocco, Tunisia, Cyprus and Turkey. It nests in Iceland, the Faeroes, Britain, Ireland and the Channel Islands, and on the mainland of Europe south from the Kola Peninsula to Stavanger, Norway, with isolated groups in Brittany and north-west Iberia. In the Mediterranean another race (*P. a. desmarestii*) breeds on islands east from the Balearics and on the coasts of the Adriatic, Turkey and North Africa and in the

Seabird colony near Marwick Head, Orkney.

ABOVE: Fulmars greeting. BELOW: nesting Cormorants

Black Sea from the Dnieper estuary to the Crimea (Vaurie 1965; Voous 1960).

Census methods

Where Shags nest in open sites, counts can be made without difficulty. Observations on the Farne Islands showed that the number of nests reaches a maximum during late May and June (Potts 1969). Even late in the season, when the adults and young idle in the vicinity, the bulky nests with their liberal guano surrounds are usually easily visible. Cave nests can often be counted from a boat, or estimates made from the number of adults flying to and fro or standing nearby. At boulder slope colonies the latter method may have to be used if searching for nests is impractical or likely to cause excessive disturbance. Potts (1971) provided useful criteria for distinguishing adults from sub-adults.

Status in Britain and Ireland in 1969–70 and past history

The Shag, with about 31,600 pairs nesting in 1969–70 in Britain and Ireland, was nearly four times more numerous than the Cormorant. The great majority, about 25,000 pairs, nest in Scotland, with particularly high numbers and some large colonies in Shetland, Orkney and the north-west from Argyll to the Outer Hebrides (Appendix Table 8; Map 10). Although numbers on the east coast of Scotland are smaller the Shag is still widely distributed there, in contrast to the Cormorant which occurs there only in the Firth of Forth and the extreme north-east. In England the Shag is restricted to Northumberland, Yorkshire, the Isle of Man and the south-west, with most in Scilly, Cornwall and the Isle of Man. In Wales, its overall distribution is much the same as the Cormorant with most in Anglesey, Caernarvonshire and Pembrokeshire and few elsewhere. In Ireland Shags are found breeding on all rocky coasts with most in Co. Donegal. They are more widely distributed and more numerous in the Channel Islands than the Cormorant. There has been no previous full survey of the Shag in Britain and Ireland, but trends in the population can be seen in many areas except in Ireland and north and north-west Scotland where former data are inadequate.

A recent decline seems to have taken place in the northern Inner Hebrides (west Inverness) where earlier counts were summarised by Evans and Flower (1967). On Rhum where a total of 75 pairs nested in 1969 there had been several colonies each with up to 100 pairs and other smaller ones during the 1950s. On nearby Eigg there were several hundred pairs in 1958 but only ten in 1969. On Muck five pairs nested in 1934 and 70 by 1963, but only 46 in 1969. Canna seems to have been the local strong-hold, with large colonies containing hundreds of pairs in the 1960s. In recent years the number has apparently fluctuated wildly with 1,060 reported in 1969, only 218 in 1970, but 1,348 in 1971. In the Firth of Clyde there was a decline from 750 pairs in 1958 to 425 in 1969. At one of the most important colonies there, on Sanda and Glunimore 475 pairs nested in 1958 but they were reduced by the systematic depredations of fishermen to 120 pairs in 1969 (Gibson 1969).

On the east coast of Scotland Shags did not nest again in Banffshire until 1947, and in Aberdeenshire not until 1950 (Watson 1954). In 1969 50 pairs nested in Banffshire and 250 in Aberdeenshire. There have been considerable increases in the Firth of Forth, especially on the Isle of May (Fife) (Table 3).

TABLE 3. *Numbers of pairs of Shags nesting on the Farne Islands (Northumberland) and on the Isle of May (Fife)*

Data up to and including 1965 from Parslow (1967)

Year	Farne Islands	Isle of May	Year	Farne Islands	Isle of May
1918	—	1	1950	59	30
1924	—	2	1953	108	140
1931	1	?	1957	164	301
1936	7	10	1961	205	550
1939	15	?	1965	362	787
1946	41	12	1969	161	880

Elsewhere here there were two pairs on The Lamb (East Lothian) in 1955, 128 in 1965 (Smith 1966), 158 in 1969 and 194 in 1970. At Craigleith (East Lothian) one colony increased from three pairs in 1961 to 38 pairs in 1965 (Smith 1966), while the total number on the island rose from 62 pairs in 1963 to between 80 and 100 in 1969. Potts (1969) noted that the Shag population of the Forth–Farnes area had grown steadily at a rate of about 11% per annum since 1905, from ten pairs to 1,900 pairs. There was, however, a sharp decrease between 1965 and 1969 on the Farne Islands (Table 3) due to an outbreak of paralytic shellfish poisoning in May 1968 (Coulson et al. 1968). Within a week 90% of the nests were deserted and some 80% of the breeding population had died, numbers being reduced to the 1950 level of about 60 pairs. By 1969 numbers had risen to 161 pairs, about the level of 1957. Further south on the east coast, Shags returned to nest on the chalk cliffs of Bempton (Yorkshire) in 1952, after being absent since the early part of the 19th century (Bunce and Fenton 1956), and in 1969 20 pairs nested there. On Lundy numbers have fluctuated considerably over the years: 12 pairs in 1922, 110 in 1939,

37 in 1950, 132 in 1956, 90 in 1963, 53 in 1965 and 58 in 1969 (Lloyd 1925, *Lundy Bird Reports*, Moore 1969, Perry 1940, Snow 1960). In south Devon 15 pairs nested at Wembury in 1960 (Moore 1969) but only three in 1969, while 25 breeding pairs at Bolt Tail and 11 at Start Point in 1967 were reduced to three and eight pairs respectively in 1969.

Elsewhere in western Britain there is little past information on Shag numbers. In Cornwall the species has generally increased, though no change has been observed in the Isles of Scilly (Penhallurick 1969). Brun (1960) recorded a decline on the Calf of Man, but Slinn (1964) found no evidence for any general change throughout the Isle of Man. The first breeding record of Shags on Bardsey Island (Caernarvonshire) dates from 1930 and 25 pairs were present in 1952 (Norris 1953); since then numbers have altered little with 28 pairs in 1969. In Northern Ireland Deane (1954) said the Shag was increasing, and a marked increase in the colony at Howth Head, Dublin has occurred recently (Parslow 1967).

To sum up, the numbers of Shags appear to have increased in almost all areas for which information is available, except for south Devon, the Clyde area and the northern Inner Hebrides. This increase has been especially marked on the east coasts of Scotland and England. Reasons for this are still disputed. Parslow (1967) suggested that a decline in human persecution may have contributed to these increases, but argued that this scarcely explained either the timing or the rapidity of the increases. He suggested that changes in abundance or distribution in the species of fish on which they feed, perhaps connected with environmental or climatic changes, provided a more plausible explanation, although direct evidence in support of this was lacking. Potts (1969) argued strongly against the food hypothesis. He pointed out that it was extremely unlikely that the vestigial Shag population scattered along eastern Britain in the latter half of the 19th century could have been held down by a food shortage of a density-governing nature. He found no clear evidence of long-term changes in the fish on which the Shag preys. Moreover, in his view, the food hypothesis failed to account for the decline in numbers of many marine species of birds during the 18th and 19th centuries, although there was much evidence of excessive human exploitation then. He found the protection hypothesis attractive because the increase of the Gannet, Kittiwake, Great Skua and Eider, as well as the Shag, began as soon as protection was afforded, mainly from the period 1880–90.

GREAT SKUA *Stercorarius skua*

Identification

The Great Skua is heavily built, about the size and bulk of a Herring Gull but with a shorter tail. Its plumage is dark brown, slightly paler beneath, while in flight a white patch at the base of the primaries is conspicuous on the bird's broad, rounded wings. The bill, which is thicker and shorter than the Herring Gull's, is dark brown; the legs are blackish. The voice of the Great Skua is a screaming 'skerr' or a gruff 'uk uk uk'.

Food and feeding habits

This species is less piratical than the smaller skuas. It often follows ships' especially those of the northern trawling fleets, to feed on garbage, offal and waste fish thrown overboard, though it can catch surface-dwelling fish itself. It vigorously harries birds as large as Gannets for the food they are carrying, and during these encounters its flight becomes quite aerobatic in contrast to the normal purposeful style. At seabird colonies Great Skuas take the eggs, young and adults of other species; they have been known to attack and kill fully grown birds larger than themselves, such as Grey Heron, Shelduck *Tadorna tadorna* and Great Black-backed Gull, while Venables and Venables (1955) recorded a Great Skua driving away two Whooper Swans *Cygnus cygnus* from a Shetland loch. From observations on Foula (Shetland), Jackson (1966) described three methods of attack, the most frequent being a determined aerial chase during which the skua strikes its victim with the feet, breast or wings in an effort to force it down. So violent are these attacks that the pursuer may itself be injured whereupon other skuas will intervene, cannibalism often being the result.

Great Skuas take Puffins by waiting by the entrances to their burrows for unsuspecting birds to emerge; a skua will also stoop low over a gathering of Puffins on their nesting slope, causing them to take flight when it will plunge like a hawk and capture a victim in its beak. At Hermaness, Unst (Shetland), Lockie (1952) found that during July and August young Kittiwakes were the main food brought to the nest, while both adults and young of this species made up most of the skuas' diet at a colony in the Faeroes (Bayes *et al.* 1964). The same situation has been noted on Fair Isle (Shetland) where young Oystercatchers *Haematopus ostralegus* are also taken in some numbers (P. E. Davis *in litt*). Burton (1970) considered that in the Antarctic Great Skuas were more opportunist feeders at sea, and that predation at seabird colonies was often overrated. This could also apply to colonies in the northern hemisphere where such predation has so often been noted because of its violent and conspicuous nature.

Breeding

Great Skuas nest on open moorland, usually in the damper areas and sometimes in loose colonies. They return to their breeding areas during late March and early April. In addition a number of non-breeding individuals, probably immatures, habitually gather in 'club' areas in the colonies, where breeding displays and even the hollowing of nest scrapes may be observed. A frequent display is wing-raising, in which the white primary patches become very noticeable; this is even performed in flight when the birds soar rather like harriers. Great Skuas are very aggressive when establishing their territories and ruthlessly drive away intruding skuas, the chases sometimes continuing for considerable distances. Stalking about their territories in a searching manner, they make scrapes at favoured spots to which the male attracts his mate with a soft squeaking call; eventually the pair choose one of these as their nest site (Perdeck 1960).

The normal clutch is of two eggs, greyish-buff to olive-brown in colour and usually with darker speckles and blotches; they are laid during May, mostly towards the end of the month, or in early June. Incubation lasts for 28 to 30 days, and newly hatched chicks are covered in light brown (almost sandy) down, somewhat paler beneath. They fledge at six to seven weeks, though their first flights are restricted by their parents who repeatedly force them to the ground, probably to prevent them from straying into neighbouring territories where they might be killed (Jackson 1966).

Movements

Great Skuas leave their colonies during August and begin to disperse out to sea and generally southwards: most early autumn ringing recoveries are from the North Sea and English Channel coasts, with a few from the west coast and from Ireland. Later in the autumn recoveries are mainly from the Bay of Biscay and Iberia. The wintering area is imperfectly known but seems to be largely restricted to the North Atlantic, with some birds penetrating the western Mediterranean (Thomson 1966). It is not known how far south in the Atlantic they wander, however, partly due to possible confusion with non-breeding birds of the Antarctic population (see below). Some intermingling is likely, since a Great Skua ringed on Foula has been recovered in Guyana at 6°30′N, while an Antarctic Great Skua from Deception Island, South Shetlands, has been found in the French West Indies at 15°50′N (Hudson 1968). Birds ringed on Foula have also been recorded in the Cape Verde Islands, and there is one re-covery south of the equator, at Paracuru, Brazil. Great Skuas have occa-sionally been recovered well inland in Europe, including France, Germany, Austria, Poland and the USSR as far east as Smolensk (34°14′E), probably due to unfavourable weather conditions after they left their breeding colonies. Thomson (1966) reported a tendency for two-year-old birds to wander far to the north during the summer, even to the west coast of Greenland where one has been recovered at 69°10′N.

World distribution

The Great Skua is the only seabird breeding both in the North Atlantic and in the polar regions of the southern hemisphere, though possibly the most southerly birds should be treated as a separate species *S. maccormicki*. It nests along the shores of Antarctica (wandering individuals having been noted well inland, even at 87°20′S by Captain Scott as he approached the South Pole in January 1912), and on many sub-Antarctic islands, extending north to about 37°S on the Chilean coast, to Tristan da Cunha in the South Atlantic and the Chatham Islands off New Zealand. In the northern hemisphere the Great Skua nests only in Iceland, the Faeroes and the very north of Scotland (Vaurie 1965, Voous 1960). A pair was reported breeding on Bear Island in 1970, the first breeding record north of the Arctic Circle (Williams 1972).

Census methods

Although observations can be made from a distance, the best way to count nesting Great Skuas is while walking slowly through the colony. Breeding pairs generally react violently to such intrusions into their territories by repeatedly diving and attacking at low level, sometimes even striking out with trailing feet. Once located, territories can be searched for eggs or chicks, the intensity of the mobbing often increasing as these are ap-proached. Those non-breeding birds which hold territories (and even, in some cases, make nest scrapes) usually do so at the edge of the breeding colony or away from it, and their reactions are much less intense (Dott 1967).

Status in Britain and Ireland in 1969–70 and past history

The Great Skua is restricted to the north of Scotland where in 1969–70 about 3,170 pairs nested. Although its population is about three times as large as that of the Arctic Skua it has a much more limited range. Its stronghold is Shetland, and in particular the island of Foula which holds 56% of the British population. Elsewhere numbers are small although Orkney was colonised as long ago as 1915 and Lewis by 1945, while more recently two other islands in the Outer Hebrides and four sites in Sutherland have been occupied (Appendix Table 10; Map 11).

There had been no previous full survey of the Great Skua in Scotland but, because of its limited distribution and small numbers, its history there is quite well documented. The first known breeding record dates from 1774 when there were six pairs on Foula and the total population, all in Shetland, was about ten pairs (Low 1879). An increase in the early 19th century was soon checked by persecution. In the 1880s small numbers nested only on Unst, Foula, Yell and the very north mainland of Shetland; their existence on the first two islands seems to have depended on the protection initiated by Dr L. Edmondston on Unst in 1831 and by the laird John Scott on Foula during the 1870s (Clarke 1892). Since those early precarious years the Great Skua has greatly increased in Shetland and spread to many other islands with 22 occupied in 1969–70, on four of which there had been no previous records (Appendix Table 9).

Great Skuas first nested in Orkney in 1915 when two pairs bred on the high moorlands of Hoy (Jourdain 1918, 1919); this has remained the most important colony in Orkney with about 20 pairs in 1941 (Lack 1942–3), 60 in 1961 (Balfour 1968) and 72 in 1969. An increase elsewhere in Orkney has been more recent, with Papa Westray first occupied about 1950 (Tewnion 1958), Rousay in 1955, Eynhallow in 1956 and Westray in 1958 (Balfour 1968). Although none nested on Eynhallow in 1969–70, there were small colonies each holding up to six pairs on some of the other islands, while six further sites with single pairs were also reported.

In the Outer Hebrides a few pairs of Great Skuas were discovered nesting in Lewis in 1945 (Campbell 1959; Cunningham 1959), and there were ten pairs at two sites there in 1969. Great Skuas first bred at St Kilda in 1963 (Pollock 1963), and by 1969 six pairs were nesting and three others prospecting. North Rona was colonised in 1965 when two pairs were noted (Slater 1965a), and there were still two there in 1969. In west Sutherland Great Skuas nested successfully on Handa in 1964 (Waterston 1965) and there were three or four pairs there in 1970. On the north coast a pair nested on Eilean Roan, off the Kyle of Tongue, in 1969 and in 1970 on the Point of Stoer. Finally Dunnet Head (Caithness) was colonised in 1949 when a single pair bred: two pairs were recorded in 1952 (Pennie 1953b) and one in 1955 (Sage and Pennie 1956), but they have been discouraged by the activities of peat diggers and lighthouse keepers and there are no recent breeding records.

The growth in the Great Skua population in Northern Scotland has taken place concurrently with a decrease in Iceland which Gudmundsson (1954) attributed to a decline in the fishing industry off the south-east coast. He estimated the North Atlantic population to number 7,200 pairs in 1954, of which 6,000 were in Iceland where the Breidamerkursandur colony alone contained 1,500 pairs, but Dickens (1964) noted only 850 successful pairs there in 1952 and less than half this in 1963. In the Faeroes the Great Skua increased from four pairs in 1897 to 71 in 1930, 200 in 1946 and 530 in 1961 (Bayes *et al.* 1964), but Williamson (1970) listed three colonies with a total population of 475 pairs and mentioned only small, scattered groups on three other islands, so that the increase there may have slowed down in recent years.

ARCTIC SKUA *Stercorarius parasiticus*

Identification

The Arctic Skua is smaller and more slender than the Great Skua, with narrower, pointed wings and the characteristic white patch on the primaries common to all members of the family. The two central tail-feathers are elongated to fine points (though these are sometimes broken off, particularly by the end of the breeding season). The Arctic Skua is dimorphic. Those of the pale form have dark sandy-brown upperparts, the crown usually darker, and a pale collar and underparts, with a darker breast-band in some individuals. Many intergradations exist between this and the dark phase which is entirely dark brown. Juvenile light-phase birds have extensive golden-buff tips to their feathers, while dark-phase juveniles have few such markings.

In the eastern North Atlantic the smallest proportion (5% or less) of light-phase birds is found in southern Norway and the Baltic, while in Scotland it ranges from 21% on Fair Isle (Shetland) to 50% in the Outer Hebrides. The proportion of pale birds tends to increase farther north: 50–55% in north Norway, 90% in Jan Mayen and 100% in east Greenland (Southern 1943). Paler coloration appears to be associated with late hatching and it has been suggested that this may be favoured in inland and northern parts of the range where the main food is small mammals, which usually become plentiful only later in the summer (Berry and Davis 1970).

Food and feeding habits

During the breeding season in Britain and other temperate maritime areas, Arctic Skuas feed largely by harrying other seabirds, in particular terns and Kittiwakes, until they disgorge and drop fish which the skuas then skilfully snatch in mid-air. These attacks are pressed home with vigorous determination, the skuas striking out with their feet and wings, a method they also use on occasions to strike small birds to the ground where they are killed. Eggs and chicks of seabirds are taken in some numbers, while dead fish and general garbage are also eaten. In tundra areas, small mammals (particularly Lemmings), small birds, freshwater fish, insects, worms and berries are taken, and on Fair Isle they eat considerable quantities of Crowberries (Peter Davis *in litt.*).

Breeding

This species usually nests in loose colonies, which in Britain are situated on open moorland: they are reoccupied in April and early May. Most birds breed for the first time when four or five years of age, though some start at only three; the same mate is often retained for a number of seasons (Berry and Davis 1970). Non-breeding birds also frequent the colonies, usually arriving after and leaving before the nesting pairs. The eggs, normally two, are laid two days apart during May or early June and take, on average, 26 days to hatch, incubation commencing with the first egg. Newly-hatched chicks are covered in sooty-brown down and leave the nest to hide in the vicinity when only a day or two old. They fledge after four to five weeks.

Arctic Skuas are most demonstrative at their colonies. Off-duty and non-breeding birds make wild flights, chasing each other with much loud calling and indulging in spectacular tumbling falls in mid-air. Intruders, whether bird or animal (including human beings), are repeatedly mobbed if they approach close to the nest, the attacking birds sweeping down to within a few inches of the head and often striking out with their feet. In an effort to lure intruders away from eggs or chicks, the adults perform elaborate distraction displays, falling and fluttering about on the ground apparently in severe distress.

Movements

The birds move south from their colonies during August and September, often accompanying migrant flocks of terns down the coasts of Great Britain and Ireland where they can best be observed in attendance on tern flocks at the mouths of estuaries and sometimes flying along the coast or passing prominent headlands. There are few distant ringing recoveries, but observations of the birds suggest that part at least of their migration is rather leisurely, though they apparently winter mainly between 30°–50°S, and records from the tropics in midwinter may result from confusion with Pomarine Skuas *S. pomarinus* wintering there during the season when the birds are moulting. Outside Europe, British-ringed birds have been recovered in Spanish West Africa, Brazil, Angola and Greenland. The last record suggests that immature birds may also wander far north in the breeding season.

World distribution

The Arctic Skua has a Holarctic breeding distribution. In North America it extends from the Aleutian chain and western Alaska along the coast and archipelagos of northern Canada east to Hudson Bay and north Labrador and south to the Great Slave and Landing Lakes. In Greenland Arctic Skuas breed in three separate areas, two on the west coast and one on the east. In Europe they nest in Iceland, the Faeroes, Scotland, Sweden, Finland, Bear Island and Spitsbergen, and on the Norwegian and Russian coasts to the Kara Sea, thence east along the coast and islands of Siberia as far as Kamchatka and the Sea of Okhotsk (Vaurie 1965; Voous 1960).

Census methods

Although the method employed for the Great Skua (see pages 102–3) can also be applied to the present species, the birds do not always mob an intruder close to their nest but move off to a distance, sometimes settling well away from their territory. Observations must then be made from a distance to locate the approximate position of the nest which can later be pin-pointed by searching. Care must always be taken not to include non-breeding birds which often resort to 'club' areas, but pairs frequently occupy territories for a season before starting to breed.

Status in Britain and Ireland in 1969–70 and past history

The Arctic Skua, with a population of about 1,090 pairs in 1969–70, is the least numerous seabird regularly breeding in Britain and Ireland. It is restricted to Scotland, where, like the Great Skua which has a population approximately three times as large, its headquarters are in Shetland, though unlike that species it nests as far south as the Inner Hebrides and on the mainland in Caithness (Appendix Table 10; Map 12).

There has been no previous complete survey of the Arctic Skua in Scotland, which in view of its small population and restricted distribution is surprising. Decreases have certainly taken place on the mainland of Scotland and in the Outer Hebrides, and possibly in the Inner Hebrides. In Orkney, although the main colony on Hoy has shown a recent decrease, the bird has generally extended its range during the last 30 years. In Shetland, still its stronghold, past information is incomplete but there is some suggestion of an increase.

In Shetland Venables and Venables (1955) reported a decrease in the numbers of those Arctic Skuas nesting in the vicinity of Great Skua colonies, specifically mentioning those on Foula, Hermaness and Noss: unfortunately, although Mainland and 18 smaller islands were used for nesting between 1945 and 1953, they provided no figures for those colonies. It is true that Great Skuas take Arctic Skua chicks (Lockie 1952; Pennie 1948) and it has been suggested that this is a possible reason for the decline of the latter in some areas. Great Skuas also arrive earlier at the breeding grounds and establish their territories in advance of the smaller species, so where they are on the increase the areas suitable for Arctic Skuas become less each year. On Foula 60 pairs nested in 1890 (Barrington 1890), 250 individuals were present in 1948 (Pennie 1948); from 1960 to 1963 130 pairs nested (Jackson 1966) and in 1969 there were 100 pairs. On Fair Isle numbers remained low until 1948; then from 15 pairs in 1949 (Davis 1965) they jumped to 180 pairs in 1969. The colony on Noss seems to have remained fairly stable: there were between 40 and 50 pairs in 1922, 60 in 1930, 37 in 1947 (Baxter and Rintoul 1953) and 40 in 1969.

The main Arctic Skua islands in Orkney are Hoy, which Buckley and Harvie-Brown (1891) considered to be their only breeding site; Papa Westray, where they first nested in 1924 or 1925 (Baxter and Rintoul 1953), and Westray. In 1941 about 80 pairs were distributed between these three islands (Lack 1942–3) while 20 years later the population numbered about 190 pairs, Hoy still being the major site, while a further eight islands besides Papa Westray and Westray then had small numbers (Balfour 1968, Bannerman 1963). By 1969–70 some 230 were nesting in Orkney, most colonies had increased since 1961 and a further eight islands, North Ronaldsay, Shapinsay, Holm of Scockness, Egilsay, Auskerry, Flotta, Cava and Fara now had single pairs, but the colonies on Hoy had decreased almost to their 1941 level:

TABLE 4. *Numbers of pairs of Arctic Skuas nesting in Orkney in 1941, 1961 and 1969–70.*

	1941	1961	1969/70
Papa Westray	18	18+	25
Westray	1	'a few'	67
Eday	—	6–8	11
Sanday	—	up to 10	9
Stronsay	—	1–2	7
Rousay	—	15–20	11
Gairsay	—	2–3	3–4
Wyre	—	2–3	3–4
Eynhallow	—	1	10
Hoy	60+	100–150	68
Mainland	—	2–3	5
Other islands	—	—	8

In the Outer Hebrides Arctic Skuas have nested for many years. A century ago Gray (1871) mentioned colonies on Lewis, North Uist, Benbecula, South Uist, Wiay and Stuala, with 'nurseries' of 40 to 50 pairs at several locations. In 1969 only 40 pairs nested, all on the main islands of Lewis, North Uist and South Uist with the majority on Lewis. Arctic Skuas have long been known in the Inner Hebrides too, as in 1772 Pennant found them nesting on Jura and Rhum; none remains on Rhum, though birds are sometimes seen in the vicinity still, and the main colonies are now on Jura, with 20 pairs in 1970, and Coll, where breeding was first reported in 1878 (Baxter and Rintoul 1953), with six pairs in 1970. The birds reported from Islay and Tiree in the past have probably joined these colonies on adjacent islands. An individual which probably came from Jura was also seen on Colonsay in 1969. In the far north-west, Arctic Skuas first nested on Handa, just off the west coast of Sutherland, in 1968, and in 1970 there were one or two pairs.

On the mainland of Scotland Arctic Skuas have nested in Sutherland, Caithness and West Inverness in the past (Baxter and Rintoul 1953). Only Caithness is still occupied; there the birds nest in scattered localities, some well inland. In 1952 21 pairs were known in four areas, indicating a decrease during the past 100 years – in 1868 it was described as a well-known and abundant species breeding in considerable numbers. Some of this decrease in Caithness has been attributed to persecution by game-keepers, though this has lessened in more recent times. One colony near the Sutherland border that was described as large at the beginning of the century contained only a single pair definitely nesting in 1952 (Pennie 1953a). About 20 pairs bred in the county in 1969, whilst in 1972 the population was probably about 30 pairs (Dr J. T. R. Sharrock *in litt.*).

BLACK-HEADED GULL   *Larus ridibundus*

Identification

The Black-headed Gull is the smallest of our resident gulls and cannot be confused with any other species regularly nesting in Britain and Ireland. The white leading edge to the wings is always characteristic, while during the breeding season adults have a chocolate-brown head, with a white orbital ring round the dark eye, and distinctive red bill and legs. From late July until the early spring of the following year the head is white with a brown smudge behind the eye, although a few individuals retain parts of their brown hood all winter. Immatures have mottled brown upperparts and flesh-coloured bill and legs. Black-headed Gulls are noisy birds, particularly at their colonies where the main cry is a harsh, grating 'kwarr'.

Food and feeding habits

Although invertebrates form a substantial part of their diet, Black-headed Gulls, like most other gulls, seek a wide range of foods. Feeding activities in rural areas may be beneficial to agriculture since the birds take large numbers of wireworms, leatherjackets and the like. Vernon (1970) stated that lowland grassland areas are particularly favoured, 75% of the flocks reported during his inquiry into their feeding habitats being on land below 200 feet and 90% on land below 300 feet. Other regular feeding habitats are stubble fields and freshly ploughed land, no farming operation which disturbs the soil being without its attendant gull flock. The birds often visit muddy estuaries to seek marine invertebrates and scavenge along the strand line. Observations in a part of Aberdeenshire showed that those feeding inland were mostly within four miles of an estuary and their numbers there depended on the state of the tide, being highest when conditions in the estuary were unsuitable (D. E. B. Lloyd *in litt.*). Feeding in urban areas is a growing habit. In London the Black-headed Gull was a rare visitor prior to the 1890s (Stubbs 1917); 165,000 roosted in the London area in December 1963, and 192,000 did so in December 1968 (Sage 1970). During the daytime some visit rural areas but many remain within the urban zone where feeding places include rubbish dumps, rivers, canals, park lakes, playing fields, city squares and gardens.

Klepto-parasitism is practised on Lapwings *Vanellus vanellus* and Golden Plovers *Pluvialis apricaria*, the gulls watching them and giving chase as soon as they discover food.

Breeding

Black-headed Gulls nest in colonies sometimes of considerable size in freshwater and salt marshes, hill lochs, moorland, sand dunes, shingle banks, coastal lagoons, settling ponds at sugar beet factories, sewage farms and gravel pits. Tree-nesting has been noted at three sites in Scotland (Baxter and Rintoul 1953), and in East Anglia some 350 pairs nested in a flooded spruce plantation in 1947 (Vine and Sergeant 1948). These examples show how the Black-headed Gull can quickly adapt to conditions suitable for breeding, even for a single season. In view of the rapid changes in land use – drainage, building, modernisation of sewage farms – which often occur in breeding areas, causing colonies to decrease in size or move away, this adaptability is a valuable asset. The building of reservoirs and sugar beet factories, the flooding of gravel and clay pits and the establishment of nature reserves all provide suitable nesting sites which the gulls are quick to exploit. There is thus a considerable movement of colonies: of the 159 reported in England and Wales in 1938 only 63 (40%) were still in existence in 1958, while a further 155 sites were used at least once during 1939–58 (Gribble 1962).

Black-headed Gulls return to their colonies in March and early April. Pair formation takes place there or close by on what Tinbergen and Moynihan (1952) termed 'pre-territories'. These are eventually abandoned as the birds begin nest building. During territorial encounters the males show a forward display posture, leaning forward to emphasise the brown hood. The same display is also used by prospective partners, when it concludes with head-flagging in which the neck is stretched upwards and the head turned so that the brown hood tends to be hidden, only the white neck being visible in an appeasing posture.

The nests, which are often close together, can be quite bulky structures of locally gathered vegetation, especially in damp sites. In marshes they are commonly placed in plants to raise them above the water level, while Bochenski (1962) noted that floating nests were considerably larger than those on firm ground and were usually among vegetation which prevented them from drifting about. Three eggs is the normal clutch and both parents take part in the incubation which lasts 23 to 24 days (Goodbody 1955). The chicks fledge at five to six weeks of age (Witherby *et al.* 1940–41).

Movements

Once able to fly, the young seem to disperse quickly, generally in a southerly direction with some reaching the Continent. After their first winter they become much more sedentary, returning to their natal colony or close to it (Radford 1962). Ringing has shown that Black-headed Gulls from Iceland, Scandinavia, Poland, Germany, the Netherlands and Czechoslovakia all occur here in winter.

World distribution

The breeding range covers a wide area of Europe and Asia, from the Atlantic seaboard to the shores of the Sea of Okhotsk and the Kamchatka Peninsula. The northern limits are reached in Iceland, Finland and the great river basins of Siberia, at 63°N on the upper Kolyma and 65°N on the Yenisei. The southern edge of the range extends from Mediterranean France through the Balkans to the Caspian Sea at about 40°N, then across central Asia to the vicinity of Vladivostok (Vaurie 1965; Voous 1960).

In western Europe there have been both an increase in numbers and a northward expansion by the Black-headed Gull during the past 100 years, although Makatsch (1952) noted a decrease in Germany. Breeding in Norway took place probably in 1865 and most certainly by 1885, and the birds have since continued to multiply and spread north (Ytreberg 1956). In Sweden and Finland the number of breeding pairs in 1950 was considered to be 100 times greater than in 1900. Black-headed Gulls were first confirmed breeding in Iceland in 1911, where they are now widespread (Voous 1960). The species has become a regular winter visitor to eastern North America since about 1930, and about 500 are now reported there annually mainly around sewage outfalls, and it has been predicted that like the Little Gull, *Larus minutus*, it may soon start to breed there (Erskine 1963). Most of these birds probably come from Iceland, but ringed birds from Europe have been recovered on the other side of the Atlantic as well, and there is an extremely closely related form, the Patagonian Black-headed Gull, *Larus maculipennis*, in South America which could be derived from an earlier colonisation across the Atlantic (Erskine 1963).

Status in Britain and Ireland in 1969–70 and past history

The Black-headed Gull breeds in a scattering of colonies on the coasts of many counties in Britain and Ireland, except in south-west England and

Kittiwakes, Guillemots (one bridled) and a Shag, Staple Island, Farnes

ABOVE: Great Black-backed Gull feeding young. BELOW: Lesser Black-backed Gull colony, Walney Island, Lancs.

most of Wales. In Ireland only small numbers nest on the coast, with most in Co. Down and Co. Wexford. The survey covered only coastal colonies in 1969–70 and the total population in these was about 74,500 pairs (see Appendix Table 11 and Map 13), the largest colonies being of 15,000 pairs at Needs Oar Point (Hampshire), 10,000 at Ravenglass (Cumberland) and 8,000 at Tentsmuir (Fife). An unknown, but probably large, number nest inland: at the time of the last full survey in 1958 some 33% (about 16,000 pairs) of the total population of England and Wales did so (Gribble 1962), but no comparable figures exist for Scotland and Ireland, although the majority there probably nest inland.

Ornithologists in Britain and Ireland have long been interested in the fortunes of our Black-headed Gull colonies. A decline in numbers took place during the mid-19th century so that J. E. Harting in 1884 considered that as a breeding species it was facing extinction (Gurney 1919). This, however, seems to have been about the nadir of its fortunes, for since then many increases have been noted. A survey organised by the British Trust for Ornithology in 1938 (Hollom 1940) showed that in England and Wales 175 new colonies had been formed since 1889, while 70 had been deserted during the same period. A revised total for the population in 1938 was 35,000–40,000 pairs (Marchant 1952). Coverage in Scotland was not so thorough, but the general impression gained was that the increase was much less marked than further south, possibly because the species was always well-established there. In the Republic of Ireland very little information was added to that contained in Gurney's list (1919), while Humphreys (1937) said that it was an increasing species with large colonies in some inland areas, though few in the south and east.

When the survey was repeated in 1958, coverage in England and Wales was considered complete except for a small number of colonies in northwest England and north Wales. A total of 191 colonies contained between 46,000 and 51,000 pairs, an increase of over 27% since 1938. The increase was particularly marked in south-east England, while more inland sites were also recorded (Gribble 1962). Some parts of Scotland were poorly covered and only 130 colonies, totalling 29,000–36,000 pairs, were visited (Hamilton 1962); except for Sutherland, where Pennie (1962) noted a great increase in the number and often in the size of colonies during the preceding 20 years, not enough information was available to assess changes since 1938.

Operation Seafarer was concerned only with coastal colonies; it is evident from Appendix Table 12 that among those on the coasts of England and Wales further expansion has taken place since 1958, by about 18,500 pairs (52%). The increase in the south-east has continued, particularly on the Hampshire coast where a vast colony, now the largest in Britain and Ireland, has been established at Needs Oar Point at the

entrance to the Beaulieu River; protection is afforded by Lord Montagu
in whose estate it lies, while since 1962 the Hampshire Naturalists' Trust
have wardened the area. Further west in the Solent two colonies which
together had contained 3,890 pairs in 1958 had increased to 7,000 pairs
by 1969. In north Kent, where the Black-headed Gull became established
as a breeding species during the 1940s, the colonies on the Rivers Medway
and Swale contained 2,500 pairs by 1958, 4,000 in 1961 (Humphreys 1962)
and 2,790 in 1969.

TABLE 5. *Numbers of pairs of Black-headed Gulls at Needs Oar Point,
Hampshire* (Taverner 1966 and *in litt.*)

1909	Founded	1961	1,200	1966	6,700
1910	16	1962	1,200+	1967	9,680
1938	75	1963	3,900	1968	10,500
1957	1,130	1964	4,000+	1969	15,000
1958	960+	1965	6,500	1970	17,000

The main coastal colony in Scotland is at Tentsmuir where nesting
commenced during the early years of the present century. Nearly 4,000
pairs nested there in 1936, 3,000 during 1953-5 (Grierson 1962) and
8,000 in 1969. In Shetland there seem to have been large fluctuations.
Only three colonies were known to Evans and Buckley (1899), but Venables
and Venables (1955) noted that a marked increase had taken place during
the previous 50 years; their largest colony, however, of 150 pairs in
Spiggie Loch, was not occupied in 1969, the largest then being of 300
pairs in a marsh on Unst where only 30 had nested in 1958. Of five
colonies on the main island of Shetland which in 1938 had contained
'hundreds' of pairs, four were completely deserted in 1969 while at the
fifth only two pairs nested.

In Ireland only small numbers nest on the coast, the main strongholds
being in Co. Down, particularly the islands in Strangford Lough where
the largest colony – on Peggy's Island – numbered 715 pairs in 1969.
Kennedy *et al.* (1954) reported the Black-headed Gull as abundant and
increasing in Ireland, with 'vast' colonies in some of the central bogs and
marshes. Whether this increase is continuing and in what numbers the
species now nests at these inland sites is not known. In Ulster Deane
(1954) said that it had greatly increased since 1920.

It seems likely, therefore, that in England and Wales there have been
further large increases since the 1958 survey, but in Scotland and Ireland
comprehensive surveys of inland colonies are necessary before any assessment of the population trends can be attempted.

COMMON GULL *Larus canus*

Identification

The name 'Common Gull' is something of a misnomer in Britain and Ireland, since this is the least numerous of our coastal-breeding gulls; the North American name of 'Mew Gull' seems much more appropriate here. Like the much larger Herring Gull, it has a pale grey back and dark-tipped wings with white spots. It measures about 16 inches in length compared with the Herring Gull's 22 inches, and has a more slender yellow-green bill and legs. The brown eyes give it a more docile appearance than its larger yellow-eyed relatives, the Great and Lesser Black-backed and Herring Gulls. Immature birds are mottled brown and white, with a dark subterminal band on the tail and with flesh-coloured legs, full adult plumage being attained in the third year. Although extremely vocal throughout the breeding season, when its high-pitched mewing calls are heard constantly over the colonies, the Common Gull is mostly silent during the rest of the year. The characteristic voice enables the species to be detected when nesting in small numbers with Herring Gulls.

Food and feeding habits

The food of the Common Gull is not as varied as that of our other breeding gulls. Besides searching the shore for small items of marine life, it spends a great deal of time on fields and moors feeding on earthworms, insects, other invertebrates and grain. In Ireland, during the breeding season, it feeds mainly on wet or partly flooded pastures, or follows the plough (Major R. F. Ruttledge *in litt.*), but most observations on its feeding habits have been made out of the breeding season. In arable areas of Aberdeenshire feeding is concentrated mainly on freshly ploughed land and the birds resort to grassland and stubble only when this is not available; also, the majority fly farther inland to feed than other gulls (D. E. B. Lloyd *in litt.*). Vernon (1970) stated that 65% of Common Gull flocks reported during his inquiry into their feeding habitats were on grassland, the majority being in drier upland areas, particularly when ploughing was in progress. There is comparatively little feeding in urban and industrialised zones, while on the coast its activities seem confined mainly to sandy shores with some birds feeding in inshore waters. Common Gulls frequently rob Black-headed Gulls, Lapwings and Golden Plovers of food, particularly during winter when the species feed in the same areas.

Breeding

In Britain and Ireland Common Gulls nest in small colonies, most containing only a handful of pairs; even the largest reported during the 1969-70 survey was of only 320 pairs at Boguille, Isle of Arran (Buteshire). Colonies may be found at any altitude from sea-level to 3,000 feet in Scotland (Baxter and Rintoul 1953) and to 4,000 feet in Norway (Voous 1960). Sites vary – small islands, sand dunes, shingle banks, marshes, moorland, cereal fields, grassy and rocky slopes above the sea are all used. In Co. Londonderry nesting was recorded on a cliff ledge between 100 and 150 feet above the sea (Hillis 1967). Common Gulls will also nest in trees and bushes: Witherby *et al.* (1940–1) mentioned occurrences in the Netherlands, Germany and Denmark. In Ireland nests have been found in low willow bushes, and once 30 feet up in a pine tree (Kennedy *et al.* 1954, Major R. F. Ruttledge *in litt.*). In Shetland Venables and Venables (1955) noted pairs nesting on stone walls, and in Perthshire Thom (1968) recorded several artificial sites – a dam wall, a post of a derelict pier and between the joining plates of a hydro-electric pipeline. In 1971 a pair attempted to nest on a building at Dalcross Airport, Inverness; the species nests on buildings in Scandinavia (Cramp 1971). In some parts of Norway, where their eggs are collected in large numbers for food, Common Gulls are encouraged to nest in boxes raised on top of poles (Haftorn 1971).

The gulls return to their colonies during February and March. The nests consist of vegetation gathered close by and used to line a shallow hollow made by the birds in the ground. Egg-laying commences normally in the latter half of May or early June, three eggs being the normal clutch. Most observations on the breeding biology have been undertaken in southern Norway, where Barth (1952, 1955) found that the incubation period varied between 24 and 28 days, both parents assisting; in Ireland it is normally 24 to 26 days, though 27 and 29 have each been recorded once (Major R. F. Ruttledge *in litt.*). The chicks leave the nest about the fourth day, remaining in the vicinity and fledging after some five weeks.

Movements

The movements of Common Gulls as shown by ringing returns have been analysed by Radford (1960). There have been only three foreign recoveries of birds ringed as nestlings in Britain and Ireland: these were ringed in Shetland, Argyll and Co. Kerry and recovered respectively in Denmark, Portugal and Spain. On the other hand, large numbers of Common Gulls ringed abroad have been recovered here in winter, the majority coming from Scandinavia and north Germany. An inquiry into the wintering of gulls in winter 1952/53 indicated that some 50,000 Common Gulls roosted at inland sites in England; coverage in Scotland was not complete, but 40,000 roosted at Gladhouse Reservoir (Midlothian) (Hickling 1954), and there are other sites which may have held as many or possibly more (D. G. Andrew *in litt.*). By 1963 the number roosting in England had risen to 125,000 (Hickling 1967). In the western Palaearctic Common Gulls tend to move west in winter and are then scarce south of their breeding range. The migration takes the form of a slow westward dispersal in late summer and autumn with a rapid high-flying passage east during the passage of a ridge in spring, which is very conspicuous on radar (Bourne and Patterson 1962). Large numbers of immature Common Gulls remain after spring passage to summer in East Anglia (Vernon 1969).

World distribution

The breeding range extends from Iceland, the Faeroes, Britain and Ireland across northern Europe and Asia to the east coast of Anadyrland, the Kamchatka Peninsula, the islands of Sakhalin and the Kurils. The northern limits are reached about the Arctic Circle, while to the south, except for isolated groups in Armenia and northern Iran, they extend to the great lakes of central Asia. The Common Gull also nests in north-west America, from Alaska south to British Columbia and into central Canada as far east as Saskatchewan (Vaurie 1965; Voous 1960). In north-west Canada the closely related and slightly larger Ring-billed Gull *L. delawarensis* overlaps with the Common Gull and farther east it replaces the smaller species ecologically.

Status in Britain and Ireland in 1969–70 and past history

Comparatively few Common Gulls nest on the coast, where some 12,400 pairs were reported in 1969–70, the vast majority in Scotland (see Appendix Table 13 and Map 14). Probably less is known concerning their total numbers than those of our other gulls, since most breed in the more remote areas of the north and west, generally in scattered pairs and small colonies, and often far inland. There has been no complete survey, but the total numbers are not likely to be very high compared with the other gulls, in view of the species' more restricted range and the fact that it does not seem to establish very large colonies in this country.

Although Saxby and Saxby (1874) stated that the Common Gull was plentiful in Shetland, Raeburn, who visited those islands regularly between 1885 and 1895, reported few nesting pairs and specifically referred to its complete absence from certain areas (Venables and Venables 1955). Nowadays the Common Gull is distributed throughout Shetland, with many in areas said to be deserted in the past. Both Buckley and Harvie-Brown (1891) and Lack (1942-3) commented on the increase of the Common Gull in Orkney, though they did not provide figures. Baxter and Rintoul (1953) remarked that it was more common there than in Shetland, a state of affairs which still exists at present.

On the mainland of Scotland the Common Gull is widely distributed, the many inland colonies outside the scope of Operation Seafarer and the virtual absence of former data making comparisons with past situations almost impossible. Baxter and Rintoul (1953) noted the southern edge of its range in the east to be in Perthshire and Angus; in the west, however, Lanarkshire, Ayrshire, Kirkcudbright and Wigtownshire all have colonies. Common Gulls have been extending their range inland in southern Scotland within recent years. A small colony discovered at Loch Arklet (Stirlingshire) in 1954 (Baxter 1957), the first recorded in that area, contained 65 pairs in 1969. In Berwickshire small numbers have nested since the first pairs in 1960 (Campbell 1961), and this applies also to Dumfriesshire where two pairs nested for the first time in 1962 (Andrew 1963). Common Gulls began breeding on St Kilda (Outer Hebrides) in 1963 (Andrew 1964) and on Fair Isle (Shetland) in 1966 (*Fair Isle Bird Obs. Bull.*, 5: 202-203), though nesting was not reported from either locality in 1969.

At Dungeness (Kent) four pairs commenced nesting in 1919. They had probably come from the Dutch colonies which were expanding at that time, rather than from our own northern ones. The numbers gradually rose to between 30 and 40 pairs by 1939, although most were unsuccessful (Axell 1956). Numbers have declined since 1952 when just under 20 pairs nested; twelve pairs seems to have been the maximum in recent years (*Kent Bird Reports*) and only four pairs nested in 1969. Since 1932 a few have bred just over the county boundary in Sussex (des Forges and Harber 1963), and a single pair did so in 1969. Elsewhere in England there have been occasional breeding records in the past: for example, on the Farne Islands (Northumberland) from 1910 to 1912 (Watt 1951) and at several localities in Cumberland between 1914 and 1940 (Blezard 1943); one pair bred in the latter county in 1969-70. On the north Norfolk coast one or two pairs have nested each year since 1965 and two pairs bred at

Blakeney Point in 1969 (*Norfolk Bird Reports*). Inland a pair nested in Nottinghamshire in 1969 (*Nottinghamshire Bird Report*). In north Wales breeding was first noted in Anglesey in 1963 (Parslow 1967) and in 1969 six pairs nested at four sites there, all in coastal Herring Gull colonies.

In Ireland the Common Gull has increased and spread since 1900, with the main strongholds on inland lakes in the western counties, particularly Mayo and Galway (Kennedy *et al.* 1954). There were only two known coastal colonies in west Donegal in the early 1950s, compared with 14 in 1969, while in Co. Galway only one coastal site was known compared with ten in 1969. Two pairs, plus possibly a further six, nesting on islands in Kenmare Bay (Co. Kerry) in 1967 were the most southerly breeding Common Gulls in Ireland (*Irish Bird Report 1967*); four islands there were occupied by twelve pairs in 1969, while four pairs breeding on an island on the Co. Cork side of the bay were the first recorded in that county. Inland colonies of Common Gulls mixed with Black-headed Gulls, especially on the Connaught lakes, frequently seem to move from place to place due to rapid growth of vegetation, but when Common Gulls nest alone the changes are by no means as rapid (Major R. F. Ruttledge *in litt.*). Common Gulls first nested in Co. Down in 1934 and on Rathlin Island (Co. Antrim) in 1946 (Kennedy *et al.* 1954); in 1969 43 pairs nested on the coast of Co. Down and six pairs on Rathlin Island.

Whether the increases which have occurred in Scotland and Ireland during the first half of this century are continuing is difficult to say, due to a scarcity of data. Certainly southward extensions of range are occurring in both countries, while the species' recent establishment in north Norfolk and Anglesey is most interesting.

LESSER BLACK-BACKED GULL *Larus fuscus*

Identification

The Lesser Black-backed Gull is one of two medium-sized gulls nesting in Great Britain and Ireland, the other being the more powerfully built Herring Gull (see pages 125–8). The adults have slate-grey backs and wings, the tips of the primaries being black with white markings (as in the Herring Gull), while the rest of the plumage is white. The bill, like that of other large gulls, is yellow with a red spot near the tip of the lower mandible; the legs are also yellow, and the eye a gleaming yellow with a bright orange orbital ring. Immature birds are mottled brown in their first year, being easily confused with immature Herring Gulls, before passing through intermediate stages to full adult plumage when four years old. The main call is a rather gruff 'kyow'; the gulls are very noisy on the breeding grounds.

Food and feeding habits

This species is much less of a scavenger than the Great Black-backed and Herring Gulls, especially during the breeding season. In Anglesey and Pembrokeshire Harris (1965b) found that in summer it fed mainly on the shore and on arable land, and none visited the fish market at Milford Haven (Pembrokeshire). On Walney Island (Lancashire) Lesser Black-backed Gulls tend to take more fish than Herring Gulls, though the diets overlap to some extent (Brown 1967). Small numbers were observed by Boswall (1960) feeding on waste fish thrown overboard from a seine netter off north-west Scotland; while Hillis (1971) noted small numbers scavenging at fishing vessels in the Irish Sea and off Co. Cork. The Lesser Black-back is the most widespread large gull at sea in summer off north-west Scotland (Dr W. R. P. Bourne pers. comm.). Overwintering birds scavenge on rubbish dumps and in urban areas, though large numbers also frequent arable land (Barnes 1961).

Breeding

Lesser Black-backed Gulls usually nest in large, often dense colonies, typically among sand dunes and on rocky islands, and inland usually on moorlands or on islands in lakes. This is more of an inland breeding species than the Herring Gull, and even on small islands it tends to occupy the summit areas away from the shore. On Skomer Island (Pembrokeshire) 3,150 pairs nested in 1966, of which only 74 were on cliff slopes, the rest being on the inland plateau. Even on Walney Island, where the habitat is much more uniform, Lesser Black-backed Gulls breed on the more level areas while Herring Gulls prefer rough uneven ground around gravel workings and coastal defences (Brown 1967). Inland breeding on the mainland of England and Wales is usually confined to hilly districts, though there have been instances in lowland areas in recent years. Dobbs (1964) summarised the breeding records in the Trent valley (Nottinghamshire) since the first in 1945, while in Essex single pairs bred at Hanningfield Reservoir in 1961 and 1962 (Hudson and Pyman 1968). Lesser Black-backed Gulls sometimes nest on roofs, though less frequently and in smaller numbers than Herring Gulls, the largest recorded colony being on a factory roof at Merthyr Tydfil (Glamorgan) from about 1946 to 1959; this was 21 miles from the sea and 23 miles from the nearest known breeding site (Cramp 1971; Salmon 1958).

Adults return to their colonies mainly during March. Nest building commences in the latter half of April, and the first eggs are laid in southern colonies by the end of that month. Nests are usually bulky and constructed from locally gathered vegetation. Some may be tucked away in hollows at the base of low bushes, where these are present at the colony, while on Steep Holm (Somerset) one nest was found three feet up in a privet bush (Vernon and Avent 1959). Three eggs make up the normal clutch, though four may be found from time to time; there is considerable variation both in ground colour – pale blue to deep olive-green – and in the degree of darker markings. Both sexes take part in incubation which lasts about 28 days. Unless disturbed, the chicks remain in the vicinity of the nest, since any that wander are liable to be killed by other adults. A great deal of mobbing takes place when the young gulls make their first flights after about seven weeks; sometimes they are forced back on to land or sea, and in the latter case may drown in stormy conditions when they are often unable to take off again easily.

Movements

In Great Britain and Ireland the Lesser Black-backed Gull is a migratory species moving south during the autumn to Portugal, southern Spain and north-west Africa (Harris 1962b). At one time few wintered here (Witherby *et al.* 1940–41), but the numbers remaining have increased, starting in the 1920s, at least in southern England. During the winters of 1949/50 and 1950/51 an inquiry for the British Trust for Ornithology showed that mainly adults were remaining and that the midwinter maximum was 310 birds (Barnes 1952). A further inquiry in 1959/60 showed a ninefold increase since the earlier investigation, with a midwinter peak of at least 2,800 (Barnes 1961). Within a further four years this had increased to 7,000, with flocks of sub-adults gathering at Midlands reservoirs during the late summer and remaining until the winter (Hickling 1967). There has been no such increase in Ireland where only ones and twos are reported in winter (*Irish Bird Report 1970*).

World distribution

The breeding range of the Lesser Black-backed Gull is restricted to Europe. It nests from Iceland to the Channel Islands, on much of the Scandinavian coast, in part of Estonia, in Finland on the inland lake complex and in the Karelia Province and the Kola Peninsula of Russia, and in smaller numbers on the coasts of north Germany, the Netherlands and Brittany (Vaurie 1965). On the Continent it has increased and expanded its range during the present century. The establishment of colonies in Denmark since 1920 and in the Netherlands since 1926 was considered by Voous (1960) to be a reoccupation of past breeding areas. In Sweden numbers are increasing and new areas being occupied (Curry-Lindahl 1961) while Iceland was colonised about 1925, although the birds are still restricted to the south-east (Timmerman 1938–49). Lesser Black-backed Gulls have recently been observed at sea off south-east Greenland (Brown 1968).

Status in Britain and Ireland in 1969–70 and past history

The Lesser Black-backed Gull is widely distributed in small numbers round the coasts of Britain and Ireland, with larger concentrations in a few areas, while there are some colonies inland which were not included in this survey. In 1969–70 the coastal population totalled nearly 47,000 pairs (Appendix Table 14 and Map 15), more than twice that of the Great Black-back but only about one-seventh that of the Herring Gull. In Scotland, where about 11,000 pairs nested around the coasts, over half were found in two areas – Argyll and the Clyde, and the Firth of Forth.

In England one colony, on Walney Island, held 17,500 pairs, and most of the remaining 5,500 pairs were breeding in Northumberland, Somerset and the Isles of Scilly. The great majority of the 10,500 pairs in Wales were in Anglesey, Pembrokeshire and Glamorgan. The numbers in Ireland (1,700 pairs) seem extremely low in comparison with Britain, though an unknown number nest inland, particularly in the western counties.

In Shetland Venables and Venables (1955) reported a huge reduction in numbers during the present century and suggested that this was due to changes in the mode of fishing; another explanation might be that they were displaced by Great Skuas or Great Black-backed Gulls. The population remains small, with only 520 pairs in 1969–70. A marked decrease occurred in Orkney during and after the 1940s which Balfour (1968) attributed partly to egg-collecting and partly to replacement by Great Black-backed Gulls, a partial recovery taking place in more recent years. An increase, from 15 pairs in 1947 to 100 in 1957 (Williamson 1958) and to 292 in 1969, has been recorded on St Kilda (Outer Hebrides), where Great Black-backed Gulls are still scarce. In western Sutherland a colony on Am Balg was replaced by one of Great Black-backed Gulls (Fisher and Piercy 1950). On the east coast of Scotland, where Great Black-backed Gulls are still lacking, there have been recent extensions of range. Lesser Black-backed Gulls were first noted nesting in Aberdeenshire in 1949 (Wynne-Edwards 1951) and in Kincardineshire in 1965 (Slater 1965b). Three pairs nested on the coast of Aberdeenshire in 1969 and an inland colony of over 100 pairs was discovered there in 1971 (Bourne *in litt.*), three pairs nested on the Kincardineshire coast in 1969, and in that same year 14 pairs nested in Banffshire where they had not been recorded previously as a breeding species (Baxter and Rintoul 1953). In Ireland, although the coastal population seems low, Deane (1954), Kennedy *et al.* (1954) and Ruttledge (1966) all referred to increases having taken place, and undoubtedly this has been the case at some inland colonies in recent years.

Despite the interest shown in the wintering of Lesser Black-backed Gulls, there has been no previous complete census of the breeding population and the 1969–70 survey covered only coastal colonies. Bearing this fact in mind, some increases seem to have taken place in England, Wales and southern Scotland. The situation in northern Scotland remains obscure, with both decreases as in Shetland and the Outer Hebrides and increases as on St Kilda. In general the species appears to be increasing except where it comes into competition with larger species which are also increasing, such as the Great Skua in Shetland and the Great Black-backed Gull along the coasts in the north and west.

HERRING GULL   *Larus argentatus*

Identification

Herring Gulls are among the best known and most numerous of seabirds nesting in Great Britain and Ireland. No coastal town is without them, while many occur inland at all seasons but particularly in winter. Adults have back and wings light grey, the primaries tipped black with large white subterminal spots; the rest of the plumage is white. The bill is yellow, with a red spot near the tip of the lower mandible; the legs are pale flesh and the eye is yellow. Immatures are mottled brown, most attaining full adult plumage by their fourth year. Like most other gulls the Herring Gull has a wide range of calls, particularly at its breeding colonies, the main one being a loud, somewhat musical, repeated 'kyow'.

Food and feeding habits

Because of concern that the Herring Gull's diet might be detrimental to fishing and agricultural interests, investigations of its food have been made in a number of countries. No evidence has been produced to confirm these fears. It has a catholic diet with a great deal of regional variation depending on local circumstances: fish, molluscs, insects, small mammals, birds, eggs, earthworms, grain, turnips, carrion and offal are all taken by this opportunist species. Some individuals and pairs have well-developed food preferences, at least in the breeding season as may be seen by examining food remains and pellets around nests. On Skomer and Skokholm (Pembrokeshire) the Herring Gull is for the most part a scavenger subsisting on waste fish and garbage, much of which is obtained from the Milford Haven fish dock area some ten miles away (Harris 1965b). In Anglesey most food is obtained from the intertidal zone and from arable land (Threlfall 1968). In Aberdeenshire very large numbers frequent agricultural land, particularly in autumn, winter and spring, following the plough and also feeding on stubble, sowings and grassland; food put out for livestock becomes more important during the summer, particularly to immatures (Lloyd 1968). Concern is often expressed at predation by Herring Gulls on the eggs and chicks of Razorbills and Guillemots. Although no quantitative studies have been made, damage is normally slight unless the auk colony is frequently disturbed directly or indirectly by man, when the gulls may quickly swoop in to obtain an easy meal of unguarded eggs and chicks. Klepto-parasitism by Herring Gulls on Puffins returning to their colonies with beakfuls of fish is referred to on pages 188–9.

Breeding

Herring Gulls are widespread, their large, noisy colonies being situated as often on low rocky skerries, shingle banks or sand dunes as on steep slopes, broad cliff ledges and sea stacks. Man-made structures, such as bridges, piers and buildings, and some other artificial sites, including quarries and china clay pits, are increasingly used for nesting in some areas. Large colonies of Herring Gulls sometimes affect those of smaller seabirds, such as terns, by physically displacing them, or as a result of increased growth of herbage, caused by their guano, making the habitat unsuitable. A certain number of birds nest inland on shingle beds, heaths and bogs, though to a lesser extent than with the Lesser Black-backed Gull, so that only a small proportion of birds are likely to have been missed for this reason.

Adults return to their colonies during early March, the males quickly establishing territories which are vigorously defended from intruders. Various hostile postures are adopted during territorial encounters; when these fail they fight, grappling with each other with wings spread, and although such battles are conducted with great ferocity blood is rarely drawn. During disputes at territorial boundaries they often pull up great beakfuls of grass or other vegetation. This habit can lead to local erosion problems which may be potentially dangerous at Puffin colonies where the soil layer is thin (Phillips 1968). The eggs are laid from mid-April onwards, three being the normal clutch; incubation usually commences with the laying of the second and lasts, on average, 28 days. The chicks generally remain in or near the nest until fledging when about seven weeks old.

Movements

The Herring Gull is one of our more sedentary seabirds. All the major colonies have well-defined dispersal areas. Those breeding in Pembrokeshire move east along the south coast of Wales to the Bristol Channel and south to Devon and Cornwall, with few recoveries elsewhere. Herring Gulls from the Anglesey colonies frequent chiefly the Liverpool Bay coasts, while those from the Isle of Man disperse along coasts on both sides of the Irish Sea. The birds tend to move towards the nearest centres of human population, where they obtain food by scavenging. There are few recoveries of British-ringed Herring Gulls abroad, and some of these may have been Lesser Black-backed Gulls misidentified when ringed as chicks (Harris 1964).

World distribution

The Herring Gull occurs in two groups each of five subspecies in Europe, Asia and North America. Birds belonging to the northern group breed from north-west Europe eastwards through Siberia to the Bering Sea, and in North America from Alaska south-east to the Great Lakes and the St Lawrence, ranging south to the vicinity of New York on the Atlantic seaboard. Those in the southern group nest on the Atlantic islands of the Azores, Madeira and the Canaries, and thence through the Mediterranean and across central Asia to Mongolia and western Manchuria. These two chains, spanning much of the northern hemisphere, are widely separated except in the basin of the Ob in western Siberia where they occasionally intermingle (Vaurie 1965).

On both sides of the North Atlantic the species has greatly increased during this century. The New England population grew from 4,000–8,000 pairs in 1900 to 110,000–120,000 in 1965 (Kadlec and Drury 1968). The number of pairs in the Netherlands increased from 10,000 to 30,000 between 1930 and 1940 (Voous 1960) and in north Germany from 10,000 to 20,000 between the late 1920s and 1960 (Goethe 1964). An impressive increase, together with the establishment of many inland colonies, has occurred in Sweden (Curry-Lindahl 1961). The colonisation of Iceland commenced in 1927 and breeding occurred later on the arctic islands of Spitsbergen and Bear Island (Voous 1960), though it does not appear to have continued on the latter (Williams 1971).

Status in Britain and Ireland in 1969–70 and past history

The Herring Gull, one of our most numerous seabirds and the second most abundant gull, is found nesting along nearly the whole coastline of Britain and Ireland, with a population in 1969–70 of about 334,000 pairs (Appendix Table 14 and Map 16). The only section with virtually no breeding Herring Gulls is the low coastline between the cliffs at Flamborough Head (Yorkshire) and those in south-east Kent, though the recent founding of a colony at Orfordness (Suffolk) is perhaps an indication of future growth even here. Elsewhere there are large colonies in many areas, particularly in north-east Scotland, the Firth of Forth, Liverpool Bay, the Bristol Channel and Dublin Bay.

It is rather surprising that there has been no previous complete survey of the Herring Gull in Britain and Ireland, particularly in view of the recent increases and evidence of damage to other seabird colonies. In most cases where there is past information to compare with that from the 1969–70 survey (see Table 1) there have been increases, sometimes very large; only in a few special circumstances have decreases been noted. In Shetland Venables and Venables (1955) considered that changes in the fishing industry had caused a decrease since the early years of the century, though they did not rule out a possible connection with the rapid increase of the Fulmar population during the same period. At Dungeness (Kent) animal and human predation was considered responsible for a decrease (Axell 1956), while on Puffin Island (Anglesey) encroachment by vegetation has restricted colony space. Parslow (1967) considered that the population in England and Wales had at least doubled during the past 20 years. In general it appears that the Herring Gull has been increasing around developed parts of the mainland coast, in estuaries such as the Bristol Channel, Morecambe Bay, Forth and Clyde, and around ports as in Pembrokeshire and Aberdeenshire, while its numbers may have remained stable in more peripheral areas such as the Hebrides, or even declined where it has come up against increasing competition from other species such as the Fulmar, Great Skua or Great Black-back, as in the Shetlands.

The habit of nesting on buildings in Britain (but not in Ireland) is quite recent. Beginning in south-west England in the late 1920s or even earlier, and in south-east England in the 1930s, it has since spread so that in 1969–70 it was reported from the west coast north to Ayrshire and from the east coast north to Shetland, with many localities occupied on the south coast. The largest colony was on rooftops in Dover where at least 225 pairs bred, but the number nesting on buildings (between 1,252 and 1,365 pairs) is only a fraction of the total population. Some local authorities, faced with complaints because these gulls are noisy and foul pavements and roofs, have tried control measures, generally with little success (Cramp 1971).

In Ireland there is an almost complete lack of information concerning past numbers of Herring Gulls, so that few changes can be measured.

Ussher and Warren (1900) stated that it was almost exclusively marine, rarely appearing inland. Changes have certainly taken place since then, for both Kennedy *et al.* (1954) and Ruttledge (1966) noted not only that numbers had increased in coastal areas but also that inland colonies had been established; these were not, however, included in the 1969/70 survey. Deane (1954) said that considerable increases had taken place in Ulster since the beginning of the century.

Nesting Shags, with Kittiwakes above

ABOVE: Puffins in flight, Fetlar, Shetland. BELOW: Gannet colony, Grassholm

GREAT BLACK-BACKED GULL *Larus marinus*

Identification

The Great Black-back is the largest gull nesting in Great Britain and Ireland. In adult plumage it can be confused only with the smaller Lesser Black-backed Gull, but its back and wings are black rather than slate-grey; in both species these contrast with the otherwise white plumage. The legs are pale flesh, the massive bill yellow with a red spot near the tip of the lower mandible. Immatures are mottled brown with paler underparts, head, neck, rump and tail, and dark brown wing tips and tail band; they do not attain adult plumage until four years old. In any mixed flock of gulls the Great Black-back is immediately conspicuous by its size, as large as a White-fronted Goose *Anser albifrons*, some 30 inches long with a wing span of five feet. Its calls are much deeper than those of other gulls and are best described as a hoarse, barking 'agh, agh, agh'.

Food and feeding habits

This is one of the most marine gulls. The bulk of the population appears to feed during much of the year on offal obtained around fishing boats, and the increasing supply seems likely to provide the main explanation of both the growing breeding population in the west, and the increasing number of birds from the Continent wintering in the east. The species is also increasingly visiting coastal and inland rubbish dumps in the winter, while in summer the chicks may also be fed on offal, fish waste, shellfish and Rabbits, and the eggs, young and adults of other seabirds. Many pairs obviously have special preferences: at one nest fish bones may predominate, at another Rabbit remains, or crab shells, or Manx Shearwater skins, for example. On Skomer Island (Pembrokeshire) Harris (1965b) found that Manx Shearwater remains formed 44% of all the food waste at nests; fish made up 21% and Rabbits 16%, while a miscellany of Puffins, young gulls, meat and bones accounted for the rest. Manx Shearwaters, being clumsy and helpless on land, are usually attacked by the gulls just before dawn, though often much earlier on moonlit nights. They are killed by vigorous shaking and pecking as feeding begins, and by the end of the meal the skin is often turned neatly inside-out, a characteristic trademark of the work of these gulls. In 1957, on nearby Skokholm Island, 27 pairs of Great Black-backs nested and the remains of 2,536 Manx Shearwaters were recovered; in 1962, after control measures, only five pairs of gulls nested and 646 Shearwater corpses were found (*Skokholm Bird Observatory Reports*). Visiting gulls from Skomer and non-breeding birds were no doubt responsible for some of the mortality.

Breeding

Great Black-backed Gulls tend to be more solitary nesters than our other breeding gulls, though large, scattered colonies flourish, for example, on Mullion Island (Cornwall), Calf of Eday (Orkney) and North Rona (Outer Hebrides). Such colonies are usually situated on the interior plateaux of islands. In general, particularly favoured sites seem to be the tops of stacks, small islands and holms, often close to colonies of other seabirds. Although, throughout its range, this gull is largely restricted to sea coasts for nesting, pairs occasionally breed inland and there are even small colonies in some inland areas. In Great Britain and Ireland these include islands in freshwater lakes in the counties of Mayo, Galway and Donegal (Ruttledge 1966), and open moorland in northern Scotland (Baxter and Rintoul 1953) and northern England (Davis 1958).

The nest is a slight depression lined with dry vegetation, often close to a boulder, low wall or other prominent feature which the off-duty bird utilises as a vantage point. The earliest clutches are laid during the second week in April, the majority towards the end of that month. The normal clutch consists of three eggs laid at about two-day intervals; incubation commences with the second. Both parents incubate and the eggs hatch after 26–28 days. The chicks are covered in down at first, and after a day or so are able to leave the nest and hide close by among rocks or vegetation, or in burrow entrances. At this stage the adults are generally less aggressive than other gulls towards human intruders, occasionally swooping low but for the most part circling, calling anxiously, until the potential danger has passed. At seven or eight weeks the chicks fledge, and within a few days they leave the colony.

Movements

During their first winter, most Great Black-backed Gulls move in a southerly direction, travelling on average about 100 miles. The very few foreign recoveries of British-ringed immatures have been mainly in north-west France and Iberia (Harris 1962c). Older birds are much more sedentary and may return year after year to nest at or near the same spot. On Skomer Island the earliest pairs always nest on the same rock outcrops, while several others can be shown to defend the same territories every year by some distinguishing feature of their eggs – more slender than usual, say, or chalky blue-green with few markings.

Each winter there is an influx of these gulls from abroad to all parts of the British Isles, especially to countries bordering the North Sea. Ringing recoveries have indicated that most of these visitors come from northern Fenno-Scandia and the Murmansk district of Russia, but there have also been a few recoveries of Icelandic birds, mostly in north-west Britain and Ireland.

World distribution

South of Britain and Ireland, Great Black-backed Gulls breed only in north-west France and the Channel Islands. North and east they nest in the Faeroes, on all coasts of Iceland, on Bear Island, in Spitsbergen (occasionally), from the entrance of the White Sea west along the Murmansk coast of Russia, on much of the coasts of Norway, Sweden and Finland, in part of Estonia and on several islands in the Kattegat. In Greenland they breed on the east coast south from about 66°N and on the west coast from about 70°N; and in North America from Labrador nearly to New York (Vaurie 1965; Voous 1960).

Like several of our other gulls (see pages 47–50), the Great Blackback has increased over much of its range within the present century, at times quite dramatically. On the eastern seaboard of the USA the first breeding record was in 1916; between 1921 and 1942 the southern limit of its breeding range there was extended by some 450 miles and the population density also increased (Gross 1955). Gudmundsson (1954) reported a pronounced rise in the Icelandic population in recent years.

Status in Britain and Ireland in 1969–70 and past history

The Great Black-backed Gull is absent as a breeding species from the east coast between Berwickshire and Hampshire. Elsewhere it is widely distributed around Britain and Ireland, with an estimated population of some 22,000 pairs in 1969–70 (Appendix Table 14 and Map 17). It has the smallest population of any gull nesting in these islands, except possibly the Common Gull whose total numbers are not known, since only coastal colonies were covered in 1969–70. It rarely breeds in large colonies, and the largest reported, on North Rona, contained only about 1,800 pairs; in comparison the Lesser Black-backed Gull, Herring Gull, Black-headed Gull and Kittiwake all have some colonies exceeding 10,000 pairs. Other large concentrations were found elsewhere in the Outer Hebrides, and in Orkney, west Sutherland, Pembrokeshire and the Isles of Scilly. Most of the population was in Scotland – about 16,000 pairs, mainly on the north and west coasts, with only 75 pairs on the east coast south of the Moray Firth. This virtual absence from eastern Scotland may be due to delay in colonisation from the west.

In Britain and Ireland marked increases and extensions of range have occurred in this century. While the Great Black-backed Gull is primarily a north and west coast species in the breeding season, occurring in the east mainly as a winter visitor from the Continent, a long-continuing increase in breeding strength in the west may now be extending to the east as well. In Scotland and Ireland there have been no previous full surveys and indeed the vast majority of colonies there had never been counted. It is evident, however, that increases and extensions of range have occurred there during the present century, with the development of colonies of hundreds of pairs along the east coast of Sutherland and the largest in the country of 1,800 on North Rona in the Outer Hebrides, for example. On the east coast of Scotland the counties of Aberdeen (*Scot. Birds* 2: 325), Kincardine, Angus and Fife (Gordon 1963) and East Lothian (Smith 1966) have all been colonised since 1960. In Ireland five new counties were colonised between 1900 and 1951, the most recent being Co. Wicklow in 1951 (Kennedy *et al.* 1954). There are more data for England and Wales. Summarising that available up to 1930, Harrisson and Hurrell (1933) showed a substantial decrease took place between 1849 and 1893, by which year nesting was restricted to six counties with a total population of only 20 pairs. The recent increase seems to have started at the turn of the century: by 1930 there were some 1,200 pairs nesting in England and Wales, of which 65% were in the Isles of Scilly and 20% in Pembrokeshire. A survey in 1956 revealed a further increase, to at least 1,600 pairs, chiefly in island populations with little change at mainland sites (Davis 1958). This figure was considered too low by Parslow (1967), since only 370 pairs were included for the Isles of Scilly where numbers increased from 600–800 pairs in 1930 to 1,200 in 1969.

Since the 1956 survey, the only county in England and Wales in which breeding has occurred for the first time is Merioneth, where a pair has nested at an inland lake, but Table 17 shows that the population as a whole has continued to rise, especially in certain areas. The main strongholds are still the Isles of Scilly and Pembrokeshire which together account for some

66% of the total. An overall increase has been noted in Pembrokeshire despite successful control measures on Skokholm and Skomer. Though primarily a north and west coast species (Map 17), the Great Black-backed Gull increasingly summers at some seabird stations in eastern England, for example the Farne Islands (Northumberland). Farther south, nesting was attempted on Havergate Island (Suffolk) in 1959 and 1962 (Parslow 1967).

KITTIWAKE *Rissa tridactyla*

Identification

The Kittiwake is a small oceanic gull about 15 inches long. The adult has a white head, underparts and tail, with a grey back and wings which end in distinctive triangular black wing-tips lacking the white mirrors present in other gulls. At the breeding colony the call of 'kittiwaak' is unmistakable, and the short black legs, waxy yellow bill and red gape can be used to confirm its identity. The immature birds are markedly different from the adults for the first year, with a black 'M' running from wing-tip to wing-tip across the back, black bill, collar and tip to the tail. They resemble immature Little Gulls but that species lacks a dark collar and is even smaller than the Kittiwake. Two-year-old Kittiwakes show a grey collar for most of the year and a greenish-yellow bill but in other respects are like the adults, which, incidentally, also have a grey collar in the winter.

Kittiwakes differ from the larger coastal gulls of the genus *Larus* in several important ways associated with adaptations for nesting on narrow cliff ledges and perhaps for an oceanic life. Walking is unimportant in their mode of life and probably because of this they have shorter legs than most other gulls. Associated with this reduction is the loss of the hind-toe which gives rise to their vernacular name in many countries of 'three-toed gull' as well as the scientific name. They normally feed well out to sea and are rarely seen inland. In one area of Britain, they penetrate up river estuaries for several miles and in many places they visit fresh-water lakes near the coast to bathe and drink. In the summer large flocks settle on the shore and these groups are often made up of a high proportion of immatures. None of these habits persists in winter when the gull becomes pelagic and ranges across the North Atlantic Ocean and normally avoids land entirely.

Food and feeding habits

The Kittiwake feeds entirely on animal material. By preference, it is a fish feeder, but at times, when fish is scarce, it will take a wide range of planktonic invertebrates. In Britain and Ireland over 90% of the food taken during the breeding season is fish, with sand-eels (*Ammodytes*) and small gadoid fish (Cod family) being taken commonly. Crustacea are the next most frequently taken food in Britain and these appear more commonly in the diet of the Kittiwake in the Arctic where they occur in very high densities in areas of upwelling caused by the meeting of waters of different salinity produced by the melting ice. In addition to these foods, the birds also take offal dumped over-board from fishing boats as well as small fish spilt from the nets, and recently they have started taking bread thrown to them in the same manner as the Black-headed, Common and Herring Gulls. There is little information on the food of the Kittiwake when it is oceanic during the winter half of the year. From what information is available it would appear that pelagic and plankton invertebrates are the main component of the food at this time and fish are of minor importance.

Food is collected by two main methods. Small items are picked off the surface either in flight or when floating on the water when the bird gyrates from side to side in the manner of phalarope. Fish are normally caught by plunge-diving from flight. Feeding in this latter manner is less spectacular than in the terns and also lacks their gracefulness as the Kittiwake keeps its wings open throughout the dive. Nevertheless, plunge-diving is efficient and the Kittiwake is usually much more successful than Herring and Common Gulls when feeding over the same area, often resulting in the other two species resorting to harassment of the successful Kittiwakes.

A great deal of food collected by Kittiwakes during the breeding season is taken well offshore and birds probably range up to 40 miles from the breeding colonies. The Sandwich Tern takes fish of a similar size but is essentially an inshore feeder and the two species do not overlap to any great extent when feeding.

Breeding

There is considerable variation between colonies in the time they are re-occupied each year. In Britain and Ireland, some colonies have birds back in early January whilst others remain unoccupied until well into March, which is more typical of colonies within the Arctic Circle. In general, breeding occurs earlier in those colonies which are reoccupied first; egg laying starts in some colonies in late April whilst in others it does not commence until mid-May or even later in the high Arctic, but in all cases laying continues into mid-June and even a little later farther north.

The nest is built annually and is a unique structure cemented to small ledges on precipitous cliffs. The nest foundation is usually formed from green algae which, mixed with guano, forms a firm attachment to the cliff. Plant débris and mud are then trampled into this and a cup is formed on top of this base from grass collected from above the tide line or from cliff tops. Nest building is often a social function in the Kittiwake and the sight of hundreds of these birds streaming backwards and forwards from a small muddy or grassy area on a nearby cliff is impressive as well as being destructive to both the soil and vegetation.

The typical clutch is two eggs and not three as in most other gulls. The lower clutch size is probably an adaptation to the restricted size of the nest-site and the need to rear the young on the small nest platform, but undoubtedly the relative safety of the nesting site has reduced predation pressure and the Kittiwake probably fledges more offspring per pair than do the other gulls. Three-egg clutches occur early in the breeding season and single egg clutches towards the end so that the mean clutch size declines in the later breeding birds. The eggs are large for the size of the gull and have a correspondingly longer incubation period – about 25 days from the completion of the clutch. Incubation is shared equally by both birds of the pair with two to four change-overs per day. Unlike the young of other British and Irish gulls, the newly-hatched young Kittiwake is covered with a uniform, pale grey down and lacks their camouflage spotting. The young remain on the nest until they can fly strongly; the restricted nature of the nest site excludes fleeing movement of the un-fledged chicks to hide from potential predators. Fledging occurs at about six weeks after hatching but the young bird is not accompanied by the parents. Many young return to the nest again after their first flight and then are fed by their parents, but none has ever been seen to be fed away from the nest. The fledged chicks rapidly leave the area of the colony and spread over the adjacent sea areas, feeding themselves. In some colonies, the adults, continue to occupy the nest site for several months after the young have fledged and have been observed there as late as November. In the Arctic, colonies are deserted in August, as soon as the young have fledged.

Movements

The Kittiwake is oceanic outside the breeding season and there is an annual movement inshore to the breeding colonies and back again to the ocean. Transects of the North Atlantic show that Kittiwakes occur across the whole ocean in winter but the central oceanic region is vacated by both the breeding and the non-breeding birds in the summer half of the year.

Young Kittiwakes return to the breeding colonies when about three years old. Most birds return either to their natal colony or to one within close proximity. Until this return, the young birds have been several hundreds or even thousands of miles away from their place of birth. Large numbers of young Kittiwakes from colonies in Britain, Norway, Denmark and the USSR spend their immature period on the west side of the Atlantic, summering off the west coast of Greenland and moving south to Newfoundland waters during the winter. Several young Kittiwakes reared in England have reached Greenland in September of the same year in which they hatched, indicating the speed with which dispersal can take place. There is no indication that any of the Kittiwakes which move to Greenland remain and breed with the native breeding birds; it seems almost certain that all of the birds retain a knowledge of the position of their natal area and return there when mature.

World distribution

The Kittiwake *Rissa tridactyla* is represented by two subspecies – *tridactyla* in the North Atlantic and *pollicaris* in the North Pacific. The only other species of *Rissa*, the Red-legged Kittiwake *R. brevirostris*, breeds in mixed colonies with the Kittiwake in the North Pacific, but has a much more restricted distribution.

In the North Atlantic, the Kittiwake breeds on both sides of the ocean. On the west, there are colonies in Newfoundland and in the Gulf of St Lawrence northwards to Baffin Island and Greenland. On the east, the southern limits are Iceland, the Faeroes and Britain and Ireland, with a few small colonies in Brittany. In the north of Europe, colonies exist along the coast of Norway, on the coast of north Russia and on the islands in the Arctic Ocean.

The southern breeding limits of the Kittiwake tend to follow the distribution of arctic water, that is, where the sea temperature does not exceed 10°C at any time of the year. The exception is in north-west Europe, including colonies in south Norway, Denmark, north France and Britain and Ireland and here the Kittiwake breeds in warmer waters than in any other part of its range.

Census methods

The Kittiwake is a relatively easy seabird to census. The nests are conspicuous and the main problem is for the observer to reach a position where he has a good view of the occupied cliffs. In many cases this can be achieved from the cliff top but, failing this, counts have to be made from the sea or from below the cliffs if this is accessible. The census unit has been taken as a fully built nest which is readily distinguishable and this ignores the non-breeding element in the colony. The size of some colonies is a further problem but this can usually be overcome by dividing the cliff into zones and areas on a sketch map and counting region by region. Repeat counting is essential for a reliable census to be made.

Status in Britain and Ireland in 1969–70 and past history

The Kittiwake is an almost completely coastal breeder and with few exceptions, nests on cliffs which have vertical, stable rock faces with small ledges. Such cliffs occur around the whole of Britain and Ireland except in much of south-east England and this is reflected in the distribution of colonies (Map 18).

By far the largest concentration of Kittiwakes occurs on the North Sea coast of Britain. The vast colony at Flamborough Head and Bempton in Yorkshire is the start of a series of colonies on the east coast which continue up through Scotland with huge ones at Foulsheugh, and many other places on the Aberdeenshire and Caithness coasts. Further large colonies occur in Orkney and Shetland and this stretch of coast along the western edge of the North Sea possesses far larger colonies and numbers of Kittiwakes than are found elsewhere in Britain and Ireland. By contrast, the colonies on the west coast tend to be smaller than those on the east and small colonies are characteristic of the Hebrides and much of the coastline of Ireland. There are very few colonies on the mainland of west Scotland, which reflects the lack of suitable cliffs along much of this coastline.

The small amount of cliff in south-east England has not deterred the Kittiwake from colonising this region. Apart from a new colony on the cliffs of the Kent coast, Kittiwakes nest on the Pier Pavilion at Lowestoft (Suffolk) and birds have also made several attempts to nest on the sand dunes in Norfolk. So far, the attempts to breed on the dunes have been unsuccessful but a colony in a similar situation has thrived for many years in Denmark and a similar one could be established in this country if given careful protection.

In addition to nesting on coastal cliffs, Kittiwakes also nest on buildings close to the coast. This occurred first at Granton, near Edinburgh, in 1932 but the colony was deserted a few years later. Another colony was established on a building at Dunbar in East Lothian and more recently new colonies on buildings have been founded at North Shields and Newcastle (Northumberland), Gateshead and Hartlepool (Co. Durham), at Lowestoft, and on the harbour wall at Scrabster (Coulson 1963; Cramp 1971). Similar colonies are also known in Norway and it is evident that the birds find buildings an acceptable alternative to natural cliffs; they also have vertical faces with small ledges (window sills) and those used usually overlook water.

The colonies on buildings at Newcastle and Gateshead are the first breeding areas in Britain and Ireland which are well away from the sea. In these cases, the birds are nesting over eleven miles from the river mouth, although still within the tidal reaches of the river. Some of these birds move up into the non-tidal stretches of the river and feed on fresh-water fish, which is a radical change in behaviour.

The first national Kittiwake census was carried out in 1959 (Coulson 1963) and the counts then made make a valuable base-line to measure the changes in the population over the last ten years. Such base-lines are one of the main reasons for Operation Seafarer and the results obtained from the Kittiwake census give an indication of the type of information which will be available for other species when repeat surveys are made in future years.

The present census indicates that there are about 370,000 breeding pairs of Kittiwakes in Scotland but this figure includes only an estimate by order of abundance for the huge colony at Marwick Head on the Mainland of Orkney which still requires a detailed census (Appendix Table 19).

England has over 50,000 pairs with the majority in the large Flamborough–Bempton area of Yorkshire. Wales now contains some 6,700 pairs and Ireland almost 43,000 pairs. The breeding population of Kittiwakes in Britain and Ireland has now almost reached half a million pairs with almost three-quarters of them nesting along the North Sea coast up to Orkney and Shetland.

A comparison of the colonies censused in 1959 and again in 1969, together with colonies known to have been established in the intervening period, show that the numbers of nesting Kittiwakes have increased by 49% over the ten-year period, which is equivalent to an annual increase of almost 4%. Regional values indicate that the rate of increase may be above this in Ireland but results will be required from a future census to establish this, as relatively few colonies were counted there in 1959.

The rate of increase in the Kittiwake population is slightly higher than that estimated in the 1959 census, but this is well within the limits of error in the methods used. It is evident that a population explosion has been taking place in the Kittiwake comparable to the expansion of the Fulmar in Britain. In both species the start of the increase on the mainland of Britain can be traced back to about the beginning of the present century, but unlike the Fulmar the increase in the Kittiwake remained undetected until the 1959 inquiry. It is perhaps a sobering thought that the Kittiwake has been increasing at a rate of about 50% every ten years for half this century without it being realised by ornithologists. One reason why this expansion remained undetected is that the Kittiwake has not established the very large numbers of new breeding stations which have been characteristic of the Fulmar's population growth. The Kittiwake, at the beginning of the century, expanded the size of existing colonies and only in the last forty years have new colonies been formed. Expansion of existing colonies from, say, 10,000 to 20,000 pairs usually remained unnoticed unless accurate counts or photographs had been taken. It is clear that accurate surveys of the breeding populations of seabirds are needed if the changes in population are to be precisely monitored.

The increase in the Kittiwake population has had other effects. New colonies have been formed on lower cliffs than those used by the Kittiwake in the last century and now several exist on rock faces which are under 30 feet high. As a consequence of this change, man-made cliffs (buildings) are now in the height range used by the Kittiwake and it is therefore not surprising that colonies have become established on buildings in certain areas. In several places, the natural cliffs are rapidly becoming saturated with Kittiwakes, yet the expansion continues in a geometric manner. It seems likely that many more unusual nesting sites will be used by the Kittiwake in the next decade; the use of more buildings and nesting away from the sea are distinct likelihoods, whilst nesting on beaches and dunes, particularly with terns, is likely to develop.

The expansion of the Kittiwake has occurred in the whole of the North Sea area as well as within Britain and Ireland. New colonies have been formed in southern Norway, Denmark, Sweden (on a structure used for warning shipping of dangerous areas), Heligoland and Brittany. There is less clear information about more northerly regions but it is doubtful if this rapid increase is occurring within the arctic. As far as the evidence is available, the Kittiwake is exploding at the southern end of its range where it has already burst out of the Arctic conditions into more temperate regions. The breeding of Kittiwakes in this region is not part of a recent spread as in the case of the Fulmar, as their bones have been found in middens many hundreds of years old. The population explosion is, however, recent and requires explanation.

The population of Kittiwakes in the British Isles decreased during the 19th century mainly as a result of human exploitation. In some regions, the breeding birds were exploited for feathers, food and for sport and the coming of the industrial revolution gave man both better weapons to kill birds and improved transport with which to reach seabird colonies. In reaction to this persecution, a series of Protection Acts were passed through Parliament at the end of the last century and the exploitation was at first reduced and then almost completely stopped. The Kittiwake now nests in many colonies where shooting and exploitation of the eggs and young would be easy but for the protection now offered. This has led to

higher adult survival rates and greater breeding success, with a consequen-
tial recovery of the population and then an expansion to beyond its previous level. Almost everywhere in Britain and Ireland the Kittiwake now
breeds without predation; Great Skuas are still relatively few and birds
of prey which feed on Kittiwakes are almost non-existent in this country.
Further, food is still superabundant and there is still no sign of the population explosion coming to an end. Seabirds can exploit only a very small
proportion of the fish in the sea because most species cannot dive far
below the surface. Most seabirds are unlikely to deplete the quantity of
fish to such an extent that it will deprive them of food and reduce their
survival rates. Only large predatory fish feeding on those species used as
food by the Kittiwake, or human exploitation of, for example, sand-eels,
seem likely to prevent the population explosion of the Kittiwake (and other
gulls) from continuing for many years. I suspect that nesting sites may
well become critical long before food shortage begins to operate.

J. C. Coulson

SANDWICH TERN *Sterna sandvicensis*

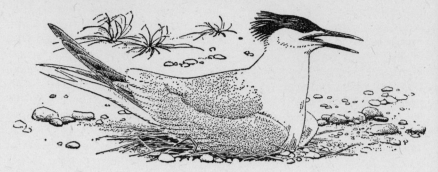

Identification

Terns are easily distinguished from gulls by their slender bodies, narrow pointed wings, fine and sharply pointed bills, elongated and usually forked tails and short legs. Their flight is generally lighter and more graceful, though that of the Sandwich Tern, the largest tern nesting in Britain and Ireland, is the most gull-like. In summer the Sandwich has the black cap typical of most terns, with the crown feathers elongated to form a crest which is raised in excitement. The bill is black, tipped yellow; the legs and feet are black. The wings and back are pale silvery-grey, and the rest of the body is white. By mid-June many birds have commenced to change to winter plumage and by late August almost all are attaining this plumage in which their foreheads become white and the black crown fringed with white. Sandwich Terns have a rasping 'kirrik' call and are among the noisiest of terns; like gulls, they are colonial nesters.

Food and feeding habits

The 'sea terns' (of the genus *Sterna*) characteristically hover and plunge for food from the wing. Sandwich Terns dive from a greater height (Dunn 1972), submerge deeper and more frequently, and often make a larger splash than do the smaller species. On Coquet Island just south of the Farnes, Langham (1968) found that Ammodytidae comprised 11% and Clupeidae 88% of their diet, although the following year, 1966, during the same period there was an increase in the former to 46% with a corresponding decrease in the latter. At the colony on the Farne Islands (Northumberland) Pearson (1968) made the following analysis, mainly of food carried by this species to feed its young –

Marine Invertebrates	2%
Crustacea	1%
Cephalopods	1%
Fish	98%
Ammodytidae (sand eels)	74%
Clupeidae (sprats etc.)	15%
Gadidae (whiting etc.)	6%
Others	3%

Smith (*in prep.*) at Sands of Forvie (Aberdeenshire) between 1960 and 1971 used the same techniques as Pearson with roughly similar results. However, Taylor (*in prep.*) at the same colony for the month of June 1972 noted equal quantities of Ammodytidae and Clupeidae being fed to chicks. The preferred food of this species seems to be clear and the observed variations in proportion reflect the relative abundance of these fish in coastal and estuarine feeding areas during the breeding season. Smith has recovered numerous fish tags from salmon smolts and silvering parr in the breeding colony at Sands of Forvie. One tag was found on a nest only 48 hours after the smolt was tagged on a river 42 miles a way. This indicates that breeding Sandwich Terns can travel far afield in search of food. In Ireland, where there are a number of colonies on inland loughs, the passage of birds to and from their marine fishing grounds is most noticeable; for example, they bring sand eels 12–15 miles overland to their colonies at Lough Conn (Co. Mayo) (Major R. F. Ruttledge *in litt.*) and Lough Erne (Co. Fermanagh) (Kennedy *et al.* 1954).

Breeding

The Sandwich Tern is exclusively a coastal breeder in Britain but (as already stated) there are colonies on several inland loughs in Ireland. It breeds in dense colonies, with the incubating birds little more than a foot apart. Nest sites are usually among sand dunes, on shingle banks or among vegetation on low rocky islands. Adults return to the colonies during late March and April. Pair formation in some birds commences as early as the end of February in Ghana and early March in Sierra Leone (Smith, *in prep.*) but for many birds seems to take place at the breeding colony. Their aerial displays at this time are most impressive, the birds in twos, threes and occasionally fours ascending to great heights until almost out of sight and then sweeping down in long glides, calling frequently. When threatening other individuals the Sandwich Tern leans forward, calling loudly, with its crest feathers raised. During greeting ceremonies male and female face each other and parade in circles with beaks half open, or stand erect with bills pointing towards the ground in the 'bent' posture. Nest sites are occupied at the very end of April or early in May, the birds arriving *en masse* and starting to lay almost at once. At Scolt Head (Norfolk) they seem to spend several evenings at the colony before remaining throughout the day, but at Sands of Forvie (Aberdeenshire) they are present in considerable numbers throughout the day although there is an increase in the numbers roosting overnight at the colony. Chestney (1970) considered that the first group of terns to arrive selects the breeding site and that the colony develops around this initial nucleus. If laying is interrupted by bad weather at this early stage, those birds which have not yet laid may form separate sub-colonies as the weather improves. At the Sands of Forvie birds in the same 'biological state' group together. Each group forms a sub-colony and achieves a remarkable synchronisation in laying with consequent high breeding success. Smith (*in prep.*) believes that a large compact colony is really a number of such groups utilising the available nesting area, which at Scolt Head and on the Farnes permits almost contiguous nesting whereas at the Sands of Forvie the nature of the dunes precludes this and clearly separates the sub-colonies (see also Langham 1968). In the event of disturbance preventing the initial establishment of the colony, the whole group may move elsewhere for the season; thus protection during these early days is essential.

Sandwich Terns often nest near or among Black-headed Gulls and other terns, and Cullen (1960) suggested that they might depend on these more pugnacious species to harass and drive away potential predators. Lind (1963) reported that Sandwich Terns associated with Black-headed Gulls derive more advantages than those associated with other terns. Nehls (1969) found that Sandwich Terns followed Black-headed Gulls when they changed breeding sites. The association has also its drawbacks, not the least of which is food parasitism by the gulls which can have serious effects on chick survival as experienced at Havergate Island and Sands of Forvie (Smith *in prep.*). Sandwich Terns normally make little concerted effort to defend their nesting colonies from predators but in a mixed colony at Needs Oar Point (Hampshire), however, many Black-headed Gulls whose nesting activities had been interrupted earlier by egg-collecting left the area where the Sandwich Terns established their colony: the latter were then quite able to guard themselves against predators, swooping close to human intruders (Taverner 1965, 1970).

The normal clutch is of one or two eggs, the ground colour ranging from white to brownish-buff and marked with spots and blotches of dark brown. They are laid in a shallow depression to which incubating birds may add small pieces of vegetation and small stones during the incubation period, which averages 25 days but may range from 21 to 29 days (Langham 1968; Smith *in prep.*). Young chicks are covered with brownish down, the ends of which stick together to give them a prickly appearance. They leave the nest within a few days of hatching; at some colonies they even-

ABOVE: Sandwich Terns, Isle of May. BELOW: Roseate Terns at the nest

A St Kildan catching Puffins, using long thin pole with a running noose at the end.

tually gather in groups which move to the sea's edge where they run from any danger that threatens, but at others they may hide within the nesting area, as observed by Taverner (1965) at Needs Oar Point. Fledging takes place at about 28 days, occasionally 26 and rarely more than 30 (Pearson 1968; Smith *in prep.*), and the young follow their parents for a long period after leaving the colony.

Movements

Juveniles initially disperse from the colonies along the coasts to areas where food is plentiful with an almost equal movement in either direction. A definite movement southwards is not obvious until late summer and the last birds depart during October. Some birds must commence migration much sooner, since ringing recoveries have been made in early September from Senegal to Ghana. The main wintering area for the western European population seems to be this part of Africa, and farther south in Angola. Some penetrate farther south and east to reach the Indian Ocean where there have been recoveries as far north as Zululand (Natal). Many recoveries of ringed birds are reported from urban centres at many of which terns are trapped for food. Trapping occurs along most of the west coast of Africa from Senegal to Angola and accounts for about 13% of ringing recoveries. Most sea terns take fish offal and dead fish in Africa and are easily attracted to a variety of traps and snares. First winter birds are more likely to be taken by this means than older birds. (Smith *in prep.*) From an analysis of ringing recoveries it appears that first summer Sandwich Terns remain in their winter quarters but colour-ringed birds of this age have been reported from the north-west of France and south-west of England during late July and August and a bird of this age was at its natal colony at Sands of Forvie in late July. In their second summer a greater number move north to European waters by June or July and several birds in this year class have bred at Sands of Forvie. They do not normally breed until the third summer when the birds are three years old (Nehls 1969; Smith in prep.). There have been a few summer recoveries in the Mediterranean where Sandwich Terns from colonies in the Black Sea spend the winter (Langham 1971; Thomson 1943, 1962).

Ringing has shown that much interchange of individuals takes place between colonies in this country, and also with those on the Continent. Birds from the Farnes (Northumberland), the Firth of Forth, Scolt Head (Norfolk) and Strangford Lough have been found breeding at the Sands of Forvie (Aberdeenshire) while others from Ravenglass (Cumberland) and Horse Island (Ayrshire) have been found at the Carlingford Lough (Co. Down) colony. In 1955 flooding at some of the large Dutch colonies caused considerable movements and one group of Sandwich Terns from the Netherlands established themselves on the Farne Islands (Cullen

1962). A four-year-old Sands of Forvie bird was also recovered having bred on the Adriatic coast of Italy. Other birds from this colony have bred on the Friesian Islands, and from the Farnes and Ravenglass colonies in new colonies on the German Baltic coasts (Nehls 1969).

World distribution

This species, first described by John Latham from specimens collected in Kent in 1787, has a very scattered world breeding distribution, accentuated locally by the instability of its colonies due to disturbance, habitat changes and possibly local food failures. It nests along the Atlantic coast of North America from North Carolina to Florida, on the coast of Mexico and Yucatan and in the Bahamas. The Old World population is split between four distinct areas: the southern and eastern shores of the Caspian Sea; the north coast of the Black Sea; the Mediterranean (where its present status is a little obscure, but birds nest or have nested in Tunisia, Sicily, Sardinia, southern France and Spain), and finally northern Europe on the coasts of both East and West Germany, Denmark (Nehls 1969) and possibly Poland, in the Netherlands, Brittany, Britain and Ireland (Vaurie 1965; Voous 1960). The largest colonies in northern Europe were formerly in the Netherlands, but pesticide poisoning during the early 1960s severely reduced these (Koeman 1971).

Census methods at tern colonies

Most tern colonies are accessible, since the birds nest on flat ground along the shore or on small islands nearby. Great care must be taken to avoid undue disturbance: terns, notably Sandwich Terns, are very prone to desert, particularly during the early part of the breeding season and at small colonies recently established. Time spent in a colony must not exceed 20 minutes per visit, though in a large colony it may be safe to work in one section without causing disturbance to birds nesting elsewhere. Since colonies are often in areas frequented by the general public, care must always be taken to avoid attracting others who might cause extra disturbance, and unknowingly trample on eggs or small chicks.

Incubating birds may be counted from a distant vantage point, unless prevented by uneven terrain or vegetation when searching may have to be employed. Roseate Tern eggs have a distinctive pyriform shape (see page 151), and the extreme sizes of those of the Sandwich and Little Terns prevent confusion with other species. The eggs of the Common and Arctic Terns are indistinguishable and at mixed colonies this causes problems. Preliminary observations made from a distance, of birds either on the ground or flying to and fro, will provide an indication of the relative numbers of each species; the total nest count can then be split proportionately. Even in mixed colonies, however, each species often occupies its own particular area within the site. The Arctic Tern tends to choose short turf, rock or sand, while the Common Tern often prefers to nest amongst vegetation. The Roseate seems to like even more cover and will nest in the entrance of a disused burrow, in a rock crevice or beneath vegetation. When eggs have hatched chicks soon leave the nest, though faecal deposits and discarded food remains still indicate their presence close by. Late counts using such criteria provide an indication of the number of successful pairs, but care should be exercised in the case of the Sandwich and Roseate Terns, since dense nesting can lead to one brood using several scrapes in succession.

Status in Britain and Ireland in 1969–70 and past history

It seems likely that the Sandwich Tern population of Britain and Ireland, 11,860 pairs in 1969–70 (Appendix Table 20), is higher now than at any time this century. As recently as the mid-1960s Parslow (1967) estimated 6,000 pairs, but in view of the limited information available from some remote areas this may well have been an underestimate. Certainly in south-east Scotland and eastern England, where the bulk of the population is found, there has been a marked overall increase since the 1920s, with no sign up to 1969–70 of any slowing down except perhaps in the Firth of Forth where irregular fluctuations occur (see Table 6).

TABLE 6. *Numbers of pairs of Sandwich Terns nesting in certain years since 1920 on the east coast of England and Scotland south of the River Tay. (Information up to and including 1964 from Parslow 1967)*

	Firth of Forth	Farne Islands	East Anglia	Hampshire	Totals
1920	Few	1,000	1	—	c. 1,000
1923	400	Nil	640	—	1,040
1932	Under 50	2,000	820	—	c. 2,850
1939	500	2,000	1,000	—	3,500
1946	1,500	120	1,900	—	3,520
1954	400	960	380	10	1,750
1957	400	800	1,520	80	2,800
1959	700	1,250	1,220	Not known	3,170+
1962	1,120	1,480	1,460	57	4,117
1964	500	1,500	2,010	5	4,015
1969	50	2,000	4,120	220	6,390

In more remote areas, particularly in Ireland and northern Scotland, the relative lack of previous data and the shifting nature of colonies, notably in response to constant disturbance in the Moray Firth area, make population trends difficult to assess. Sandwich Terns are very sensitive to disturbance and habitat changes, but nearly all the largest southern colonies are protected in nature reserves; provided this protection is maintained and the birds are not affected by pollution, as happened in the Netherlands, or by food shortages, they should continue to thrive.

The history of many colonies, especially on the east coast of Britain, is well documented. Although Sandwich Terns have nested occasionally in Shetland (Venables and Venables 1955), Orkney is the most northerly regular breeding area in Britain and Ireland, and indeed in the world; nesting was first noted there in 1893 (Marples and Marples 1934) and a number of different sites have been and still are used, not all annually. Sandwich Terns have nested in the past at sites in the Moray Firth and in Easter Ross and east Sutherland, most regularly on the Moray-Nairn border where 150 pairs attempted to nest in 1970 but were totally unsuccessful (*Scottish Bird Report 1970*). 1,000 pairs appear to have been more successful at a site used by smaller numbers in Easter Ross at least since 1966, but they are apparently often disturbed there as well, and this whole area is apparently too unsettled now for a permanent colony to survive and moreover increasing numbers of gulls are also using the sites. In 1971 the birds tried to breed again at the Moray-Nairn site, but eventually appear to have moved on, late in the season, to the main headquarters for northeast Scotland on the Sands of Forvie in eastern Aberdeenshire. This colony was first noted by A. Landsborough Thomson in 1910 but nothing further was heard of it until 1935 and 1936. It was much disturbed during the 1939–45 war (Baxter and Rintoul 1953); except for 14 pairs in 1951, none nested there from 1947 to 1953, but 100 pairs returned in 1954 and since then they have nested annually although without success in 1959 (see Table 7).

TABLE 7. *Numbers of pairs of Sandwich Terns breeding at Sands of Forvie (Aberdeenshire) from 1954–1971((A. J. M. Smith)*

1954	100	1963	382
1955	29	1964	565
1956	110	1965	724
1957	224	1966	743
1958	208	1967	743
1959	13	1968	1,345
1960	165	1969	740
1961	63	1970	1,281
1962	357	1971	2,100

In Fife, Sandwich Terns bred at Tentsmuir from 1906 (perhaps earlier) until 1939 in very variable numbers, averaging 300–400 pairs annually. Once again disturbance during the 1939–45 war drove the birds away, and although they returned in 1945 successful nesting was not achieved until 1951 and then only a single chick fledged from 22 pairs (Grierson 1962). None nested from 1956 to 1968 when 500 pairs returned but were unsuccessful due to gales, high tides and blown sand (*Scottish Bird Report 1968*); there was none in 1969. Various sites, usually on islands, have been used in the Firth of Forth, Fidra (East Lothian) and Inchmickery (Midlothian) being the main strongholds: again, large annual fluctuations have occurred (see Table 8).

TABLE 8. *Numbers of pairs of Sandwich Terns on Fidra (East Lothian) and Inchmickery (Midlothian) from 1959 to 1971 (Information supplied by R. W. J. Smith)*

	Fidra	Inchmickery		Fidra	Inchmickery
1959	70	630	1966	Nil	315
1960	?	298	1967	Nil	300
1961	300+	353	1968	Nil	405
1962	519	608	1969	Nil	46
1963	35	161	1970	225	3
1964	254	95	1971	300	Nil
1965	38	246			

Fifty miles south on the Farne Islands Thomas Bewick noted Sandwich Terns nesting in 1802 and they have apparently bred almost annually ever since. Numbers were low after the Second World War – for example, 120 pairs in 1946 (Sandeman 1963) – but except for 600 pairs in 1958 they have fluctuated between 1,000 and 2,000 pairs since 1950 (*Farne Islands Reports*) with 2,000 in 1969. The main centre in Britain and Ireland, however, is now the north coast of Norfolk where breeding has been recorded annually since 1920. Five sites have been used at different times with a maximum up to 1966 of 2,700 pairs (Seago 1967). Large fluctuations have occurred; for instance 1,900 pairs nested in 1946 but only 80 in the following year (Fisher and Lockley 1954); the number recorded in 1969, 3,950 pairs (3,850 at Scolt Head), was far higher than in any previous season. In Suffolk Sandwich Terns have taken advantage of two reserves established by the Royal Society for the Protection of Birds: on Havergate Island 30 breeding pairs in 1951 increased to 350 by 1960 (Payn 1962) and to 800 in 1962, but in 1968 there was none and in 1969 150 pairs bred, while at Minsmere they first nested in 1965 – 110 pairs – following the construction of shallow lagoons, but in 1969 only 13 pairs bred. They are said to have bred in the Blackwater estuary (Essex) in 1834 but Hudson and Pyman (1968) gave only one recent breeding record in the county, and in 1969 17 pairs nested at Foulness Point. Ironically Sandwich Terns ceased to nest at the type locality, Sandwich Bay in east Kent, by the mid-19th century (Harrison 1953). On the Solent (Hampshire), where several areas are now protected, they first nested in 1954 – ten pairs (Cohen 1963) – and had increased to 220 pairs by 1969.

In Anglesey the species breeds only irregularly. An influx of some 50 pairs at one site in 1970 occurred during mid-season, perhaps due to displacement from elsewhere. In Lancashire Sandwich Terns have nested in Furness since about 1843, with peaks of some 300 pairs in 1930, 1948 and 1949 (Oakes 1953) and a count of 157 pairs in 1969. On the Cumberland coast 25 miles farther north is Ravenglass where they have nested since at least 1864: there were 15 pairs in 1888, 21 in 1889, 71 in 1891, 104 in 1906, only 15 in 1915, 7 in 1924, and a jump to 370 by 1932 (Marples and Marples 1934); from 1954 to 1960 360–480 pairs nested (Stokoe 1962), and 460 pairs did so in 1969. It seems likely that the terns shift their colonies between Furness and Ravenglass, judging by the recorded fluctuations. Sandwich Terns have nested at five or possibly six sites in the Firth of Clyde, though at the present time only two are used regularly, while in 1969 three pairs nested at a third, now a reserve of the Scottish Wildlife Trust. A decline in numbers in the Clyde has possibly taken place during recent years: 280 pairs were recorded in 1951, 300 in 1958, 230 in 1960 and 1964, and 170 in 1968 (Gibson 1969); there were 190 in 1969.

In Ireland they were first discovered nesting in 1850, on Rockabill (Co. Dublin) where they last bred in 1935 (Kennedy et al. 1954). Although they nest in many other counties, the main stronghold in Ireland seems to be Co. Down where they first bred in 1930 (Kennedy et al. 1954). Deane (1954) reported a maximum population of 500 pairs on islands in Strangford Lough, and Ruttledge (1966) said that small colonies continue to flourish there, while Carlingford Lough to the south then had 100 pairs. In 1969 660 pairs nested in Strangford Lough and 470 in Carlingford Lough, while two offshore islands in the county together held a further 68 pairs.

ROSEATE TERN *Sterna dougallii*

Identification

Though the Roseate Tern may be confused with the Common and Arctic Terns at long range, it differs in some important respects. The adults' red legs are noticeably longer; the bill is rather longer and finer and largely black, though breeding adults have a little red at the base. The upperparts are a much paler grey, while the underparts appear whiter with the breast tinged pale rose for a short period in spring. The tail streamers are longer, extending well beyond the closed wings. Roseates may be picked out in flight from Common and Arctic Terns by their much whiter appearance, shorter wings (appearing relatively broader), longer tail streamers, slightly smaller bulk and more buoyant flight with shallower wing-beats. Their characteristic calls, a long rasping 'aak', a softer 'kaa' or 'kyaa', and a squeaky 'chuvick', are very distinctive, though they also have a chattering 'kekekekek' like the Common and Arctic.

Food and feeding habits

The Roseate Tern has very similar feeding habits to those of other terns but is rather more marine, flying slowly along with head looking intently down ready to swoop to catch small fish and sand eels swimming near the surface. On the Farne Islands (Northumberland) Roseate Terns have been observed stealing fish carried back to the colony by Arctic Terns (Watt 1951).

Breeding

This is essentially a coastal nesting species, with colonies usually on small rocky or sandy islands and only occasionally on the mainland shores of Britain and Ireland. Although the nests may be as densely packed as those of Sandwich Terns when on open ground, they are often hidden in rock crevices or vegetation, a favourite spot being beneath the hanging fronds of marram and lyme grass.

Roseate Terns return to their colonies later than other terns, mostly arriving during the second half of May. Nests may be quite large; at a Co. Down colony Williamson and Rankin (1943) found that they consisted mainly of dry vegetation, though one was lined with Rabbit droppings and another with stalks and flower-heads of thrift, while a third pair had taken over an abandoned Black-headed Gulls' nest. The clutches are normally of one or two eggs which are generally easily recognisable even in a mixed colony by their straight-sided pyriform shape. Their colour varies from light stone to light brown, spotted more frequently than the eggs of Common and Arctic Terns with dark brown and sepia and with greyish-blue undermarkings. Incubation lasts 23 to 25 days. Although smaller, the young chicks are similar to those of Sandwich Terns in that the filaments of their down stick together, giving them a somewhat spiny appearance. They fledge when about 28 days old.

Movements

Roseate Terns leave European waters rapidly during September, and by November all are concentrated in their winter quarters between the equator and 10°N on the coast of West Africa. Immatures remain in this area during their first summer and although some second-summer (two-year-old) birds migrate north they generally do not breed until their third summer (Langham 1971). Most ringing recoveries are from Ghana, where 67 ringed birds from Britain and Ireland were recovered in the three years 1967–69 compared with only 19 elsewhere in Africa.

World distribution

This species has a highly fragmented breeding range covering all continents save Antarctica. In North America it breeds along the coast from Nova Scotia to Virginia and southern Florida, in Central America in Yucatan and British Honduras and on many islands through the West Indies (and formerly Bermuda) and in South America on islands off Venezuela. It nests in the Azores, on islands off West Africa, in Mauretania and formerly Tunisia and in a scattering of colonies down the east coast of Africa to Cape Province, and in the Indian Ocean in the Seychelles and Carajos Cargados. In Asia there are scattered colonies on islands from the Ryu Kyus in the South China Sea through the East Indies to the Straits of Malacca and the Molucca Sea and Ceylon and islands off the south-eastern and west coasts of India. In Australasia Roseate Terns nest in northern Australia, New Guinea, the Solomons and New Caledonia.

Britain and Ireland are without question the European headquarters, but there are also colonies in Brittany and pairs breed occasionally in northern Germany and Mediterranean France (Vaurie 1965, Voous 1960).

Census methods

See Sandwich Tern (page 146).

Status in Britain and Ireland in 1969–70 and past history

The population of Britain and Ireland in 1969–70 – 2,367 pairs – is small compared with those of most other seabird species. The majority nest around the Irish Sea coasts, Ireland having 1,714 pairs, or 72% of the total population (Appendix Table 20; Map 20). Even in Ireland the Roseate Tern is very locally distributed, most breeding either in Ulster or in Co. Wexford where a single colony contained 1,200 pairs in 1969. In view of the small number of colonies, it is rather surprising that, as with nearly all our other seabirds, again no previous complete survey has been attempted; indeed, a veil of secrecy has been drawn over the species in certain areas. This, together with the wide annual fluctuations which often occur at tern colonies, makes it difficult to assess clearly any overall trends in the population. Parslow (1967) noted a large increase during the present century but was unsure whether this was still continuing. He calculated that in 1962 the British and Irish population was approximately 3,500 pairs, including an estimated 2,000 pairs at the main Co. Wexford colony. If this 1962 total was correct, there appears to have been a decline.

The first Roseate Terns known to science were obtained as recently as 1812, shot by a Dr McDougall, hence the specific name *dougallii*, and reported by Montagu (1813). The colony from which the birds came, on the small islands in Millport Bay, Great Cumbrae (Buteshire), ceased to exist about 1850. Elsewhere in the Firth of Clyde the species has nested at seven sites, most being occupied only sporadically. The two main colonies there are now on Lady and Horse Isles off the Ayrshire coast. On Lady Isle Roseate Terns nested possibly in the late 1930s but not certainly until 1942 when a few pairs bred (Onslow 1943); 90 pairs in 1953 had decreased to eight by 1968 (Gibson 1969) and only a single adult was seen in 1969. On Horse Isle they were discovered nesting in 1952 and twelve pairs were present in 1969. In the Firth of Clyde as a whole, at least 65 pairs nested in 1958 (Gibson 1969): by 1969 these had been reduced to the twelve on Horse Isle.

Roseate Terns nest only infrequently or in small numbers on the east coast of Scotland except in the Firth of Forth. Here the main colony has hitherto been on Inchmickery (Midlothian) – up to 450 pairs in the late 1950s and early 1960s (Sandeman 1963), but only 50 pairs in 1969.

On Fidra (East Lothian) there were 50 pairs in 1953–54 with smaller numbers later (Sandeman 1963) and 100 pairs in 1969. In eastern England Northumberland is the only county where Roseate Terns regularly nest. On the Farne Islands small numbers bred at least since 1818 but until 1950 the number never exceeded 30 pairs; the colony then expanded to 94 pairs in 1961 (Sandeman 1963), but subsequently declined to 60 in 1969. On Coquet Island, where a few nested as long ago as 1830 (Hewitson 1831–42), 130 pairs bred from 1965 to 1967 (N. P. E. Langham *in litt.*) and there were as many as 230 in 1969.

Roseate Terns reoccupied the Isles of Scilly in 1920 after a lapse of 50 years but numbers never seem to have been large; Penhallurick (1969) considered the maximum to have been twelve pairs, but in 1969 20 nested. Anglesey is the main breeding area on the east side of the Irish Sea: Forrest (1919) reported one colony containing 300 pairs in 1918; there were 250 pairs distributed between seven sites in 1961 and 200 in 1965 (*Merseyside Nat. Assoc. Rep.*); and in 1969 there were two colonies with a total of 200 pairs.

For a period about the end of the last century the Roseate Tern ceased to breed in Co. Wexford, but several important colonies have since been established there, the largest of which, on Tern Island (which was declared a reserve of the Irish Wildbird Conservancy in 1969), held 1,600 pairs in 1961, 2,000 in 1962 (Ruttledge 1966) and 1,200 in 1969. Rockabill (Co. Dublin) is an old-established colony with 'hundreds' in 1844 and 70–80 pairs in 1847, but nesting ceased soon after 1850 (Marples and Marples 1934); there were 200 pairs there in 1949, 68 in 1958 (Ruttledge 1966) and 60 in 1969. Roseate Terns ceased to nest in Ulster about 1880 but returned in 1908 when a few pairs nested in Strangford Lough (Co. Down) (Marples and Marples 1934); in 1969 20 pairs nested at three sites in the Lough, but the main Ulster areas are now Carlingford Lough in Co. Down (230 pairs) and Larne Lough in Co. Antrim (190 pairs).

COMMON TERN *Sterna hirundo*

Identification

The Common Tern, one of three medium-sized terns nesting in Britain and Ireland, most closely resembles the Arctic Tern. Both have the body-plumage pale grey above and white below; adults in summer have black caps and napes, while in winter the forehead and front of the crown become mottled white. In summer the bill of the Common Tern is orange-red with a distinct black tip, while the Arctic Tern has an all-red bill (though a few individuals retain some black at the tip which is, however, by no means as distinct as in the former species). In winter the bills of both species are blackish with a red base. The Common Tern has longer legs and stands higher. There is also a slight difference in the length of the tail streamers: in the Common Tern they do not project beyond the tips of the closed wings, while in the Arctic Tern they usually project slightly. In flight the two may be separated by the extent of the dark areas on the wings: in the Arctic Tern the wings are almost translucent with a darker band along the posterior edge, while in the Common Tern the fifth and sixth primaries are darker than the rest of the wing, so that a narrow dark patch is visible near the wing tip. Further the Common Tern has a longer head which projects further forward of the wings in flight and a more slender silhouette (Vande Weghe 1966). Until quite recently juvenile Common and Arctic Terns were considered very difficult to separate in the field, but Grant and Scott (1969) have provided criteria by which, with care under reasonable conditions, they can be specifically identified. The voice of the Common Tern, a long, grating 'kree-err', is rather similar to that of the Arctic Tern.

Food and feeding habits

Terns catch fish and other marine life by diving down, sometimes barely touching the surface but often partially submerging and on occasions completely disappearing from view, though they do not swim underwater. In feeding flight they move slowly along with deep wing-beats, head inclined down, watching for movement in the water, and then dive from a semi-hovering position some feet up. The catch may be eaten straight away or taken in the bird's bill to land where it may be presented in display or, later in the season, fed to the chicks. Collinge (1926) found that about 25% of the food taken by Common Terns at Blakeney Point (Norfolk) was food fish (Whiting, Herring etc.), 14% sand eels, 26% crustacea and marine worms, 10% molluscs, 20% insects and about 5% unidentifiable animal matter. Baxter and Rintoul (1953) observed them hawking over arable land in Fife, probably seeking crane-flies which were unusually abundant at the time.

Breeding

Common Terns nest in a variety of sites – sand and shingle beaches, sand dunes, saltings, freshwater marshes, marine islands and islands in coastal lagoons and freshwater lakes. In 1949 some were found nesting on reserve coal dumps overgrown with grass at Ringsend Power Station, Dublin (Kennedy *et al.* 1954); in 1967 30 pairs nested (*Irish Bird Report*) and a similar number did so in 1969. Common Terns breed inland more frequently than other terns, occurring high up river valleys in northern Scotland (Baxter and Rintoul 1953) and recently in such lowland Scottish counties as Lanarkshire, which was colonised in 1955 (Meiklejohn and Palmar 1958), and east Stirlingshire, colonised in 1957 (Baxter 1958). In Ireland, however, the once-flourishing inland colonies have now ceased to exist except for the occasional scattered pair (Major R. F. Ruttledge *in litt.*). During recent years there has been an increasing tendency in England for Common Terns to nest inland at such places as gravel pits, with small numbers in many eastern counties. In the Trent valley (Nottinghamshire) they have nested since 1950, with a maximum of 19 pairs in 1955, up to six different sites having been used in a single season (*Nottinghamshire Bird Reports*). They can be attracted to nest in suitable areas by the provision of moored rafts, as at Ranworth Broad (Norfolk) where 24 pairs bred in 1966 (Seago 1967), and at the John Summers steelworks, Deeside (Flintshire), where ten pairs nested in 1969.

Courtship commences soon after arrival at the colonies, one of the main displays being fish-carrying in which the birds fly noisily about with fish dangling from their beaks. The fish is presented to a prospective mate who often flies straight off followed by its partner, while during the early days fish may be passed between a number of birds. Gradually pairs form as males continually return with food for their mates. Females beg for food prior to copulation, which normally takes place at the nest site. The birds hollow out the nest scrape by thrusting themselves forward on their breasts and throwing out débris with their feet, turning in a tight circle as they do so. Males make scrapes early in the season and females enlarge these or make new ones alongside. During incubation they line the nest with material from close at hand: if this is plentiful quite a substantial nest platform results (Marples and Marples 1934).

Two or three eggs is the normal clutch, replacements being laid if these or young chicks are lost. Their ground colour ranges from greenish or bluish-white to dark buff, with markings of brown. Incubation, undertaken by both parents, lasts on average 24 days. Chestney (1970) reported that when the terns at Scolt Head (Norfolk) are frequently disturbed incubation may extend to 29 days, and the chicks which hatch are weaker and have less chance of survival during the first critical days of life. Leaving the nest within a few days of hatching, chicks do not wander far. They are fed on small fish brought ashore by their parents who often have to run the gauntlet of other terns intent on stealing their catch. Robbing activity seems to start when birds lose their own young and before they lay replacement clutches. Chestney noted that up to 55 minutes may normally elapse between feeds for the chick, but where robbing is severe this may be extended to 90 minutes and only one fish in ten may reach a chick, with as many as twelve adults attempting to steal from a single parent. The extent to which these activities may be related to local food shortages is not clear. Fledging takes place when the chicks are about 30 days old (Palmer 1941). At first they are still fed near the colony by their parents, but gradually they begin to accompany them on fishing sorties.

Movements

Dispersal away from the colonies by juvenile Common Terns is slower than that of Arctic and Sandwich Terns. Initially it occurs along coastlines in any direction from the natal colonies, but as the autumn proceeds movement to the south begins. The main wintering area for both adults and juveniles seems to be the west coast of Africa from about 20°N to the equator, a few moving farther south, with some ringing recoveries in Angola. There are, however, two remarkable recoveries of European-ringed Common Terns in Australia: one was of Swedish origin, the other was ringed as an adult on the Copeland Islands (Co. Down) in May 1959 and found in Victoria in October 1968 (Spencer 1969). Juveniles remain mainly in their wintering area during their first summer, while in their second those that do move north do not seem to arrive in the breeding areas until at least mid-June; most Common Terns do not breed until three years old (Langham 1971).

World distribution

Common Terns nest over a wide area of the northern hemisphere. In central North America they are found from Hudson Bay and the Great Slave Lake south to Alberta, the Great Lakes and the St Lawrence, on the east coast from south-east Canada to North Carolina and islands off Florida and Texas, and also on Bermuda, in the Bahamas and Virgin Islands and off Venezuela. They nest on the Atlantic islands of the Azores and Madeira, in Africa on the Tunisian coast, in Mauretania and the Niger delta, and across most of Europe and Asia to Kamchatka, the Kuril Islands and Manchuria. Although the Common Tern breeds as far north as 70°N on the Norwegian coast, inland its northern limit seems to be reached at about 67°30'N in Siberia, whence it extends south to Iran and Tibet (Vaurie 1965; Voous 1960).

Census methods

See Sandwich Tern (page 146).

Status in Britain and Ireland in 1969–70 and past history

In 1969–70 at least 14,700 pairs of Common Terns nested in Britain and Ireland (Appendix Table 20; Map 21). This total represents only a minimum, since an unknown number, particularly in Scotland, nest at inland sites not included in the survey. There had been no previous full survey of the Common Tern in Britain and Ireland. In England and Wales, where 6,407 pairs nested in 1969–70, counts are made annually at many sites, but as with most of our other seabirds such information is available from Scotland and Ireland only for a few well-watched colonies. The marked fluctuations which frequently occur at tern colonies make population assessments difficult, but despite local increases it seems that in England the Common Tern may be decreasing. Parslow (1967) estimated 5,500 to 6,000 pairs in England and considered this to be lower than in the 1930s; in 1969–70 there were 6,117 pairs.

Information concerning the past status of the Common Tern in Scotland is very sparse. At Tentsmuir (Fife) large numbers nested during the first half of this century but were virtually eliminated following the establishment of a firing range in the 1939–45 war. New colonies were later founded and 200 pairs in 1953 were followed by 100 in 1954 and 1955 (Grierson 1962), while the 200 pairs in 1969 represent a recovery over more recent seasons. On the Isle of May (Fife), following an absence from the middle of the last century until after the 1914-18 war, numbers have fluctuated greatly, with a maximum of 5,000-6,000 pairs in 1946-7 and none since 1956 (Eggeling 1960), though numbers still nest elsewhere around the Firth of Forth

In Northumberland there has been a remarkable increase on Coquet Island, from two pairs in 1958 to about 1,500 pairs in 1965 (N. P. E. Langham *in litt.*) with a similar number in 1969. In Norfolk, Blakeney Point remains a stronghold of the Common Tern, but despite protection measures numbers have declined from over 2,000 pairs during 1935–40 and 1950–52 (Seago 1967) to 1,200 pairs in 1969. At Scolt Head 17 pairs nested in 1922, increasing to 2,470 by 1938; by 1958 the maximum was 1,000 and numbers have since dropped further (Chestney 1970), with only 500 pairs in 1969. In Suffolk, Payn (1962) noted a big decrease since about 1930; the largest colony is at Minsmere where in 1969 250 pairs nested on islands in a man-made lagoon which was first occupied in 1962. In Essex there has been a decline in the breeding population since the 1939–45 war (Hudson and Pyman 1968), the largest colony being on Great Cob Island with usually 50–60 pairs but with only 20 in 1969. The colony at Dungeness (Kent), which contained up to 1,000 pairs in the 1930s, declined to a maximum of 40 pairs in 1952–5 (Axell 1956), recovering slightly to 200 in 1967 (*Kent Bird Report*) and falling again to 110 in 1969. In Hampshire, Cohen (1963) reported an increase during the 1950s in the colonies along the Solent to 127 pairs in 1960; in 1969 260 pairs bred there. Two or three pairs in Poole Harbour (Dorset) in 1952 and 1953 (*Dorset Bird Report*) increased to 75 in 1969, the birds nesting on a man-made lagoon. On the Lancashire coast 900 pairs nested at one time in the Ainsdale dunes, but a gradual decrease took place and by 1950 breeding success was virtually nil (Oakes 1953); none nested there in 1969. Foulney Island once contained the largest Common Tern colony in north-west England – for example, 1,100 pairs in 1963 (*Lancashire Bird Report*) – but this has since been greatly reduced and only ten pairs nested in 1969. Meanwhile the number nesting on the Ribble Marshes has increased from 100 pairs in 1964 (*Lancashire Bird Report*) to 420 in 1969, and on Walney Island, where none nested in 1963, there were 140 pairs in 1969.

The Common Tern colony on the Copeland Islands (Co. Down) was described as 'large' by Kennedy *et al.* (1954) and in 1958 1,050 pairs of mixed Common and Arctic Terns were nesting, but success was low and none has nested since 1966 (*Copeland Bird Obs. Report*). In Co. Dublin Kennedy *et al.* noted that the 'celebrated' colony at Malahide was usually 'very large', but none nested there in 1969, while on Rockabill off the same coast 250 pairs nested in 1949 but only 34 in 1969. The largest colony in Ireland in 1969 was on Tern Island (Co. Wexford) with 800 pairs; elsewhere in that county only 50 pairs nested at coastal lakes on the south coast where Kennedy *et al.* had noted this species as very numerous, as well as reporting 75 pairs on the Keeragh Islands where none nested in 1969. In Co. Kerry, which formerly had only a few scattered pairs, there were 16 colonies in 1969–70 on coastal islands with a total of 500 pairs. This apparent increase in the south-west is of interest, particularly in view of the decline inland compared with recent inland expansions in England and Scotland. On the west coast many small colonies were recorded in 1969–70, but details of past status are lacking.

ARCTIC TERN *Sterna paradisaea*

Identification

The Arctic and Common Terns, as already mentioned (page 155), may be easily confused. The best distinguishing features of the Arctic Tern in summer are its distinctive silhouette in flight with a round head which does not project far in front of the wings, slightly shorter scarlet bill, very short red legs, slightly longer tail streamers projecting a little beyond the tip of the closed wing, and pale, almost translucent primaries. The usual call, a loud 'kee-yair', can be distinguished from the similar calls of the Common Tern only with experience.

Food and feeding habits

At the Farne Islands (Northumberland) Pearson (1968) noted that the main fish taken by Arctic Terns were sand-eels, small Herrings and Sprats, while small amounts of crustacea and cephalopods were also eaten. On average, the birds spent 50 minutes away from the nest on fishing trips, up to 19 hours per day being so occupied when feeding young. About 25 meals per day were delivered to broods consisting of only a single chick and about 46 to broods of two. In Spitsbergen Burton and Thurston (1959) observed Arctic Terns fishing up to about 100 yards offshore and over lakes on the tundra; most were found from stomach analyses to be eating small crustacea. In Novaya Zemlya this species has been recorded taking small fish, crustacea, flies, dragonflies and beetles (Belopol'skii 1961). On West Ellesmere Island in arctic Canada, adults fed mainly on amphipods and small squids while unfledged chicks contained only small fish (Parmelee and MacDonald 1960). In Iceland large numbers of flies are taken by Arctic Terns from the surfaces of lakes (Bannerman 1962) and they often feed over fields there. Insects figured in the diet of Arctic Terns at the Farne Islands, though forming only about 1%; they were mainly lepidoptera taken on the wing over the nesting area (Pearson 1968). Many insects are of course blown out to sea with offshore winds and are also likely to be caught by terns.

Breeding

Arctic Terns nest colonially on low rocky skerries, sheep-grazed holms, shingle and sand banks and open ground near the shore. Inland nesting is somewhat infrequent in Britain and Ireland where the breeding ranges of the Arctic and Common Terns overlap. Farther north, where only the Arctic Tern occurs, inland nesting on shingle banks in rivers, on islands in freshwater lakes, in marshes and on the open tundra is common. At mixed colonies Arctic Terns tend to nest in areas of little or no vegetation, but where there is no competition for sites they will nest amongst lush vegetation.

On returning to their breeding sites during the latter half of April and early May, the terns make fish-carrying flights to attract mates. During territorial disputes they stretch their entire bodies forward, including the head and bill. In greeting ceremonies between the sexes the head and bill may be pointed skywards, with the bird in an erect posture, or inclined steeply down with the neck somewhat withdrawn and the body bent. Human intruders at colonies are mobbed, some birds swooping low enough to strike a person's head with their wings or bill.

Two or three eggs are laid from late May or early June, with replacements as late as July should the first clutch fail or young chicks be lost. The eggs are indistinguishable from those of the Common Tern and are incubated by both parents in turn for about 22 days (Fisher and Lockley 1954). Work at the Farne Islands has shown that Arctic Terns do not breed until they are three years old and their success rate is low during the first year of nesting, the most productive birds being five to ten years old (Horobin 1969). Having dried out after hatching, the chicks are covered in fluffy brown down. For the first few days they are brooded on the nest by one parent while the other searches for food, but later both adults go fishing and the chicks hide near the nest. They fledge when between three and four weeks old (Fisher and Lockley 1954).

Movements

The Arctic Tern is one of the greatest of bird migrants. Some individuals make round trips of 20,000 miles or more each year, breeding far to the north in the Arctic and wintering among the pack-ice at equally high Antarctic latitudes, thus enjoying more hours of daylight than any other creature. At one time it was not known how far south Arctic Terns travelled, since confusion is possible with the rather similar Antarctic

Tern *S. vittata* which nests on islands in the southern oceans. Collected specimens and, more recently, ringing recoveries have shown the full extent of the species' southward penetration: for example, an adult ringed in Denmark in May 1958 was recovered in February 1959 at 65°08's (Johansen 1959), and a chick ringed on the Farne Islands in July 1961 was recovered in December 1961 at 56°20's (Spencer 1963). The moult is postponed during these lengthy migrations and takes place rapidly in the presence of an exceptionally rich food supply in the Antarctic from late December until late February, unlike that of other terns which moult right through the non-breeding months, since they migrate much shorter distances at a slower pace (Stresemann and Stresemann 1966).

Two main routes are used by Arctic Terns as they move south, one along the west coasts of Europe and Africa, the other along the west coasts of North and South America, while it is not clear what route is followed by birds from northern central Asia, which may join one of these streams or filter south through the Middle East, where a number of Arctic Terns are reported on migration from time to time. Birds nesting in eastern North America cross the Atlantic in autumn with the aid of the prevailing westerly winds and then turn south; together with birds from northern Europe they arrive in South African waters by October and November. The final stage of their great journey is across the southern ocean where in the westerly airflow they move south-east towards the pack-ice. Some have been carried as far as Australia and New Zealand; thus a chick ringed on Anglesey in June 1966 was recovered in New South Wales at the end of December the same year, a minimum journey of 12,500 miles in six months (Spencer 1967). In the Antarctic they feed on krill found in the vicinity of convection currents around the pack-ice. At first the terns continue to move eastwards with the prevailing wind, but as the Antarctic summer progresses the ice retreats south until a zone of continental easterlies is encountered. They may take advantage of these at the start of their long journey north, moving west at first along the edge of the ice before turning north into the Atlantic and Pacific oceans (Salomonsen 1967). It seems likely that one-year-old Arctic Terns remain in the southern hemisphere, possibly circumnavigating the world in the westerly drift or moving northwards off the southern land masses. In their second summer they move north towards their breeding areas but arrive too late to nest, and breeding does not commence until their third summer (Langham 1971).

World distribution

The Arctic Tern has a circumpolar breeding distribution, replacing the Common Tern in high latitudes. In North America it nests from Alaska

to the Atlantic coast south to Massachusetts, and it breeds on all Green-
land coasts even to within 20 km. of the most northerly point, Cape Morris
Jessup at 83°40′N. In Europe the species nests in Iceland, the Faeroes,
Britain, Ireland and Brittany, on the mainland coasts of the Baltic, and
in Norway, Spitsbergen and north Russia, and it extends across Arctic
Asia to the Bering Sea and Sea of Okhotsk (Vaurie 1965; Voous 1960).

Census methods

See Sandwich Tern (page 146).

Status in Britain and Ireland in 1969–70 and past history

The Arctic Tern is the most numerous tern nesting in Britain and Ireland
with a population in 1969–70 of at least 30,773 pairs (Appendix Table
20; Map 22). Although some large colonies were reported, most were small
and often close together. The majority nest in the north and west of
Scotland and especially the Orkneys and Shetlands, with particularly
large colonies inland on the fields and moorland on Westray, and Papa
Westray, which, owing to their erratic distribution, proved exceptionally
difficult to count, with fourfold variations in the number reported by
different people in different years. For the time being we have accepted a
very cautious estimate of the number of pairs present in this area, which
may well need to be greatly increased after further study. Only small
numbers breed in England, Wales and Ireland. In England the Arctic
Tern is virtually confined to the north-east and north-west coasts, and in
Wales it nests only on Anglesey. In view of the lack of information on
tern numbers in many areas in the past, together with the rapid fluctuations that can take place due to the shifting nature of colonies, it is impossible at this stage to assess any overall changes which might be taking
place in our Arctic Tern population.

In Scotland the historical record is reasonably complete only for the
well-watched areas of Tentsmuir and the Isle of May, Fife. At Tentsmuir,
where Arctic Terns have nested since at least 1885, numbers reached a
peak of 500 pairs in 1953, falling to 150 in 1959 (Grierson 1962) and to
only 20 in 1969, lower than the pre-war level of about 50 pairs. On the
Isle of May, where 800 pairs nested in 1936 and 400–550 in 1946, numbers
ranged from 20 to 180 pairs until 1955 (Eggeling 1955), but none has
nested since 1957.

In England Northumberland is the stronghold. The largest colonies
are on the Farne Islands where the species has been known since at least
1687 (Marples and Marples 1934); 3,200 pairs nested there in 1969. A
little farther south on Coquet Island 800 pairs nested in 1969. The only
other part of England with sizeable colonies is the north-west. In 1963

Foulney Island (Lancashire), with 150–200 pairs, was considered to be the only regular colony; there were 105 pairs there in 1967 (*Lancashire Bird Report*), but only ten in 1969. At Walney Island (also Lancashire) Oakes (1953) reported a decrease from a maximum of about 100 pairs in 1913 to a mere handful in the 1940s, but in 1969 100 pairs were again present.

There seems to be no doubt that the Arctic Tern has undergone a severe decline in Ireland (Kennedy 1961; Kennedy *et al.* 1954; Ruttledge 1966). Ruttledge noted that, except on Lower Lough Erne (Co. Fermanagh), all inland colonies were deserted. During recent years the largest Irish colony was on Inishmurray (Co. Sligo) where at least 500 pairs nested in 1955 (Major R. F. Ruttledge *in litt.*) and 400–450 in 1961 (Cabot 1962), but none in 1970. A century ago it was said to outnumber the Common Tern in Ulster, but more recently there has been a relative decline there (Deane 1954); at two of the largest colonies in 1969 – Swan Island (Co. Antrim) and Green Island (Co. Down) – there were 370 pairs of Common and five of Arctic, and 370 of Common and 150 of Arctic respectively.

LITTLE TERN *Sterna albifrons*

Identification

The Little Tern is only eight to nine inches in length and is thus the smallest tern nesting in Britain and Ireland. It has the typical pale grey upperparts and white underparts of sea-terns, but the black cap is incomplete, the forehead being white, and a black eyestripe runs to the base of the bill. Its legs and feet are dull yellow and its bill is brighter yellow with a black tip. It has a rather characteristic flight, more fluttering than that of other terns. The main call-notes are a distinctive 'kik-kik' and a quicker 'kirri-kirri-kirri'.

Food and feeding habits

Little Terns seem to fish closer to their colonies than the other species and may often be seen flying slowly over creeks and shallow pools left by the receding tide on sandbanks and salt-marshes. Like other terns, their method of fishing is to drop quickly down when prey has been sighted. Small fish seem to figure less in their diet than in that of the larger sea-terns. From a small sample from Blakeney Point (Norfolk), Collinge (1926) found that they took mainly crustacea and annelids with small amounts of fish and marine mollusca.

Breeding

In Britain and Ireland the Little Tern is almost exclusively a coastal nesting species. Most sites are on shingle and shell beaches, generally in exposed positions and with little or no vegetation. Norman and Saunders (1969) reported that 64 colonies out of 89 for which such information was available were less than five feet above high-water mark, while 27 out of 95 for which such information was available were less than five yards inland from high-water mark. Colonies are occasionally found on coastal lagoons and gravel pits, and one site in Argyll is on the crumbling foundations of old RAF hangars not far from the shore. Inland sites have included Abberton Reservoir (Essex) where a number nested for several years until 1950 and ten pairs returned in 1965 (Hudson and Pyman 1968); the Stour valley (Kent) where a pair nested successfully on a gravel island in 1962 and attempted to do so in 1963 and 1964 (W. G. Harvey *in litt.*); and Hickling Broad (Norfolk) where two pairs nested in 1969 (*Norfolk Bird Report*). Abroad, Little Terns often nest inland on shingle banks alongside rivers and on the shores of lakes.

Little Terns return to their colonies during mid-April and engage in much the same pre-nesting activities – fish-carrying, aerial chases and high flying – as the larger terns. Two or three eggs are laid, varying in colour from pale stone to brown drab and thickly marked with spots and blotches of darker brown. Incubation takes 19 to 22 days, and the chicks fledge after spending about four weeks in the vicinity of the nest (Fisher and Lockley 1954).

Movements

Far fewer Little Terns have been ringed in Britain and Ireland than our other breeding terns, a total of 2,981 by the end of 1969 compared with 51,540 Common Terns, 44,072 Arctic, 14,285 Roseate and 71,362 Sandwich (Spencer 1971). There have been only 41 recoveries, some in the Netherlands, France, Spain and Portugal; those in Iberia presumably included birds moving south to their winter quarters. The most southerly recovery is from Cadiz, Spain; while a juvenile ringed at Bradwell (Essex) in August 1966 was recovered at Leixoes, Portugal, not more than seven days later, a journey of about 1,000 miles by the shortest sea route. There have been no recoveries of British-ringed Little Terns outside Europe, but this species has been reported in winter on the west coast of Africa.

World distribution

Little Terns have the widest breeding range of all our nesting terns. They nest along the Atlantic and Pacific coasts of the United States and inland along the Colorado, Mississippi and Missouri river valleys, on the coasts of Central America and through the West Indies to the only South American colonies, on islands off Venezuela. In Africa they breed along much of the Mediterranean coast, in the Gulf of Guinea, inland along the rivers Niger and Benue, and on the Red Sea and Somali coasts. In Europe they nest from the Gulf of Bothnia to the Black Sea and inland on many of the larger rivers. Their range extends over a wide area of central Asia east to Afghanistan, the Yarkland and western Altai, and south to the Persian

Gulf, the west coast of India and the river systems of that sub-continent. In the Far East they breed from Manchuria and Japan south to the Straits of Malacca, Java, New Guinea and the Bismarck Archipelago, and on the north and east coasts of Australia (Vaurie 1965; Voous 1960).

Census methods

See Sandwich Tern (page 146).

Status in Britain and Ireland in 1969–70 and past history

The Little Tern population of Britain and Ireland in 1969–70, 1,809 pairs (Appendix Table 20; Map 23), is the smallest of any of our regularly breeding seabirds except the Arctic Skua. Most Little Terns nest in south and east England; elsewhere colonies are generally small and often well scattered. The decreases which have occurred in many areas (Appendix Table 21) seem to be due mainly to human disturbance in one form or another; their tendency to nest on bathing beaches makes them particularly vulnerable. Special protection measures have been found necessary to prevent further declines at some colonies; these have usually resulted in improved fledging success and increasing populations. Protection is usually arranged by the Royal Society for the Protection of Birds and/or county naturalists' trusts: more efforts will be required, even in some remote areas, if further reductions in numbers are to be avoided.

Little Terns decreased at many colonies during the 19th century but then increased to a peak in the 1920s or early 1930s (Parslow 1967). Their subsequent decline led to a special inquiry during the summer of 1967 (Norman and Saunders 1969). Coverage was generally good, although as usual in such inquiries some of the more isolated colonies in the west of Ireland and north of Scotland were not visited. The total known population in 1967 was about 1,600 pairs, of which between two-thirds and three-quarters nested in eastern and south-east England from Lincolnshire to Kent. Most colonies were small, 113 of the total of 133 containing 25 pairs or less, and only four colonies had more than 50 pairs. The results of this inquiry confirmed the growing concern for the future of the Little Tern as a breeding species in many parts of south-east England and in north Wales. Unfortunately a lack of data for many colonies in Scotland and Ireland prevents any proper assessment in these countries, although Kennedy et al. (1954) considered that a decline had taken place in Ireland.

RAZORBILL *Alca torda*

Identification

Razorbills are stout, short-winged birds, with white underparts contrasting with a black head, back and wings in summer, though from August to March the chin and side of the head become white and this may be retained into the summer by some young birds. The wings have a white line along part of the trailing edge, formed by light tips to the secondaries. The laterally compressed bill from which the name of the species is derived is broad and heavily grooved with, in adults, a conspicuous white line crossing it half-way along and another from the base to the eye, which is deep brown. The legs and feet are dark grey. At their breeding colonies, particularly during territorial disputes, Razorbills are noisy birds with deep burring calls. They stand like penguins and waddle somewhat clumsily on their broad tarsi. When taking off from cliffs, they simply flutter down until full speed is attained, usually just before reaching the sea, but flight from the sea is more difficult, particularly during calm conditions when they splash along for many yards before gaining enough momentum to lift them clear. Their flight is fast and direct, their torpedo-shaped bodies being propelled on small, swiftly whirring wings.

Food and feeding habits

Razorbills can only dive from the surface of the sea in their hunt for food, but they are expert swimmers, both wings and feet being used underwater for propulsion. Prey species include sand-eels, small sprats, crustacea and mollusca. During the breeding season they often feed closer inshore than the Guillemot, though they also range far out to sea. Fish are held firmly in the bill and are sometimes still alive when brought to the nest site.

Breeding

Razorbills return to their colonies in January and February. The first visits are irregular, birds arriving early in the morning and leaving before midday and on some occasions within an hour or so of daybreak. Numbers gradually increase as the visits become more frequent and prolonged in March and April. Their displays at this time – line formations, mass diving, pivoting – are similar to those of the other auks. A great deal of billing takes place; Conder (1950) considered that this occurred only between pairs. Head-shaking, the bill partly open to reveal the yellow interior, is another display frequently seen. Birds leaving the ledges often perform a 'butterfly flight', in which the wings are beaten in slow motion, for up to a minute before normal flight is resumed. Fights break out from time to time on the sea and there is much chasing among the flocks.

When nesting on cliffs, Razorbills prefer crevices and corners of ledges rather than the exposed positions favoured by Guillemots. Other common sites are holes amongst boulders at the bases of cliffs, on cliff slopes and on sea stacks, and even enlarged burrow entrances close to cliff tops. Thus many Razorbills nest singly rather than in a jostling crowd, though where conditions are suitable, particularly amongst boulders, large numbers will nest in close proximity. A single large egg is laid during late April or early May; it is usually white, sometimes green or blue, and is liberally marked with brown and black. Normally no nest is made, though plant fragments have been found beside eggs and on Skokholm (Pembrokeshire) Plumb (1965) noticed that sandstone chippings were frequently piled around the egg when these were available close by. Both parents take part in the incubation which lasts 34 to 39 days (Plumb 1965). The newly hatched chick is covered with short, almost velvety down, light brown on the body, grey on the head. This is soon moulted and it then looks similar to the adults, black above and white beneath with its feathers now completely waterproof, but with a smaller and more pointed bill and with legs and feet large and out of proportion to the rest of its body. Chicks leave the nest site, fluttering down on partly grown wings, usually accompanied by an adult, about dusk some 18 days after hatching. Though barely a third the size of their parents, they quickly leave the vicinity of land for they can swim and dive expertly even at this early stage. How long they are dependent on their parents is not known, but family trios each comprised of two moulting adults and a chick are a familiar sight during any boat journey near large seabird colonies in late summer.

Movements

Recoveries of Razorbills ringed at colonies in the south-west of Britain and Ireland show a southerly movement in winter to the Bay of Biscay and Iberia and into the western Mediterranean as far east as the Gulf of Genoa. Some from southern Britain, especially first-year non-breeding birds, move into the North Sea where there have been recoveries on continental coasts north to southern Norway. Birds from colonies in Scotland travel to Scandinavian waters in large numbers in late summer and autumn, few moving south (Mead in press.; see Map 29).

World distribution

Razorbills are restricted to the North Atlantic region. On the western shores they breed from Labrador south to Maine, and on the west coast of Greenland from Melville Bay southwards, while as recently as 1953 a colony was discovered on Baffin Island in the Canadian Arctic. In Europe they occur on Bear Island, from the White Sea west and south to the vicinity of Stavanger (Norway), in Iceland, the Faeroes, Britain, Ireland, the Channel Islands, Brittany and Heligoland, and on some islands in the Baltic (Vaurie 1965; Voous 1960).

Census methods

When Razorbills nest in cliff crevices or burrow entrances an accurate count of the number of pairs is often possible. Incubating birds, eggs or chicks may be searched for amongst accessible colonies in scree and boulders, though care must always be taken to ensure that disturbance is kept to a minimum. When such colonies are inaccessible, counts can only be made of off-duty birds flying or resting on prominent vantage points, preferably neither early nor late in the day. The considerable daily and seasonal fluctuations at colonies are as yet little understood, however, and much more research is required before such counts can be used to assess the number of breeding pairs.

Status in Britain and Ireland in 1969–70 and past history

Razorbills are found nesting on most coastlines in Britain and Ireland, except between Flamborough Head (Yorkshire) and the Isle of Wight, where there are few suitable cliffs. Counts and estimates for 1969-70 suggest that the total population may have been some 144,000 pairs, and possibly more, as minimum figures have been taken for some colonies, including Horn Head (Co. Donegal) and Clo Mor (Sutherland). Since the proportion of colonies where accurate crevice or burrow counts were possible is not known, these figures must be regarded as indicating only the approximate order of abundance. They suggest, however, that Razorbills may be only about one quarter as numerous as Guillemots. Most Razorbills breed in Scotland and Ireland, with small numbers in England, Wales and the Channel Islands. Even in Scotland there are few on the east coast south of Caithness, except in Kincardineshire, and Razorbills appear to outnumber Guillemots in very few areas of Britain and Ireland (see Appendix Table 22).

There has been no previous overall survey of Razorbill numbers; indeed, there is no information, even in the vaguest terms, concerning the past size of most colonies. The limited historical information available (see Appendix Table 23) suggests that decreases have occurred, mostly in recent years, in south-west England (where the colonies are mainly rather small, although numbers on the Isle of Wight fell from 1,000 pairs in 1937 to 6 pairs in 1969–70 and on Lundy from 10,500 pairs in 1939 to 580 pairs in 1969–70), at some colonies in south Wales, Great Saltee in southern Ireland and at some colonies in northern and western Scotland. There seems to have been either little change in numbers or even indications of some increase at several places where Guillemots have decreased in numbers during the same period. So it appears possible that Razorbill numbers may not have been as markedly affected as those of the Guillemot, except in the southern parts of its range.

GUILLEMOT *Uria aalge*

Identification

The Guillemot is a little larger than the Razorbill, slimmer in build and with head, neck, back and wings brown-black and underparts pure white. Its bill is slender and pointed, black with an orange interior. The chin and a stripe behind the eye become white in adults after the onset of the moult in August, but old birds start to resume the dark head from about October, though young ones may retain it into the summer. Its short wings are beaten rapidly, so that flight is swift, though not particularly powerful, and it uses its legs and feet as rudders and air brakes, especially while manoeuvring to land. The wings are used for propulsion underwater and the birds can remain beneath the surface for up to a minute (Tuck 1960). The legs, so well adapted for life on and beneath the surface of the sea, have ceased to be efficient on land, and Guillemots are capable only of an upright trotting waddle, using their wings when negotiating obstacles. At colonies this is the noisiest of the British auks, rarely silent even during the hours of darkness, uttering a garrulous trumpeting call of varying pitch.

Food and feeding habits

Like the Razorbill, the Guillemot dives from the surface of the sea when searching for food, which is probably caught mainly near the surface, though birds have been trapped in fishing gear set at depths of 40 fathoms (240 feet) off Newfoundland (Tuck and Squires 1955). The food consists mainly of small schooling fish such as sand-eels and sprats, though invertebrates (crustacea, annelids and mollusca) are also consumed, sometimes in quantities sufficient to stain the excrement. On the Farne Islands (Northumberland), Pearson (1968) calculated that the mean weight of the fish brought ashore by Guillemots was 7.5 gm., though there was a considerable size variation. Off Newfoundland Tuck (1960) found that Razorbills and Guillemots consumed similar food – mainly Capelin – except in winter, when the Razorbills turned more to crustacea.

Breeding

Guillemots return to their colonies before the turn of the year. According to Pembrokeshire fishermen, they are always back on the ledges before Christmas; while visits in November and December have also been noted in Sutherland, Berwickshire, Northumberland and Dorset (*Seabird Bull.*, 3: 20). During these visits, which occur mainly in the early morning, the birds seem nervous when ashore and quickly take off at the sight of a distant observer or a boat passing beneath the colony, occurrences which cause no concern later in the breeding season. They tumble off the ledges, hurtling down in a curtain of brown and white bodies before gaining height and circling back to swirl past the cliff and out to sea once more. These circular flights continue for some minutes before slowly breaking up as the birds return to land.

Though some Guillemots nest in crevices or caves, most use exposed sites on cliff ledges, or on the tops of sea stacks where the centre of the colony may be several yards from the edge. They prefer to nest in close proximity to one another: the density on some ledges is such that the incubating birds huddle side by side while those landing have to force a passage through the throng. Every bird seems to be continually bowing its head and this almost nervous action becomes more pronounced at the slightest disturbance, when their trumpeting calls rise to a crescendo. Coition usually takes place on the cliff, rarely at sea (Tuck 1960).

Guillemots lay a single large pyriform egg which usually has a pale green or blue ground colour and is marked with streaks and splashes of brown. Brightly coloured when fresh, the egg rapidly becomes coated with guano slime which assists in preventing it from rolling about too much on the ledge, though many are lost nevertheless. Uspenski (1958) demonstrated that, as incubation progresses, the egg becomes more stable and rolls less due to an increase in the size of the air cell at the wide end which shifts the centre of gravity towards the narrow end. Both parents take part in the incubation which lasts between 32 and 34 days (Tuck 1960). The chick is at first covered in short brownish down and is brooded continuously. By the time it is five or six days old it begins to move around, though still seeking shelter under the wing of an adult, not necessarily its parent. Fish is brought ashore carried lengthways in the adult's bill. Feathers appear on the chick within a day or two of hatching, and before it is three weeks old its first plumage is complete and waterproof.

Young Guillemots leave their nest site when they are between 18 and 25 days old, and a third grown. Food requirements have been suggested as a primary factor in this early departure (Greenwood 1964), but the hazards chicks face on ledges must also be important as they are in continuous danger from boisterous adults, who may knock them over the edge or into inaccessible cliff crevices. Tuck (1960) found that 53% of chick mortality at a colony of the closely related Brünnich's Guillemot was from this cause. Gulls and skuas prey on unguarded chicks, especially those of isolated pairs. Adverse weather is yet another factor in chick mortality, especially of older individuals which are unable to shelter beneath adults.

Before the young leave the ledges they exercise their wings and wander about, while adults (not only those with chicks) become excited and begin deep bowing movements. The chicks utter loud 'peep-peep-peep-peep-peep-peep' calls and eventually flutter down on their growing wing-coverts (the flight feathers not yet having developed) with their large feet spread out, usually accompanied by a parent. This departure takes place usually within a short period about dusk; on Lundy (Devon) Greenwood (1964) found that during the first two weeks of July it occurred between 20.45 and 22.00 hours. The failing light reduces the activities of predators while still allowing enough visibility for the descent, and the birds can then leave the vicinity of the colony and its attendant dangers under cover of darkness. The chicks continue to call on the water, enabling them and their parents to be swiftly reunited; together they move away from the colony, the chicks already capable of swimming and diving expertly. Tschanz (1959) reported that they are able to catch their own food soon after.

Movements

The distribution of Guillemots during the winter is still imperfectly known. The majority probably do not move far from our shores, though birds from colonies in northern Scotland have been recovered in Denmark and Norway. Most of the distant recoveries of Guillemots ringed in the south-western colonies have been in France, particularly on the Biscay coast; a few have been found in northern Spain, while a juvenile ringed in Pembrokeshire in 1958 was recovered off Gibraltar in 1964 (Spencer 1965; Mead, in press).

World distribution

Guillemots breed in both the North Pacific and North Atlantic oceans. In the Pacific they are found from Oregon to Alaska, then through islands in the Bering Sea and south to Hokkaido, Japan. In the western North

Atlantic they breed from Newfoundland and the Gulf of St Lawrence to about 56°N in Labrador, with a small colony in Greenland just south of the Arctic Circle. In the eastern Atlantic their range extends farther north to include Iceland, Bear Island, Novaya Zemlya and the Murmansk coast, and they also nest on the Norwegian coast south to Bergen, on islands in the Baltic, in Heligoland, the Faeroes, Britain, Ireland, the Channel Islands, Brittany and islands off western Iberia as far south as the Berlengas (Tuck 1960; Vaurie 1965; Voous 1960). Two subspecies breed in Britain and Ireland: brown-backed *U. a. albionis*, which ranges from Iberia north to southern Scotland, and *U. a. aalge*, which is black, not brown, above and slightly larger, and is found throughout the rest of Scotland, in Norway, the Faeroes, Iceland, west Greenland and eastern North America.

A variant form known as the 'bridled' Guillemot occurs in Atlantic (but not Pacific) colonies. It has a white eye-ring from which a white line runs towards the nape. Three surveys of its distribution have been carried out. In 1938–9 the proportion of 'bridled' birds was found to increase with higher latitude – less than 1% in the south of England rising to 26% in Shetland, 34% in the Faeroes and 50–70% in south Iceland (Southern 1939; Southern and Reeve 1941). In 1948–50 the proportion of 'bridled' birds had declined at some colonies and increased at others and it was suggested that the decreases might be due to the climate becoming warmer (Southern 1951). Ten years later the changes had been reversed so that the situation was similar to that in 1938–9. The lines joining areas with similar proportions of 'bridled' birds slope steeply from south-west to north-east and appear to follow surface-water isotherms (Southern 1962).

Census methods

Since Guillemots nest in open positions individuals are relatively easy to count, though deep crowded ledges and densely packed sea stacks demand care. Assessing the number of breeding pairs is much more difficult. Birds incubating or brooding young chicks can be recognised by their half-crouched stance (Gibson 1950), though this is often difficult at a distance, while a closer approach may disturb them so that they leave their eggs. Moreover, since many eggs are lost, later counts will give fewer birds incubating than have laid, even allowing for relaying. Counting eggs and chicks in a sample part of the colony, as used by Brun (1969), has similar limitations.

Direct counts of birds present were used in Operation Seafarer. Joensen (1963) suggested that the mean number present during incubation and brooding is about half the breeding population; Southern *et al.*

(1965) found the proportion was 0.5–0.6, while more recent observations by J. J. D. Greenwood (pers. comm.) suggest it may be a little higher still. Greenwood has also shown that during June the mean number of birds at a colony varies by little more than 10% from day to day, that the minimum count each day is usually more than 80% of the mean, and that maximum counts occur during brief peaks in the early morning and late evening: thus seasonal and hourly variations may be less important than was suspected. The most satisfactory counts are obtained between about 09.00 and 15.00 hours during the late incubation or early young stage (early to mid-June). Counts late in the year are liable to be biased first in one direction by the appearance of non-breeding birds at the colonies, and then in the other by the departure of fledglings and their parents, some of which may already be leaving by the beginning of July.

Status in Britain and Ireland in 1969–70 and past history

Though the Guillemot has much the same overall breeding distribution as the Razorbill in Britain and Ireland, it appears to be more numerous in nearly all areas (Appendix Table 22 Map 25). While the counts for the smaller colonies are likely to be more accurate than with the Razorbill, difficulties are encountered in dealing with the largest colonies, which contain enormous numbers of birds, more than with any other species, and especially with the largest colonies of all along the west coast of the Orkneys. Several different people were unable to estimate the number at the colony at Marwick Head on the west coast of Mainland there more accurately than as lying between 10,000 and 100,000 pairs from the ground, while from the air it appeared to equal the largest colonies elsewhere such as Handa, Noss, east Caithness and Foulsheugh, in which case it may contain at least 25,000 pairs. The largest colony of all on the east coast of Westray to the north appeared at least two or three times larger from the air and was estimated to contain 70,000 pairs by N. Hammond on the ground. If these estimates are accepted, the total population would have been nearly 577,000 pairs in 1969–70, four-fifths of them in Scotland and over a quarter in the Orkneys. It is thus probably the most numerous of our seabirds and, unlike the Razorbill, large numbers nest all down the east coast to the English border and beyond it in Northumberland and Yorkshire. In Wales the major colonies are in Caernarvonshire and Pembrokeshire which, with those in the counties of Dublin and Wexford, make the Irish Sea and St George's Channel an important Guillemot area. Major colonies are found in Ireland in several west coast counties (for example, Kerry, Clare and Donegal), but the largest is on Rathlin Island off the coast of Co. Antrim.

There has been no previous complete survey of Guillemot numbers in

Britain and Ireland and past information is available only for a limited number of colonies, mainly in southern areas (Appendix Table 24). This suggests that there have been considerable decreases, mainly in the last thirty years, at most colonies in the south, and these are apparently still continuing. Thus nearly all the colonies surveyed in the Isle of Wight, Dorset, Devon, Cornwall, and as well as both south and north Wales, have suffered declines in population, the most marked being on Lundy, which held an estimated 19,000 pairs in 1939 but only 1,647 pairs in 1969–70. There have also been decreases farther north, with the population on Ailsa Craig falling from some 5,000 pairs in 1910 to 4,180 in 1969–70, and at colonies on Mull and Tiree. On the other hand, numbers have increased, sometimes markedly, at a number of other Scottish colonies, including St Kilda, Fair Isle, the Isle of May and St Abb's Head. There are only limited data available from Ireland, though the colony at Great Saltee has diminished since the early 1960s. To sum up, despite the limited data and the problems of estimating numbers, especially at the larger colonies, the Guillemot appears undoubtedly to have declined in southern England and Wales and locally elsewhere, though in Scotland the decreases at some colonies may have been counter-balanced by increases elsewhere. Although England, Wales and Ireland together contain only about 20% of the Guillemot population of Britain and Ireland, it should not be forgotten that these all belong to the subspecies *U. a. albionis* which has a restricted range elsewhere.

BLACK GUILLEMOT *Cepphus grylle*

Identification

The Black Guillemot is a striking bird in breeding plumage, sooty black with conspicuous white wing patches, a black bill (the interior of which is bright vermilion) and coral-red legs and feet. It is mid-way in size between the Guillemot and the Puffin. In winter the head, neck and underparts are white, the back is barred light grey and white, and the diagnostic white wing patch is retained; its whole appearance then has been described as ghostly. It flies low and with quick wing-beats like the other auks, but its stance on land is more crouching and its voice is a high-pitched, plaintive 'sphee-ee-ee-ee'.

Food and feeding habits

The Black Guillemot is an efficient diver, using both wings and feet underwater and capable of remaining submerged for over a minute. Feeding mainly on the bottom in shallow waters, it frequently occurs high up sea lochs and voes, places not normally visited by other auks. Most of the population on Fair Isle (Shetland) nests on the east coast, where the sea-bed is shallow, rather than on the west side which shelves much more steeply. The food consists of small fish, crustacea, mollusca, worms and seaweed. In Anglesey the only fish observed to be caught was the Butterfish, a species primarily found in the *Laminaria* zone close inshore (E. I. S. Rees *in litt.*).

Breeding

Black Guillemots gather on the sea near their breeding sites during the early spring, joining in striking communal displays vividly described by Armstrong (1940). Pairs swim round each other in obvious excitement, tails cocked up like fins, heads bobbing and beaks held open to expose the vermilion interior. Pursuits develop both on and just below the surface, the birds barely submerging so that their backs show in a flurry of broken water. Whole groups may engage in this activity; frequently they form into long straggling lines all gently swimming the same way, and then, as if by some signal, they turn and move in another direction, or dive and indulge in a mass submarine chase. Although lacking the vigour of the pre-breeding season gatherings, line formations may be seen later during August and September, when young birds also take part, and small parties may even perform in midwinter.

The species prefers hidden sites for nesting, choosing crevices among boulders, in cliffs and in caves, usually less than 100 feet above the sea. On Fair Isle, out of 73 nests examined in 1966 50 were among boulders or in small caves just above high-water mark while the remainder were in cliff holes well out of reach of the sea (Dennis 1966b). Cavities in man-made structures are used in some areas, for example harbour walls at Port-patrick (Wigtownshire) and Bangor (Co. Down), a hole in a wooden pier at Greenore (Co. Louth), the great stone broch on Mousa (Shetland), and ruined buildings 100 yards from the sea on North Rona (Outer Hebrides). The largest colony recorded in 1969–70 was of 340 pairs on Auskerry (Orkney), but most are considerably smaller, many containing but a hand-ful of pairs. Two eggs are normally laid, though frequently only one and occasionally three; the other British and Irish auks lay a single egg, though both the Razorbill and the Puffin have two brood patches, perhaps relics from a time when they, too, laid two eggs ? Black Guillemot eggs, white, often tinged with green, cream or buff and marked with brown or grey blotches, are laid on the bare rock or earth of the crevice, without nesting material. Both parents take part in the incubation which lasts, on average, 29 days, the chicks fledging at five to six weeks of age (Winn 1950).

Movements

This is one of the most sedentary of our seabirds, few individuals moving far from their colonies even in midwinter. The most distant recovery in Britain and Ireland involved a Fair Isle bird found in the Blackwater estuary (Essex), but this was exceptional and most recoveries are much more local, mainly following the post-breeding dispersal of juveniles between adjacent areas such as Orkney and Shetland. Arctic populations move no farther than the edge of the pack-ice, or remain in leads among it in winter.

World distribution

Black Guillemots have a nearly circumpolar distribution. They occur in very high latitudes: the doomed Andrée and his companions, struggling southwards from their wrecked balloon across the pack-ice, observed Black Guillemots at 81°47′N, while the crew of the *Fram* saw some as far north as 84°N. In North America they breed from Maine to the Canadian Arctic and into the Polar Basin, on the west Greenland coast from Cape Farewell north to the Thule district and in east Greenland from Scoresby Sound northwards. In the eastern Arctic they nest on many islands from Jan Mayen to Wrangel and on the Chukotski peninsula; and in Europe on the coasts of the White Sea, the Kola Peninsula, Norway, Sweden, north Denmark, Finland, Estonia, Iceland, the Faeroes, Britain and Ireland (Voous 1960; Vaurie 1965).

Census methods

Since nests are hidden, any census is difficult. Nests may occasionally be searched for at accessible sites, but normally the only counts possible are of birds visible. Counts early in the season, when displays are frequent, provide a good measure of the population. When the chicks have hatched, adults may be noted returning with fish to the nest sites. Direct counts of birds on the sea or resting on rocks can only provide some indication of numbers and distribution.

Status in Britain and Ireland in 1969–70 and past history

The number of Black Guillemots recorded nesting in Britain and Ireland, 8,340 pairs (Appendix Table 25), is a great deal smaller than those of the the other auks and could be an underestimate, though it would not be surprising in view of the species' more restricted range, confined to a narrow belt offshore in the north and its smaller, more widely scattered colonies. There has been no previous full survey in Britain and Ireland; indeed, the Black Guillemot has attracted little attention in the past. Some extensions or recolonisations seem to be taking place around the Irish Sea, while in Scotland, where the bulk of the population nests, decreases have been recorded in west Ross and northern parts of west Inverness, and increases farther south in the latter county and in the Firth of Clyde. Further censuses are required before population trends can be adequately assessed.

The Black Guillemot (see Map 26) has a predominantly northern and western distribution in Britain and Ireland, and its complete absence from the east coast of Britain south of Caithness, except for a single pair in Banffshire, is surprising. According to Nelson (1907), it once nested as far south as Bempton Cliffs (Yorkshire), where a pair was present in 1938 (Chislett 1952). In south-east Scotland it disappeared as a breeding species during the last century, and Baxter and Rintoul (1953) knew of none nesting south of Caithness except for a pair in Kincardineshire.

There is very little information on past numbers in the main breeding areas. North Ronaldsay (Orkney) was colonised in 1938–40 (Lack 1942–3) and 45 pairs nested there in 1969. On Handa (Sutherland) the species ceased to breed in 1891 (Baxter and Rintoul 1953), and, though four pairs nested again in 1962 (R. H. Dennis *in litt.*), none did so in 1970. Between 70 and 100 pairs bred on Priest Island (west Ross) in 1938 (Darling 1940) but there were only ten pairs in 1969; while on Raasay (west Inverness), where the Black Guillemot was described as numerous in 1936–7 (Temperley 1938), only a single pair was reported in 1970. Farther south, however, the increases reported on the Small Isles by Evans and Flower (1967) seem to be continuing, the number on Muck having risen from eight pairs in 1963 to 14 in 1969, and on Canna from 17 pairs in 1961 to 40 in 1969. Similarly, in the Firth of Clyde, where the Black Guillemot was first discovered nesting in 1898, the total population rose from 40 pairs in 1951 to 100 in 1969 (Gibson 1969).

On the shores of the Irish Sea there are signs that an expansion of range has occurred in recent years, though some of this could be the recovery of lost ground. In 1940 breeding was proved in Cumberland at St Bees Head, where birds had been observed previously and may have nested undetected (Stokoe 1962); in 1969 there were two pairs. In north Wales Thomas Pennant, the great 18th-century naturalist, knew of Black Guillemots nesting on the Great and Little Orme Heads (Caernarvonshire) and in Anglesey. They recommenced nesting in Anglesey in 1962 and at least eight pairs were present in 1969, but despite recent sightings off the Caernarvonshire coast there are as yet no modern breeding records for that county. In Pembrokeshire, where Montagu (1802) recorded a few pairs breeding near Tenby, there have been recent sight records and a pair has summered.

On the north-west coast of Ireland Ruttledge (1966) noted that an increase had taken place in Co. Donegal. In the far south-west, the population on Cape Clear Island (Co. Cork) fell from 44 pairs in 1963 to 16 in 1967 (Sharrock and Wright 1968), but rose again to 39 pairs in 1969. In Ulster the Black Guillemot bred for the first time on the Copeland Islands (Co. Down) in 1959 (*Copeland Bird Obs. Report*), and five pairs were recorded there in 1969.

PUFFIN *Fratercula arctica*

Identification

Many people are familiar with the Puffin from paintings and photographs, even if they have never been fortunate enough to visit a breeding colony; with its large, brightly coloured bill and curious waddling walk, it is a most amusing bird to watch. It stands some eight inches high and has a black back, grey cheeks, white underparts and orange-red legs and feet. The remarkable triangular bill, with blue, red and yellow bands, is unusual in that some parts of the casing of both mandibles are lost during the winter, as are the fleshy yellow rosette round the mouth and the red and grey eye-patches. The voice of the Puffin, a deep purring 'aar', is heard chiefly from birds in their nest burrows and appears to vary from angry to ecstatic.

Food and feeding habits

Puffins dive for their food from the surface of the sea using their wings for propulsion and their feet as rudders. Their winter food is not known. During the summer, however, there are excellent opportunities at the colonies to observe the food taken as the adults bring back beakfuls of small fish – sand-eels, Whiting and Sprats – to feed to their chicks. The fish are carried cross-wise in the adult's beak, though not in the neat heads-and-tails arrangement that has been suggested. Most fish loads are brought to the colony in the early morning and in the afternoon. Myrberget (1962) found at a Norwegian colony that the average number of fish per load was 5.2, though up to eleven at a time were recorded. How such numbers are held in the bill has always been a matter of interest: the backward-pointing serrations on the interior of both mandibles probably play an important part.

Breeding

Puffins return to their colonies – usually on islands but also on remoter sections of mainland cliffs – during mid-March in the south, but not until the end of the month or early April farther north. At first they gather in flocks or 'rafts' on the sea close to the colony, and it may be up to two weeks before any land. Until laying begins they may desert the colony for several days at a time, especially in bad weather.

One of the most exciting events at a seabird colony is the spring arrival of the Puffins, which usually occurs at the end of several days during which the number on the sea has gradually increased. Previously activity in the rafts had been minimal but now the birds become restless, whirling in great flocks around their section of the coast. A few land and walk nervously after being at sea for seven months; gradually more alight until eventually most are ashore, and all the while there is a continual coming and going so that the air is full of flying birds. At the slightest disturbance the whole assembly will take flight and circle round again before slowly returning. After spending several hours on land they will just as swiftly depart and the procedure may not be repeated for some days.

Although Puffins often nest in crevices on cliffs or among boulder scree, the favourite sites are burrows excavated in soft ground on cliff slopes or tops, on wide ledges with steep grass banks above the sea or on more level summits of islands. They sometimes share a common entrance to the burrow with Manx Shearwaters or Rabbits. Soon after arriving at the colony they begin to investigate old burrows which may have become choked with vegetation or loose soil. Showers of earth erupt from the entrance as they commence their clearing operations, an activity which quickly attracts others, for Puffins are inquisitive birds. Although no real nest is built, large amounts of dry grass and other vegetation may be placed in the nest chamber, and sometimes a tug-of-war develops over large items like feathers.

The main courtship display is a clashing or rubbing of bills which takes place both on land and on the sea throughout the breeding season. Other birds in the vicinity are often stimulated to commence billing and on occasions it becomes general among small groups. Head-flicking, when they jerk their heads as if with hiccoughs, is also seen throughout the breeding season and is considered to be an appeasement ceremony (Fisher and Lockley 1954). Fights are usually brief but occasionally they may be prolonged affairs with the combatants falling many yards down a slope or even over a cliff edge before parting; the birds become so engrossed while fighting that it is often possible to walk up and catch them. Mating usually occurs on the sea. The single white egg, laid at about the end of April, is incubated by both parents in turn, hatching after 40–43 days. The chick is covered with dark grey down and is fed on small fish brought into the burrow and dropped on the floor by its parents.

The chick is deserted and left to fend for itself at about six weeks of age. After fasting for some eight days, during which time it uses up accumulated fat reserves, it leaves the burrow and makes its own way to the sea; at this stage it looks like a smaller, greyer version of its parent with a much more slender bill. During evenings in late July young birds may often be seen standing by burrow entrances, viewing the outside world for the first time. Most leave after dusk in order to avoid predators, particularly the larger gulls and skuas. Many will have to walk only a few feet before making their first flight down to the sea; others may have to travel several hundred yards to find a suitable take-off point.

Movements

The colonies are rapidly deserted during early August with the departure of the young birds; indeed, this happens as suddenly as the spring arrival. The whole winter is spent at sea, but at present little is known of this important part of their lives, though they appear to be highly marine and keep well away from land. Birds ringed on the north-east coast of Britain appear to remain in the North Sea, whereas birds from western Britain and Ireland have been recovered south to the Straits of Gibraltar and into the Mediterranean (C. J. Mead in press). Puffins wrecked on the northeast coast of Britain in the early spring in 1969 and 1970 were in various stages of wing moult (W. R. P. Bourne, J. J. D. Greenwood and R. Yule), and they have also been found in moult as far south as the Balearic Islands in March and April (Stresemann and Stresemann 1966), though most of the birds wintering in the south appear to return north through the Straits of Gibraltar and up the west coast of Europe in a short period in early April (Pettitt 1972; E. F. J. Garcia *in litt.*). At least two ringed on St Kilda have made transatlantic crossings and been recovered off Newfoundland.

World distribution

In North America the Puffin is found southwards from about 55°N in Labrador to New Brunswick and eastern Maine. In Greenland it occurs on the west coast from the Thule district southwards to about 60°N, and on the east coast in Scoresby Sound, while the Arctic islands of Bear Island, Jan Mayen, Spitsbergen and Novaya Zemlya all have colonies, although the exceptionally large Arctic race *F. a. naumanni* is not as numerous as the smaller birds occurring farther south. It breeds westwards from the Kola Peninsula to southern Norway and on Swedish islands in the Kattegat; elsewhere, colonies are found in Iceland, the Faeroes, Britain, Ireland, the Channel Islands and Brittany (Vaurie 1965, Voous 1960).

Census methods

Breeding Puffins are difficult to count accurately because of their habit of nesting in burrows. The best method is to count the occupied burrows, which are usually recognisable from their worn entrances liberally splashed with droppings, but great care is necessary when Manx Shearwaters and Rabbits occupy the same area. Complete counts of occupied burrows are only practicable in small, easily accessible colonies. At larger sites selected sample areas may be counted and, with a knowledge of the density in the sample and the total area of the colony, overall estimates can be made. When even this is not feasible, direct counts of birds ashore or sitting on the sea close to the colony can be made before egg-laying commences (subsequently many birds are incubating, and there may be an influx of non-breeding individuals). Since there can be considerable daily variation in the number of Puffins ashore, several such counts are required, and even then it is impossible, on the basis of our present knowledge, to relate such counts to the number of breeding pairs with any accuracy. As a rule, maximum numbers may be seen ashore during the evening. None of these methods is applicable where Puffins nest on the grass slopes of very high cliffs, such as are encountered on Foula (Shetland), Hoy (Orkney) and Clo Mor (Sutherland) and in such cases only crude estimates can be attempted. In view of the difficulty in counting Puffins, information on the number recorded in each county is given (Appendix Table 25) in the form of orders of abundance. Where Puffins are scattered along extensive sections of coast, two colonies have been separately defined when a clear uninhabited mile of coast exists between them.

Status in Britain and Ireland in 1969–70 and past history

It is clear from the foregoing that no accurate method of counting the numbers of breeding Puffins, except sometimes at the smaller colonies, has yet been found. In 1969–70 most observers were able to make numerical estimates using one or more of the methods described above, but for just under one-fifth of the colonies only the order of size was attempted. A total figure has been obtained by summing the numerical estimates and adding to this a figure for the other colonies based on the averages for each order obtained from the first group. (These averages were, in all cases, less than the arithmetic mean.) This method gave a total for Britain and Ireland of some 490,000 pairs, of which the overwhelming majority were in Scotland.

This figure must obviously be treated with the utmost caution. Even

at colonies where numerical assessments were made the most accurate
method of counting or sampling burrows was feasible only in a relatively
few cases. All other assessments were based on counts of birds present
and, as has been stressed, the relationship of such counts to breeding pairs
is complex and so far little understood. Moreover the total figure depends heavily on the accuracy of the counts at the few very large colonies.
The problems here are vividly illustrated in the St Kilda group where, as
described later, although the best estimate was 163,000 pairs in four
colonies (and this figure has been used in the calculations), the numbers
might have been some 50% higher.

Although counts or estimates of the numbers at many colonies have
been made in the past these refer in general to the smaller southern
colonies. Some north and north-western colonies have never previously
been surveyed; at best such phrases as 'vast numbers' or 'innumerable'
have been used to give an idea of their size. Parslow (1967) noted that
decreases had been occurring for many years in the south-west but found
little evidence of marked changes (locally even some increase) in the
north during the present century, though reliable data from the large
northern colonies were scarce. The 1969–70 survey confirmed that decreases had been taking place in the west and showed that they were not
confined to the south-west (Appendix Table 27). The only area where an
increase has been recorded is the Firth of Forth, notably on the Isle of
May where 2,500 pairs were recorded compared to 50 just over thirty
years previously. An increase may also have occurred on Papa Stour on
the west side of Shetland in an area where the trend is otherwise for a
decrease.

The decreases which have been occurring in south-west England, the
Irish Sea area and south-west Scotland since the end of the last century
seem in many cases to be continuing and a crash from an estimated
population of about 25,000 pairs in 1964 to 7,500 in 1969 was reported by
Evans (1972a) from Inishtearaght in south-west Ireland. Until the present
survey the giant north-western colonies were thought to be holding their
own, an impression reinforced for the casual observer by the immense
numbers of birds still present and the difficult terrain. More detailed
surveys have confirmed that the decline is now accelerating in the
north-west as well.

It was postulated that there might be anything from one to three million
Puffins at St Kilda in the last century and as recently as 1947 Fisher
(1948) considered that each of the three main colonies at Carn Mor, the
Cambir and Conachair on the main island of Hirta was larger than any
colony elsewhere in Britain, while the colonies on the outlying islands of
Dun, Soay and Boreray were even larger. The decline here was first
noticed by Donald Baird in 1960, who pointed out that the birds were

deserting the mainland slopes overlooking Village Bay on Hirta, where many can be seen in old photographs. The numbers in the other colonies there were also by no means so large, and the birds had begun to leave the centre of the landward end of Dun, though vast numbers could still be seen visiting the far end and the slopes of Soay in the distance (Bourne 1971 and pers. comm.). Surveys of Hirta and Dun in 1969 indicated that the decline was becoming more marked, and fewer birds could now be seen visiting Soay. When a full survey of the St Kilda group was completed in 1971 (Flegg 1972), it was found that while millions of burrows were still present only about 163,000 and certainly not more than 250,000 were still occupied. The areas deserted by the Puffins on Dun had become colonised by a dense growth of sorrel, and it was also noticed that this had extended rapidly along the island as the Puffin colony contracted between 1969 and 1971, until they occupied only a narrow belt around the outside of the island and about a fifth of its western end.

Another vast Puffin colony used to exist on the Shiant Islands in the Minch between the Hebrides and the mainland of Scotland, where the birds used to nest all round the periphery of the islands. In 1969 it was found that considerable areas were already deserted here too, and that the population, formerly estimated to number hundreds of thousands, had shrunk to 77,000 pairs. By the following year these had diminished by another fifth as well (Brooke 1972). A similar decline has occurred at an equally large colony on the cliff slopes at Clo Mor on the north coast of Sutherland (I. D. Pennie *in litt.*), and a decrease is also becoming visible at Foula in the Shetlands to the north (M. J. Wareing *in litt.*).

Several factors may have important effects on particular colonies. Brown Rats are thought to have seriously depleted Puffin numbers by eating eggs and young chicks at some colonies, including those on Lundy Island (Devon), St Tudwal's (Caernarvonshire), Puffin Island (Anglesey) and Ailsa Craig (Ayrshire), although they seem to have had less effect on the Shiant Islands (Outer Hebrides). Great Black-backed Gulls and Great Skuas kill adult Puffins emerging from burrows or young birds venturing close to the entrance or leaving for the sea during the daytime. It is hard to estimate the mortality from such causes since the birds are often taken down to the sea to be eaten, which may explain why few bodies are to be found at many of the northern colonies frequented by these predators; in any case it seems unlikely that the Puffins are caught by more than a few rogue birds, or otherwise they would fail to survive at sites such as North Rona or Am Balg at all. Klepto-parasitism, especially the tactics of Herring Gulls and, in some northern areas, Common Gulls in harrying Puffins taking fish to the burrows may also have an effect on numbers. At a Newfoundland colony Puffins nesting on more level ground were more affected by this than those on cliff slopes, due to the greater difficulties the birds had of landing swiftly and close to the burrow on level ground, and in the worst affected areas, the young received fewer feeds and consequently left for the sea lighter in weight than those reared on cliff slopes (Nettleship 1972). In many areas in Britain and Ireland where they have become reduced Puffins now nest in cliffs or cliff slopes. However, a good many still survive in some areas with large gull colonies.

Erosion has been blamed for the decrease at some Puffin colonies, as at Grassholm (Pembrokeshire), where the birds burrowed the soil so extensively that the roofs of tunnel systems collapsed (Lockley 1957) and in Shetland (Venables and Venables 1955). On the Farne Islands (Northumberland) digging activities by Puffins and grass pulling by gulls denude some areas of vegetation by late summer, then Grey Seals cause further erosion by using these areas for autumn nurseries (Bonham and Hickling 1971). On East Wideopens (Farne Islands) although this island is not used by seals, erosion has reduced the area available for Puffins and many of the remaining burrows are short – some no more than twelve inches long and liable to flooding, and here chicks are especially vulnerable to gull predation. Between 1962 and 1970 the population declined from 2,830 pairs to 760 pairs (N. Brown *in litt.*).

Such local events cannot explain the major declines now affecting so many areas for which there appears to be no single convincing reason. Lockley (1953a) suggested that climatic changes in the North Atlantic might have affected the food supply of Puffins nesting in the southern parts of their range, but this seems unlikely to be responsible for the major declines which have occurred more recently in the north. The increasing pollution of the seas might be affecting Puffins adversely, though they contain comparatively small amounts of pollutants such as organochlorines and heavy metals (Parslow 1972; Bourne and Bogan 1972). They may be more vulnerable to oil pollution at sea, for they spend much of their time swimming on the sea and are then at serious risk from oil slicks. Yet they are seldom common among oiled birds washed ashore in Britain and Ireland. It may be that Puffins are not so obviously affected as other auks because they winter much farther offshore and to the south to a greater extent, and their small bodies sink or disintegrate before they reach beaches (see Hope Jones *et al.* 1970). If many birds are killed then it might be expected that evidence would be found on local beaches, but it is notable that the number of Puffins at the main French colony on the Sept Iles decreased from 2,500 pairs before the *Torrey Canyon* disaster to 400 pairs afterwards, with little sign of the mortality along the shore (Monnat 1969).

Scarcer Species and Vagrants

MANY seabirds travel great distances, so it is hardly surprising that in addition to the 24 species now breeding every year on the coasts of Britain and Ireland there are 36 others which have been accepted as having occurred naturally in these islands and surrounding waters, besides some for which the evidence of natural occurrence is not conclusive. The latest official list of the accepted species (*The Status of Birds in Britain and Ireland*, published by the British Ornithologists' Union in 1971) contains full details, but a brief summary may be of interest.

Four of these scarcer species have bred in Britain and Ireland in historical times. The most famous of these is the Great Auk *Pinguinus impennis*, which almost certainly nested on St Kilda and perhaps elsewhere on islets in the north and west before man exterminated it throughout the world in the first half of the last century (Greenway 1958). The three others have all bred in England within the last 25 years. The Gull-billed Tern *Gelochelidon nilotica*, a nearly cosmopolitan species which has occurred in small numbers every year recently, nested on an Essex reservoir in 1950 and probably also in 1949. The Mediterranean Gull *Larus melanocephalus*, a species which has been extending its range northwest across Europe, started breeding in Hampshire in 1968 among a colony of Black-headed Gulls *Larus ridibundus*, with which it tends to hybridise. The Black Tern *Chlidonias niger*, one of three marsh terns which usually nest away from the coast, but which may perhaps be considered as a seabird because it spends much of the rest of the year at sea, has bred erratically on inland waters in England and Ireland in recent years and may be attempting to re-establish itself after its extinction here in the middle of the last century.

There are two other seabirds which might one day nest in these islands. They are the Little Gull *Larus minutus*, which breeds locally and often sporadically in Europe and Asia, some in the Netherlands, and visits us on passage and in winter, recently occurring more frequently at all seasons (and has even bred in Canada since 1962), and perhaps, if it found a suitable site, the almost cosmopolitan Caspian Tern *Hydroprogne caspia*, which nests as near as the Baltic and has also been observed more recently, mainly on the coasts of southern and eastern England, often in the summer months.

Then there are a number of seabirds which occur regularly as visitors either on passage or in winter. They include six species from the Arctic – the Glaucous Gull *Larus hyperboreus*, which has a circumpolar breeding distribution, the Iceland Gull *L. glaucoides*, which nests in Greenland and north-eastern Canada, and the Little Auk *Alle alle* nesting in the far north of Canada and Greenland across to Europe and Asia, which appear in varying numbers each winter, and the Pomarine and Long-tailed Skua, *Stercorarius pomarinus* and *S. longicaudus* and Sabine's Gull *Larus sabini*, all of which occur on passage between their breeding haunts over large areas of the Arctic and their winter quarters farther south. Then what are probably non-breeding populations of Cory's Shearwater *Calonectris diomedea* and the very distinct Balearic race of the Manx Shearwater *P. puffinus mauretanicus* which breed in the Mediterranean and Atlantic archipelagoes, and the Great and Sooty Shearwaters *Puffinus gravis* and *P. griseus* which nest in our winter in the South Atlantic, all occur in variable numbers in late summer along our western coasts; some, mainly Sooty Shearwaters, also reach the North Sea.

Finally, there is a very mixed group of vagrant species which have occurred less than 100 times and some only on one or two occasions. With the shearwaters mentioned above, which appear in late summer in the waters off our western coasts, some rarer petrels breeding on the Atlantic archipelagos may occur out at sea; most commonly the Little Shearwater *P. assimilis* and very infrequently Bulwer's Petrel *Bulweria bulwerii*, the Madeiran Storm-petrel *Oceanodroma castro* and the White-faced Storm-petrel *Pelagodroma marina*, as well as Wilson's Storm-petrel which nests in the Antarctic, though most of these are less easy to detect, partly owing to confusion with commoner species.

The albatrosses are unmistakable but often it may be far from easy to determine the exact species concerned. Only one species has been identified with certainty so far in Britain and Ireland, the Black-browed Albatross *Diomedea melanophris*, an oceanic species of the southern hemisphere which has been observed at sea on a number of occasions, whilst a single bird has frequented the gannetry at the Bass Rock during recent breeding seasons. Frigate-birds are also quite distinctive, but problems of identity again arise, and only one, the Magnificent Frigatebird *Fregata magnificens*, a tropical and oceanic species whose nearest breeding places are in the Cape Verde Islands and the West Indies, has so far been officially accepted as occurring naturally. Also from the West Indies is the Capped Petrel *Pterodroma hasitata*, which has been recorded once, as long ago as 1850.

Several gulls have occurred as vagrants and, with greater attention now being paid to their sometimes confusing plumages, more reports may be expected. Two are from northern waters – the Ivory Gull *Pagophila eburnea*, which breeds in scattered colonies on Arctic coasts and islands, formerly occurred relatively often, especially in Scotland, but has become much rarer in recent years, and Ross's Gull *Rhodostethia rosea*, a much scarcer gull from distant north-east Siberia, though it has once been recorded nesting in Greenland. Two of these gulls are from the Palaearctic region – the Great Black-headed Gull *Larus ichthyaetus*, whose breeding range extends from the Crimea to central Asia and beyond, and the more southerly Slender-billed Gull *L. genei* which may be found nesting locally as near as southern Spain and Tunisia, but is more common farther east. The last three gulls are vagrants from across the Atlantic – Bonaparte's Gull *L. philadelphia*, breeding in Alaska and Canada; the Laughing Gull *L. atricilla*, breeding farther south along the Atlantic coast of Canada and the USA and in the Caribbean, Mexico and California, and the most recent of all, not recorded until 1970, Franklin's Gull *L. pipixcan*, the breeding gull of the prairies of Canada and the USA (*British Birds* 64: 310–313).

The three vagrant terns include two which are widespread breeders in tropical seas, from the Pacific and Indian Oceans to the Atlantic and the Caribbean. The most frequently recorded, though still uncommon, is the pelagic Sooty Tern *Sterna fuscata*, which nests off the Antilles, Ascension and St Helena, while the more coastal Bridled Tern *S. anaethetus*, of much rarer occurrence, breeds still nearer on the Banc d'Arguin off the coast of Mauritania. The third, the Royal Tern *S. maxima*, has a more northerly distribution, nesting, in addition to Mauritania, from Maryland and Baja California south to the Caribbean, yet it is the most infrequently recorded of the three. Finally, among the seabird vagrants is Brünnich's Guillemot *Uria lomvia*, which nests on coasts and islands in the North Atlantic, the western Arctic and the North Pacific, but, although its breeding range overlaps with its close relative the Guillemot as near to Britain and Ireland as Iceland, it has been recorded only infrequently in our waters.

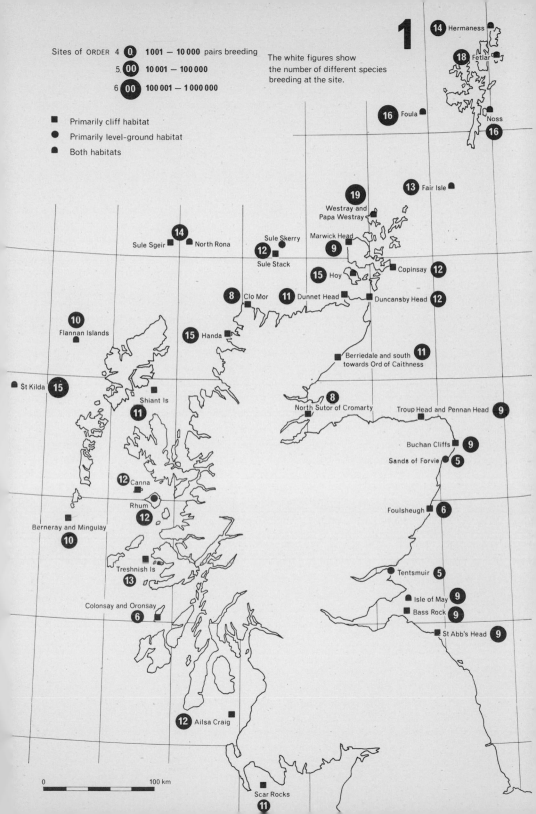

1

Sites of ORDER 4 **0.** **1001 — 10 000** pairs breeding

5. **00** **10 001 — 100 000**

6 **00** **100 001 — 1 000 000**

The white figures show
the number of different species
breeding at the site.

■ Primarily cliff habitat

● Primarily level-ground habitat

⬢ Both habitats

14 Hermaness

18 Fetlar

16 Foula

Noss

16

13 Fair Isle

19
Westray and
Papa Westray

14 Sule Sgeir ● North Rona

12 Sule Skerry
Sule Stack

Marwick Head
9

15 Hoy

Copinsay **12**

8 Clo Mor **11** Dunnet Head

Duncansby Head **12**

10
Flannan Islands

15 Handa

Berriedale and south
towards Ord of Caithness **11**

St Kilda **15**

11
Shiant Is

8
North Sutor of Cromarty

Troup Head and Pennan Head **9**

Buchan Cliffs **9**

Sands of Forvie **5**

12 Canna

Rhum

12

Foulsheugh **6**

Berneray and Mingulay

10

Treshnish Is

13

Tentsmuir **5**

Isle of May **9**

Bass Rock **9**

Colonsay and Oronsay

6

St Abb's Head **9**

12 Ailsa Craig

0   100 km

Scar Rocks

11

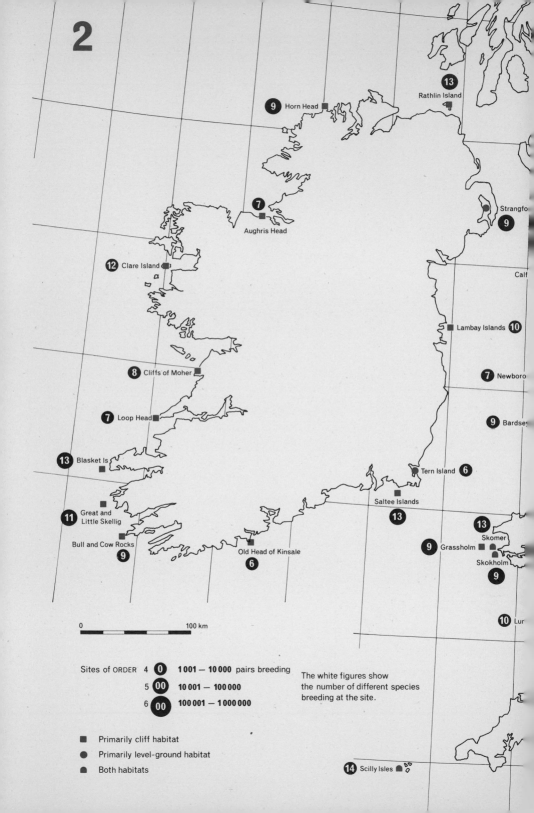

2

9 Horn Head

13 Rathlin Island

7 Aughris Head

9 Strangfo

Calf

12 Clare Island

10 Lambay Islands

7 Newboro

8 Cliffs of Moher

7 Loop Head

9 Bardse

13 Blasket Is

6 Tern Island

11 Great and
Little Skellig

13 Saltee Islands

13 Skomer

Bull and Cow Rocks

9 Grassholm

9

Skokholm

9

6 Old Head of Kinsale

10 Lur

0   100 km

Sites of ORDER 4   **0**   **1 001 — 10 000** pairs breeding

5   **00**   **10 001 — 100 000**

6   **00**   **100 001 — 1 000 000**

The white figures show
the number of different species
breeding at the site.

■   Primarily cliff habitat

●   Primarily level-ground habitat

⬣   Both habitats

14 Scilly Isles

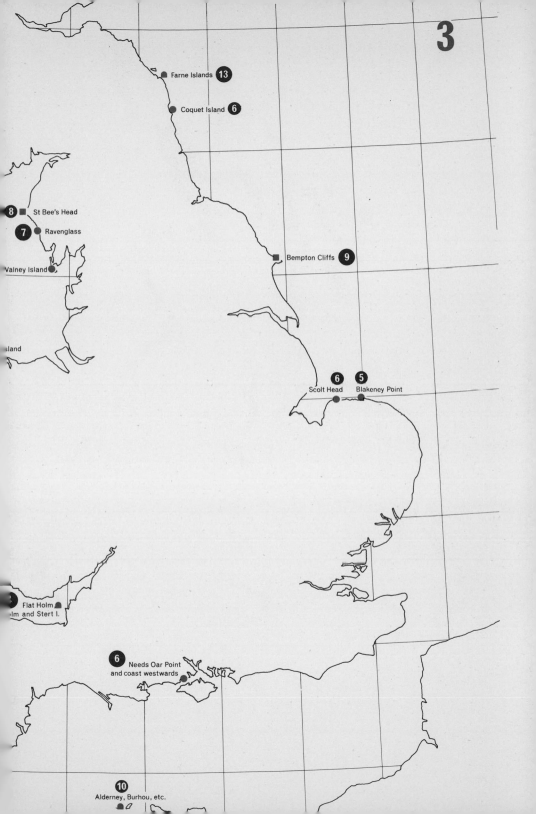

3

Farne Islands 13

Coquet Island 6

8 St Bee's Head

7 Ravenglass

Walney Island

Bempton Cliffs 9

6 5
Scolt Head Blakeney Point

Flat Holm
olm and Stert I.

6 Needs Oar Point
and coast westwards

10
Alderney, Burhou, etc.

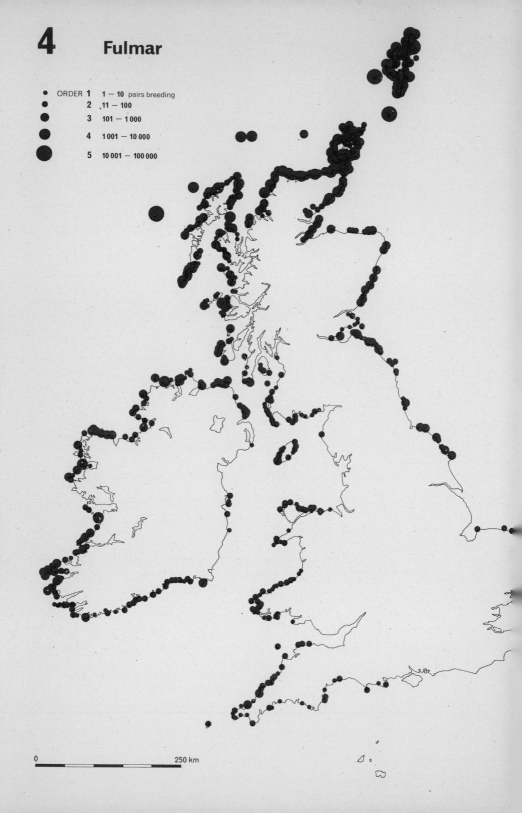

4 **Fulmar**

ORDER **1** 1 — 10 pairs breeding
2 11 — 100
3 101 — 1 000
4 1 001 — 10 000
5 10 001 — 100 000

0   250 km

Manx Shearwater

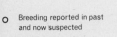

* For reasons of security, the exact
locations of the sites in Anglesey
and Carnaervonshire are not defined.

250 km

6 Storm Petrel

ORDER **1**   **1 — 10**   pairs breeding
     2   **11 — 100**
     3   **101 — 1 000**
     4   **1 001 — 10 000**
     5   **10 001 — 100 000**

▲ Breeding ; order not known

○ Breeding reported in past
and now suspected

□ Breeding reported in past;
present status unknown

? Breeding never proved;
now suspected

0   250 km

Leach's Storm-petrel

● Breeding in 1969

□ Breeding reported in past;
   present status unknown

? Breeding never proved;
   now suspected

○ Breeding reported in past
   and now suspected

7

0   250 km

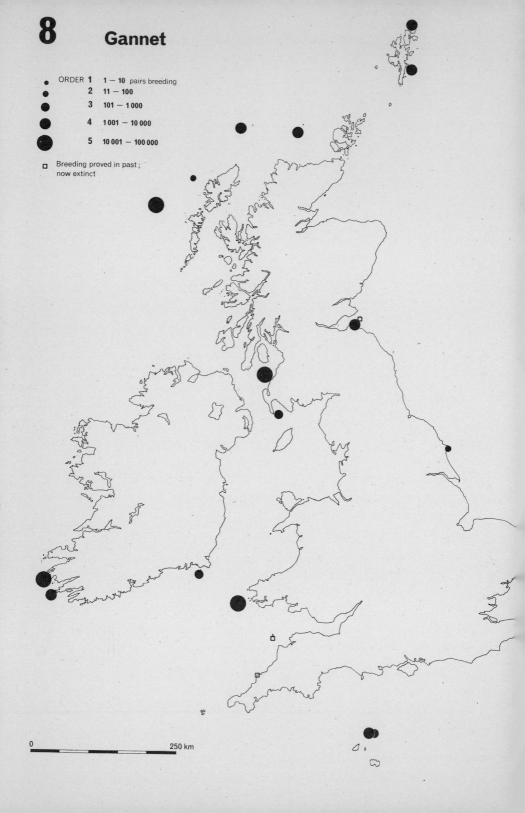

8 Gannet

ORDER **1** **1 — 10** pairs breeding
2 **11 — 100**
3 **101 — 1 000**
4 **1 001 — 10 000**
5 **10 001 — 100 000**

□ Breeding proved in past ;
now extinct

0   250 km

Cormorant

ORDER **1** **1 − 10** pairs breeding
2 **11 − 100**
3 **101 − 1 000**
4 **1 001 − 10 000**
5 **10 001 − 100 000**

0   250 km

10 Shag

0   250 km

Great Skua

11

ORDER **1** **1 – 10** pairs breeding
2 **11 – 100**
3 **101 – 1 000**
4 **1 001 – 10 000**
5 **10 001 – 100 000**

0   250 km

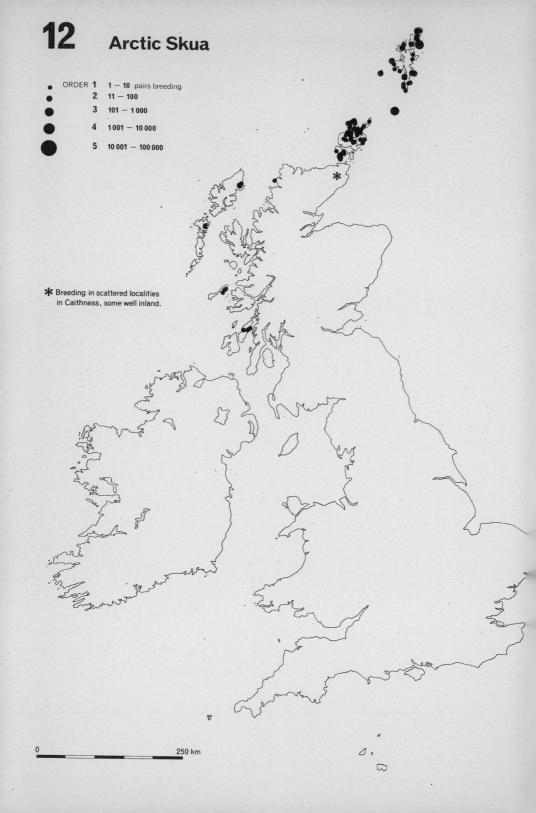

12 Arctic Skua

ORDER **1** 1 — 10 pairs breeding
2 11 — 100
3 101 — 1 000
4 1 001 — 10 000
5 10 001 — 100 000

✳ Breeding in scattered localities
in Caithness, some well inland.

0   250 km

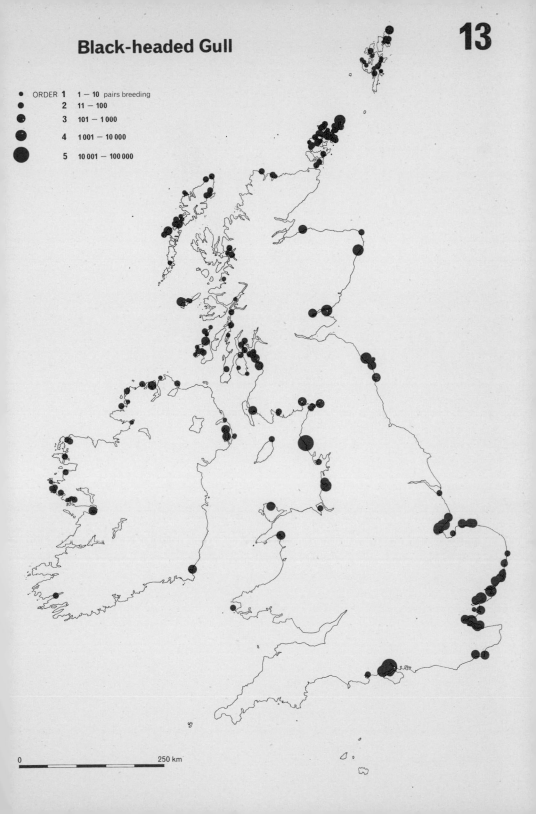

Black-headed Gull

ORDER **1** 1 — 10 pairs breeding
2 11 — 100
3 101 — 1 000
4 1 001 — 10 000
5 10 001 — 100 000

13

0   250 km

14 Common Gull

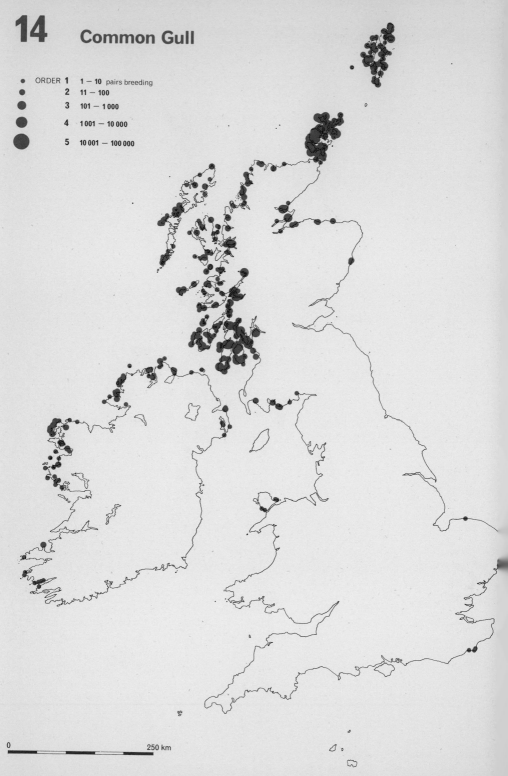

ORDER **1** **1 — 10** pairs breeding
2 **11 — 100**
3 **101 — 1 000**
4 **1 001 — 10 000**
5 **10 001 — 100 000**

0   250 km

Lesser Black-backed Gull

15

ORDER 1 1 — 10 pairs breeding
2 11 — 100
3 101 — 1 000
4 1 001 — 10 000
5 10 001 — 100 000

0   250 km

16   Herring Gull

ORDER **1** 1 — 10 pairs breeding
2 11 — 100
3 101 — 1 000
4 1 001 — 10 000
5 10 001 — 100 000

0   250 km

Great Black-backed Gull

17

ORDER
1 1 — 10 pairs breeding
2 11 — 100
3 101 — 1 000
4 1 001 — 10 000
5 10 001 — 100 000

250 km

18 Kittiwake

ORDER **1** 1 — 10 pairs breeding
2 11 — 100
3 101 — 1 000
4 1 001 — 10 000
5 10 001 — 100 000

0   250 km

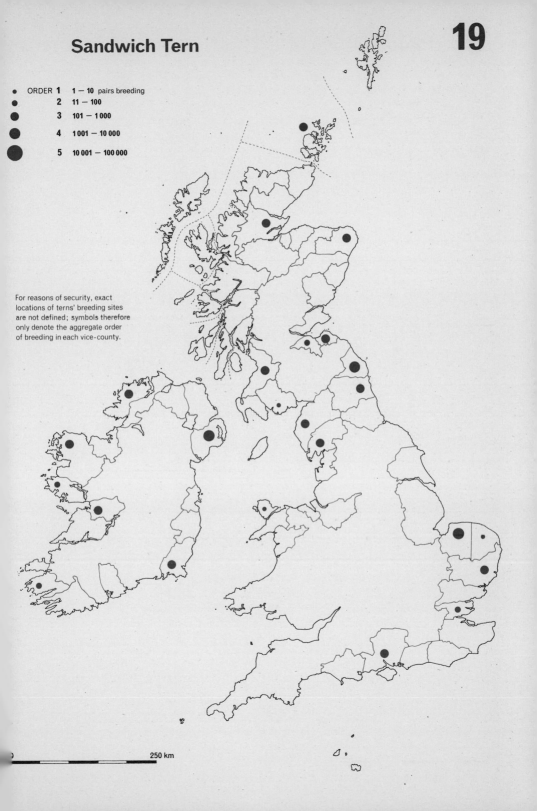

Sandwich Tern

ORDER **1**   **1 — 10**   pairs breeding
      2   **11 — 100**
      3   **101 — 1 000**
      4   **1 001 — 10 000**
      5   **10 001 — 100 000**

For reasons of security, exact
locations of terns' breeding sites
are not defined; symbols therefore
only denote the aggregate order
of breeding in each vice-county.

250 km

20 Roseate Tern

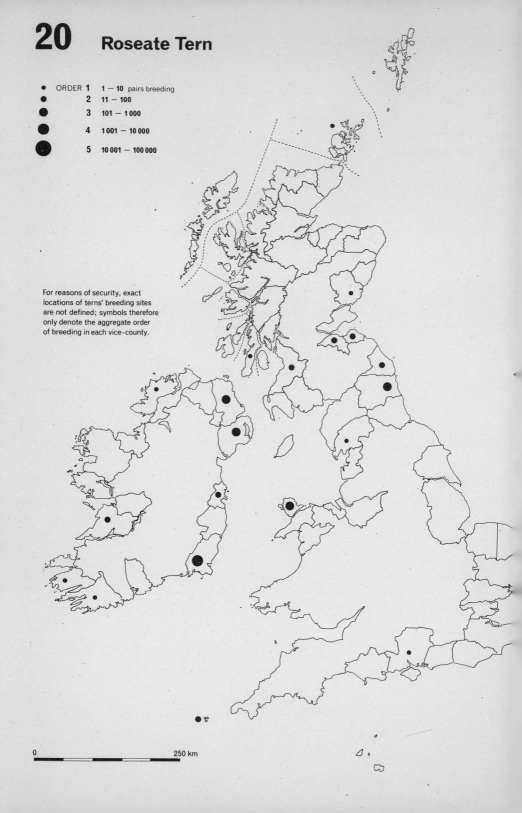

ORDER **1** 1 — 10 pairs breeding
2 11 — 100
3 101 — 1 000
4 1 001 — 10 000
5 10 001 — 100 000

For reasons of security, exact
locations of terns' breeding sites
are not defined; symbols therefore
only denote the aggregate order
of breeding in each vice-county.

0   250 km

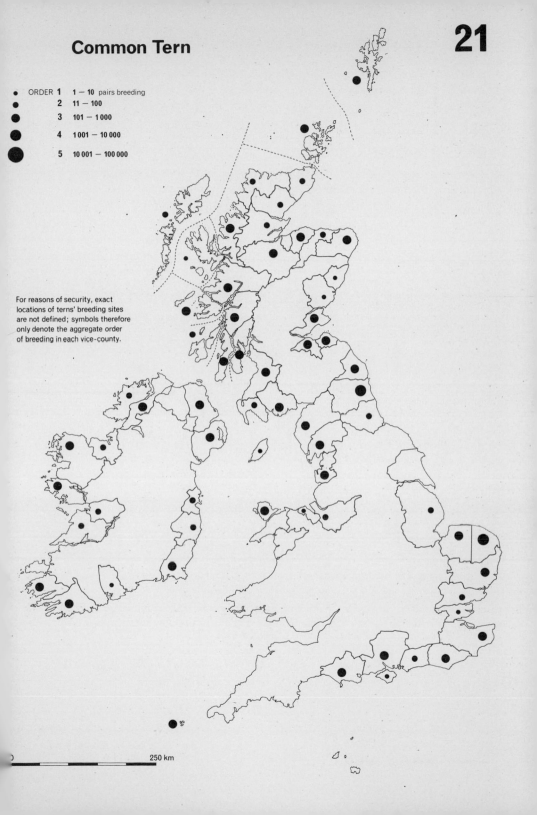

Common Tern

ORDER **1** **1 — 10** pairs breeding
2 **11 — 100**
3 **101 — 1 000**
4 **1 001 — 10 000**
5 **10 001 — 100 000**

For reasons of security, exact
locations of terns' breeding sites
are not defined; symbols therefore
only denote the aggregate order
of breeding in each vice-county.

250 km

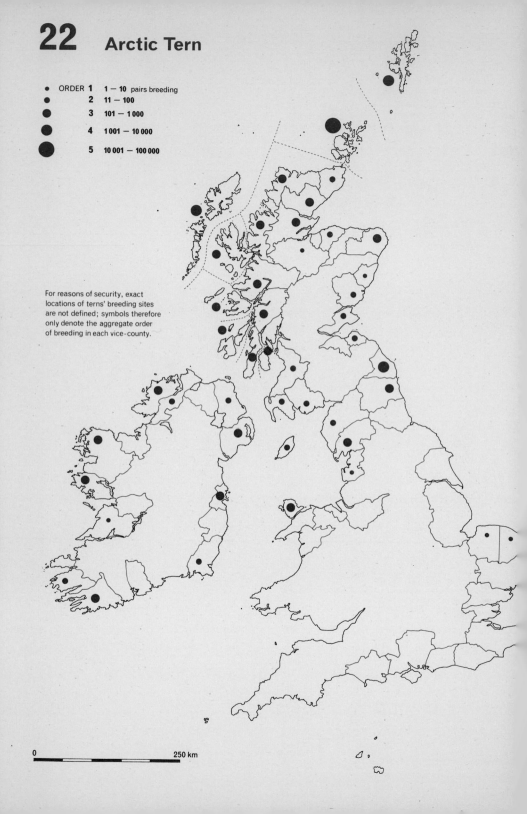

22 Arctic Tern

ORDER **1** 1 — 10 pairs breeding
2 11 — 100
3 101 — 1 000
4 1 001 — 10 000
5 10 001 — 100 000

For reasons of security, exact
locations of terns' breeding sites
are not defined; symbols therefore
only denote the aggregate order
of breeding in each vice-county.

0   250 km

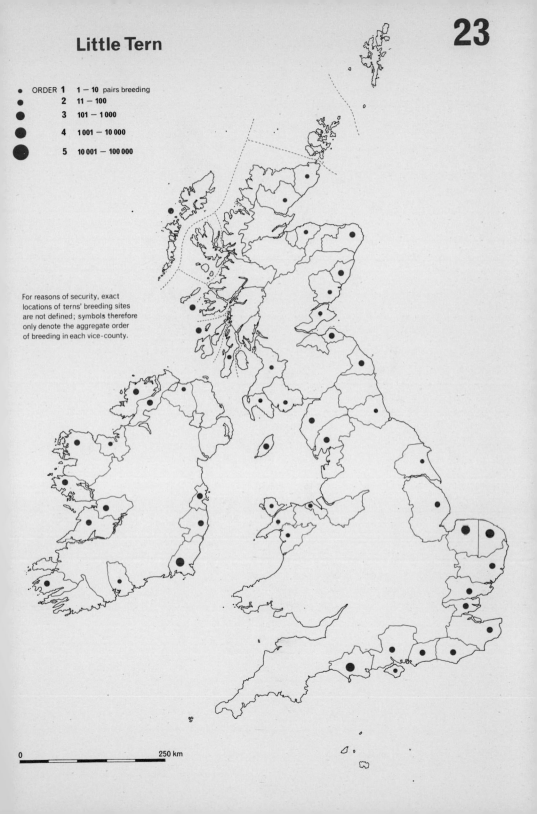

Little Tern

ORDER **1** **1 − 10** pairs breeding
       2 **11 − 100**
       3 **101 − 1 000**
       4 **1 001 − 10 000**
       5 **10 001 − 100 000**

For reasons of security, exact
locations of terns' breeding sites
are not defined; symbols therefore
only denote the aggregate order
of breeding in each vice-county.

0   250 km

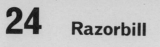

24 Razorbill

ORDER **1** 1 — 10 pairs breeding
2 11 — 100
3 101 — 1 000
4 1 001 — 10 000
5 10 001 — 100 000

0   250 km

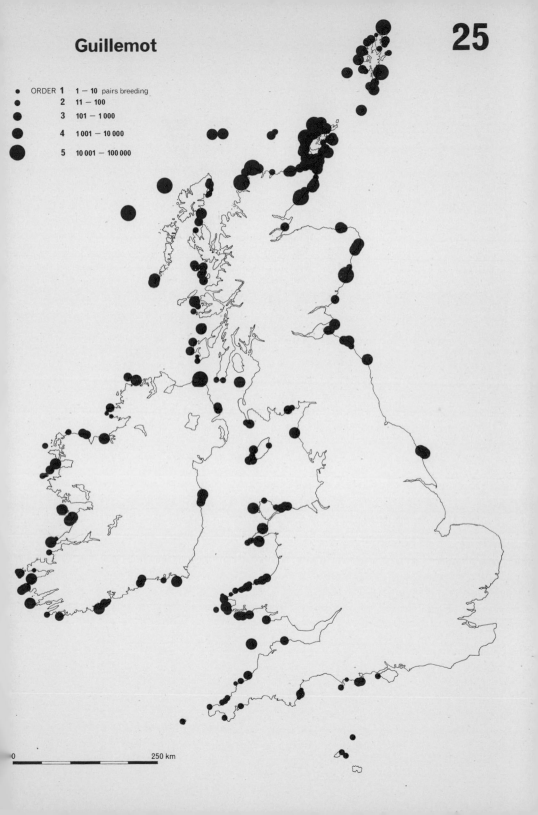

Guillemot

0   250 km

26 Black Guillemot

ORDER **1** **1 — 10** pairs breeding
2 **11 — 100**
3 **101 — 1 000**
4 **1 001 — 10 000**
5 **10 001 — 100 000**

0   250 km

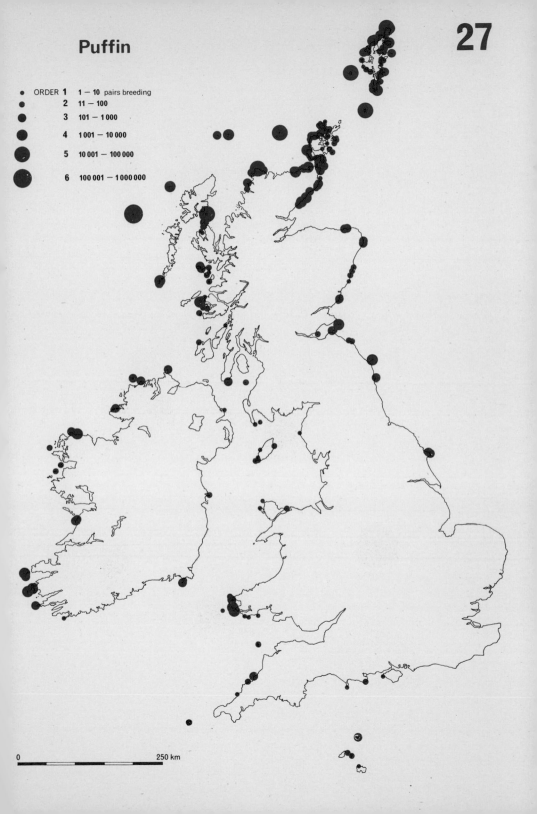

Puffin

ORDER 1   1 — 10   pairs breeding
      2   11 — 100
      3   101 — 1 000
      4   1 001 — 10 000
      5   10 001 — 100 000
      6   100 001 — 1 000 000

27

0   250 km

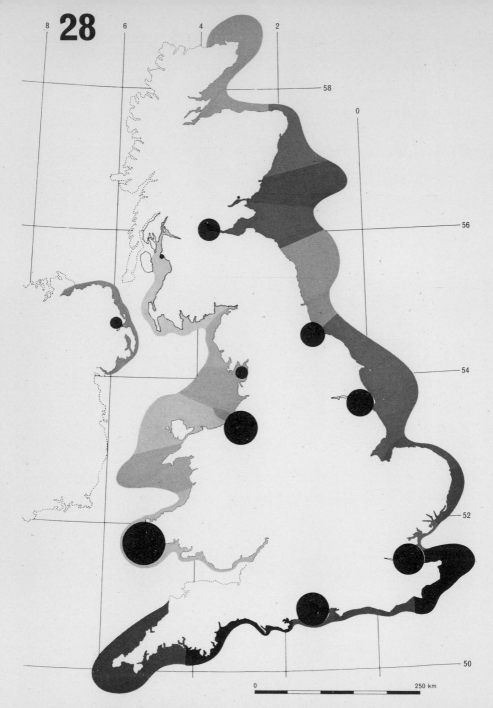

Map showing quantities of dead auks picked up on beaches 1968-70 and the proportions found oiled. The area of coastal colour represents the number of dead auks in the vice-county(-ies) off whose shore that colour lies; thus 273 dead auks were found in Cornwall. The shading of the coastal colour is proportionate to the percentage of auks oiled, taking pure black as 100% (e.g. Kent), and the palest grey as 21% (e.g. Ayrshire). The red circles represent tanker-handling terminals; the area of each circle is proportional to the number of metric tons handled in 1970 (e.g.: Ardrossan 300,000 and Milford Haven 33,000,000). (Based on information supplied by C. J. Bibby).

Recoveries of Razorbills ringed in Britain and Ireland up to 1970, to show the extreme form of movement from breeding colonies facing the Atlantic to winter quarters along the continental coasts found in British auks. Red dots represent recoveries of individual Razorbills more than 150 km from breeding places in the Irish Sea, and black dots those recovered more than 150 km from breeding places elsewhere in Britain and Ireland. Young birds tend to move farther than older ones, while many Scandinavian recoveries are due to shooting in the autumn. (Based on information supplied by C. J. Mead).

30   Water temperature and salinity in January. Fresh coastal water contracts towards the coast, as it sinks when cooled in winter. Black isotherms show mean surface temperature in degrees C. The pink area represents sea in which surface salinity exceeds 35 parts per thousand. (Based on I.C.E.S. Temperature and salinity at the surface of the North Sea and adjacent waters: Provisional monthly mean charts, 1955).

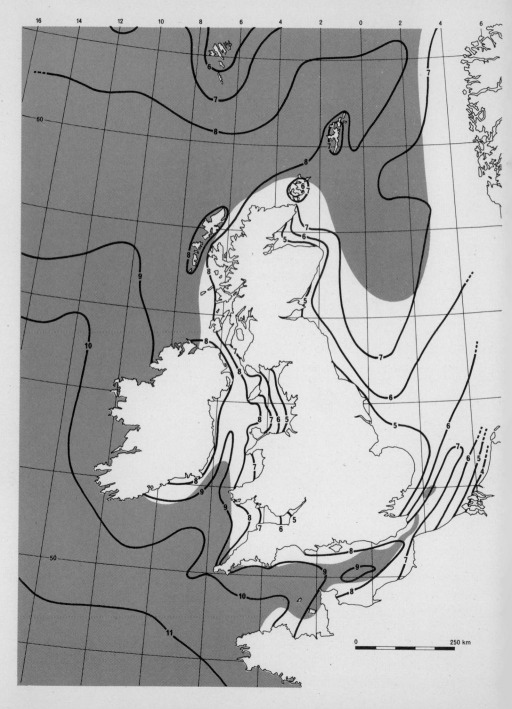

Water temperature and salinity in July. The fresher coastal water starts to spread outwards as a distinct layer on top of the cooler oceanic water as it is warmed during the summer, except where strong currents cause water mixing in such areas as the Minch and down the east coast of Scotland (see also text figure B, p. 27), associated with increased plankton production and turn-over of floating food organisms so that they become available to birds. (Based on I.C.E.S. Temperature and salinity at the surface of the North Sea and adjacent waters: Provisional monthly mean charts, 1955).

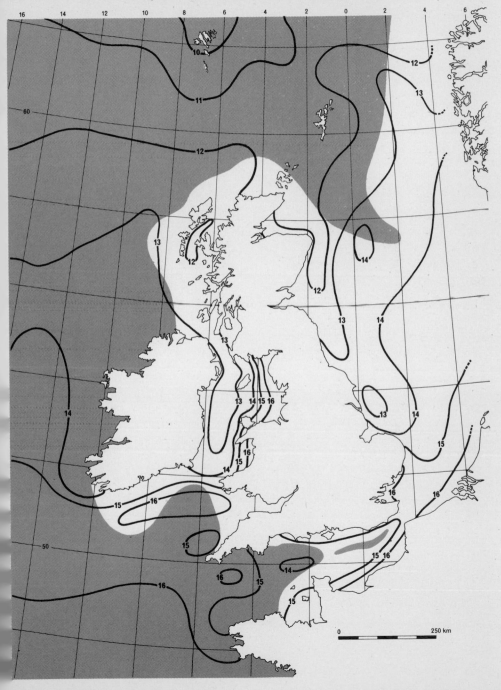

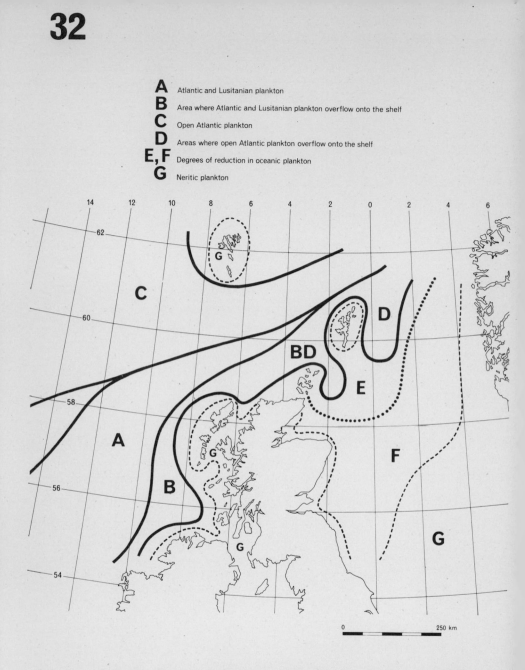

A   Atlantic and Lusitanian plankton
B   Area where Atlantic and Lusitanian plankton overflow onto the shelf
C   Open Atlantic plankton
D   Areas where open Atlantic plankton overflow onto the shelf
E,F   Degrees of reduction in oceanic plankton
G   Neritic plankton

Oceanic plankton in waters off Scotland. Variations seasonally, annually, long-term and in depth are so great that this map cannot truly be representative of any one species or at any one time; there are no boundaries so sharply defined that they may be represented by lines. Nevertheless this idealised chart gives an indication of the distribution of plankton in the area. (Based on information supplied by Dr. J. H. Fraser).

Appendices

18. Changes in numbers of breeding pairs of Great Black-backed Gulls at certain colonies.

19. Number of pairs of Kittiwakes breeding in Britain and Ireland in 1969–70.

20. Number of pairs of Sandwich Terns, Roseate Terns, Common Terns, Arctic Terns and Little Terns breeding on the coasts of Britain and Ireland in 1969–70.

21. Changes in numbers of breeding pairs of Little Terns in certain counties of England and Scotland and north and south Wales.

22. Numbers of pairs of Razorbills and Guillemots breeding in Britain and Ireland in 1969–70.

23. Changes in numbers of breeding pairs of Razorbills at certain colonies.

24. Changes in numbers of breeding pairs of Guillemots at certain colonies.

25. Number of pairs of Black Guillemots breeding in Britain and Ireland in 1969–70.

26. Number of Puffin colonies (in Orders of Abundance) in Britain and Ireland in 1969–70.

27. Changes in numbers of breeding pairs of Puffins at certain colonies.

TABLE I. *Increase of the Fulmar population (occupied sites) in Britain and Ireland between 1879 and 1969–70 (1879–1959 figures from Fisher (1966))*

Group	1879	1889	1899	1909	1919	1929	1939	1949	1959	1969/70	% changes 1959–1969/70
Shetland	24	75	405	1,516	4,367	8,871	17,741	29,262	35,857	116,865	+226%
Outer Hebrides	—	26	73	266	672	1,362	4,454	10,688	19,824	25,158	+ 27%
Orkney	—	—	—	132	548	1,701	6,258	13,557	13,917	47,304	+240%
North Highlands (Caithness–West Ross)	—	—	—	125	206	959	3,902	9,467	13,514	43,525	+222%
Atlantic Ireland (Donegal–Wexford)	—	—	—	—	151	227	864	2,889	4,665	15,468	+232%
Eastern Scotland (East Ross–Berwick)	—	—	—	—	25	155	566	1,350	3,827	6,689	+ 75%
Inner West (Londonderry–Wicklow West Inverness–Merioneth)	—	—	—	—	—	84	964	2,266	3,816	10,488	+175%
Eastern England (Northumberland–Kent)	—	—	—	—	—	123	474	681	945	1,690	+ 79%
Low South-West (Cardigan–Sussex)	—	—	—	—	—	—	—	312	674	1,852	+175%
Total other than St Kilda	24	101	478	2,039	5,969	13,482	35,223	70,472	97,039	269,039	+177%
St Kilda	NOT KNOWN						c. 20,780	38,178	c. 37,500	c. 36,600	(—c.3%)
Grand Total	NOT KNOWN						56,003	108,650	134,539	305,639	+126%

TABLE 2. *Manx Shearwater colonies in Britain and Ireland censused in 1969–70*
Approximate estimates of sizes of colonies are sometimes indicated by 'Orders
of Abundance': Order 1 = less than 10 pairs; Order 2 = 10–99 pairs; Order
3 = 100–999 pairs; Order 4 = 1,000–9,999 pairs; Order 5 = 10,000 - 99,999
pairs.

Colony	Status in 1969–70	Previous history when known
Treshnish Islands, Argyll	Breeding	Breeding since late 19th century (Baxter and Rintoul 1953)
Eigg, Inverness	Order 2	Up to six miles of cliff occupied in late 19th century, decreased since 1930; c.100 pairs in late 1950s, less than 50 pairs in 1964 (Evans and Flower 1967)
Rhum, Inverness	c.70,000 pairs	Nesting in large numbers since at least 1716 (Evans and Flower 1967)
Canna, Inverness	Order 4	Breeding since 1881, always considered a large colony (Evans and Flower 1967)
St Kilda, Outer Hebrides	Breeding	Possibly breeding in 1698, breeding since at least 1840, but said to have decreased about 1900 (Baxter and Rintoul 1953)
Hoy, Orkney	Two colonies, Order 1 and Order 2	Breeding in 19th century (Baxter and Rintoul 1953); three colonies in 1933 (Serle 1934)
Foula, Shetland	A few pairs	Breeding in 1774; considerable numbers in 1837. Decreased at one colony 1938–48; total population c.50 pairs; 30–40 pairs in 1956 and 1963 (Jackson 1966)
Fetlar, Shetland	c.100 pairs	Bred in 19th century (Venables and Venables 1955)
Isles of Scilly	c. 1,000 pairs	Probable decrease (Parslow 1967)
Lundy, Devon	c. 100 pairs	Small colonies (Davis 1954)
Skokholm Island, Pembrokeshire	30,000–40,000 pairs	c. 20,000 pairs (Lockley 1942); c. 35,000 pairs in 1964 (Harris 1966a); 35–37,000 pairs in 1967 (Perrins 1967)
Skomer I. and Middleholm, Pembs.	c. 60,000 pairs (c. 95,000 pairs in 1971 – Corkhill 1973)	c. 25,000 pairs in 1946 (Buxton and Lockley 1950)
Bardsey, Caernarvonshire	c. 2,500 pairs	Increase between 1913 and 1930 (Norris 1953)

Colony	Status in 1969–70	Previous history when known
Calf of Man	Very small numbers	Noted in 1586, ceased to breed late 18th or early 19th century (Williamson 1940). Rediscovered breeding 1967 (birds heard previously) (Alexander 1968)
Great Saltee, Wexford	c. 20 pairs	Small colony since at least 1943 (Kennedy et al. 1954)
Skellig Michael, Kerry	Order 4	Large numbers (Kennedy et al. 1954); 3,000+ pairs (Lovegrove et al. 1965); 5,000 pairs in 1966 (Lovegrove in prep.)
Puffin Island, Kerry	Order 5	Breeding (Kennedy et al. 1954); 10,000–20,000 pairs in 1955 (Ruttledge 1966)
Inishvickillaun, Kerry	Order 3	Three well-established colonies (Alexander 1954); 500 pairs in 1966 (Lovegrove in prep.)
Inishnabro, Kerry	Order 3	Breeding abundantly in 19th century (Alexander 1954); 1,000 pairs in 1955 (Ruttledge 1966)
Inishtearaght, Kerry	Order 3	200 pairs in 1968 (Lovegrove in prep.)
Inishtooskert, Kerry	Order 3	Several hundred pairs in 1966 (Lovegrove in prep.)
Slyne Head, Galway	c. 15 pairs	No information
Inishbofin, Galway	Order 3 (low)	Breeding since at least 1920, though numbers considered small (Ruttledge 1957)
Inishturk, Mayo	4 occupied burrows	No information
Tory Island, Donegal	Not found	Said to breed (Kennedy et al. 1954), but this was a misprint (Ruttledge 1966)
Rathlin Island, Antrim	Order 4	Former great colonies overestimated (Kennedy et al. 1954); c. 150 pairs in 1953 (Deane 1954)
Copeland Islands, Down	c. 300 pairs	Small numbers breeding since 1939 (Kennedy et al. 1954)

TABLE 3. *Manx Shearwater colonies in Britain and Ireland known from past records, or suspected, but not censused in 1969–70*

Colony	Situation in 1969–70	Previous history when known
Staffa and Iona, Argyll	No information	Breeding in 19th century (Gray 1871)
Tallisker Rocks, Skye	No information	Breeding in 1886–87; not found in 1945 (Baxter and Rintoul 1953)
Islands off Skye, Inverness	No information	Breeding in 1945 (Baxter and Rintoul 1953)
Berneray, Outer Hebrides	No information	Ceased to breed by 1843 (Baxter and Rintoul 1953)
Mingulay, Outer Hebrides	No information	Decreased in 19th century and not found in 1888 (Baxter and Rintoul 1953)
Sandray, Outer Hebrides	No information	Possibly breeding (Diamond *et al.* 1965)
Pabbay, Outer Hebrides	No information	Decreased in 19th century (Baxter and Rintoul 1953)
Bearasay, Outer Hebrides	No information	Breeding in 1962 (Robson and Wills 1963)
Papa Westray, Rothiesholm (Stronsay) and Walls (Hoy), Orkney	No information	Breeding in early 19th century (Baxter and Rintoul 1953)
Westray, Orkney	Seen offshore and thought to breed in Rapness Cliffs	Breeding in 19th century (Baxter and Rintoul 1953)
Bressay, Shetland	Seen offshore	Seen offshore and possibly breeding (Venables and Venables 1955)
Yell, Shetland	110 on water at dusk off SE cliffs	Possibly breeding in 19th century (Venables and Venables 1955)
Unst, Shetland	No information	Bred in 19th century (Venables and Venables 1955)
Marsden Rock, Durham	No information	Egg found in 1939 (Temperley 1951)
Caernarvonshire	One bird seen at suspected site	Suspected at several sites (E. I. S. Rees *in litt.*)
Anglesey	Heard calling at a known site	6–8 pairs in 1966 (E. I. S. Rees *in litt.*)
Lambay, Dublin	Thought still to breed	Less than 10 pairs in 1950s (Kennedy *et al.* 1954)

Colony	Situation in 1969–70	Previous history when known
Ireland's Eye, Dublin	Up to 20 likely burrows seen from boat	Several pairs in 1950s (Kennedy *et al.* 1954)
Howth Head, Dublin	Several likely burrows seen from boat	Less than 10 pairs in 1950s (Kennedy *et al.* 1954)
Bray Head, Wicklow	*c.* 10 likely burrows	Small numbers (Kennedy *et al.* 1954)
Scariff Island, Kerry	Thought to breed	No information
Great Blasket, Kerry	Thought to breed	50–100 pairs suspected (Alexander 1954)
Corrigeenagowlra, Galway	No information	Small number thought to be breeding in 1942 (Major R. F. Ruttledge *in litt.*)
Inishshark, Galway	No information	Breeding (Ruttledge 1957); 450 seen offshore in 1968 ('Operation Seafarer' records)
High Island, Galway	No information	At least 10–99 pairs (Major R. F. Ruttledge *in litt.*)
Clare Island, Mayo	One heard calling	No information
Kid Island, Mayo	No information	Less than 10 pairs (Major R. F. Ruttledge *in litt.*)
Aranmore, Donegal	No information	Breeding (Kennedy *et al.* 1954)

TABLE 4. *Storm Petrel colonies in Britain and Ireland visited in 1969–70*
Approximate estimates of size of colonies – Order 1 = 1–9 pairs; Order 2 = 10–99 pairs; Order 3 = 100–999 pairs; Order 4 = 1,000–9,999 pairs; Order 5 = 10,000–99,999 pairs.

Where breeding suspected – Smell = Characteristic musky smell from possible nest site; Sound = Birds churring from possible nest site; Sight = Birds seen at night over suitable terrain.

Colony	Status in 1969–70	Previous history when known
Lunga (Treshnish Is.), Argyll	Suspected – Smell and Sound	Breeding in 1865, 1892, 1937 (Baxter and Rintoul 1953)
Canna, West Inverness	Suspected – Sound	Breeding (Gray 1871)

Table 4 continued

Table 4 continued

Colony	Status in 1969–70	Previous history when known
Longa (Gairloch), West Ross	Breeding	Breeding in 1918 (Baxter and Rintoul 1953)
Priest Is. (Summer Is.), W. Ross	Breeding	Breeding (Darling 1940)
Faraid Head, Sutherland	Suspected – Sight	Not known
Island Roan, Sutherland	Breeding	Breeding in 1884 (Baxter and Rintoul 1953)
Shillay (North Uist), Outer Hebrides	Suspected	Breeding 1830 (Baxter and Rintoul 1953)
Boreray (North Uist), Outer Hebrides	Suspected – Sight	Not known
Shiant Is., Outer Hebrides	Suspected – Sight	Not known
St Kilda, Outer Hebrides	Breeding	Breeding records since 1697 (Baxter and Rintoul 1953)
Sula Sgeir, Outer Hebrides	Breeding	Present in 1958 (Bagenal and Baird 1959)
North Rona, Outer Hebrides	Breeding	First breeding record 1886; *c.* 1,000 pairs at the main colony in 1958 (Bagenal and Baird 1959)
Sule Skerry, Orkney	Breeding	Large colony (Balfour 1968)
Muckle Skerry, Ork.	Breeding	Breeding (Balfour 1968)
Auskerry, Orkney	Order 3	Thriving colony (Balfour 1968)
Muckle Green Holm, Orkney	Suspected – Smell	Probably breeding (Balfour 1968)
Switha, Orkney	Suspected – Smell	Probably breeding (Balfour 1968)
Rusk Holm, Orkney	Order 2	Breeding (Balfour 1968)
Wart Holm, Orkney	Order 2	Not known
Skea Skerries, Ork.	Order 2	Not known
Fair Isle, Shetland	Order 2	Breeding records since 1809 (Baxter and Rintoul 1953)
Mousa, Shetland	Breeding	Breeding (Dunn 1837)
Hoy, Junk and Hogs of Hoy, Shetland	Order 1	Breeding on Scalloway Islands (Evans and Buckley 1899)
Foula, Shetland	Order 3 (two known colonies)	Breeding since first recorded by Hewitson (1831–42)
Papa Stour, Shetland	Suspected – Sound	Breeding (Evans and Buckley 1899)
Samphrey, Shetland	Suspected – Sound	Breeding on four islands in Yell Sound (Evans and Buckley 1899)

Colony	Status in 1969–70	Previous history when known
Bigga, Shetland	Suspected – Smell	
Yell east, Shetland	c. 20 pairs	Not known
Fetlar, Shetland	Breeding	Breeding (Venables and Venables 1955)
Linga (off Yell)	Breeding	
Haaf Gruney, Shet.	Order 2	⎫
Urie Lingey, Shet.	Order 2	⎬ Breeding on islets north of Fetlar in 1941 (Baxter and Rintoul 1953)
Sound Gruney, Shetland	Suspected – Smell	
Daaey, Shetland	Order 2	⎭
Stroma, Caithness	Suspected	Not known
Annet, Isles of Scilly	Order 4	Breeding first reported 1903 (Penhallurick 1969)
Gorregan, Scilly	Order 1	Breeding in 1964 (Penhallurick 1969)
Skomer Island, Pembrokeshire	Order 3	First noted by Mathew (1894): c. 30 pairs in 1946 (Buxton and Lockley 1950)
Middleholm, Pemb.	Order 1	Not known
Skokholm Island, Pembrokeshire	5,000–7,000 pairs	Breeding since at least 1931 (Lockley 1932)
Bardsey, Caernarvonshire	Breeding	Breeding first proved in 1953 (Norris 1954)
Great Saltee, Wexford	Order 2	None proved to breed (Kennedy et al. 1954)
Bull Rock, Cork	Order 4	c. 150 pairs in 1955 (Ruttledge 1966)
Skellig Michael, Kerry	Order 4	Enormous numbers (Kennedy et al. 1954); 4,000 pairs in 1955 (Ruttledge 1966); 10,000 pairs in 1967 (Irish Bird Report)
Puffin Island, Kerry	Order 4	Less than 1,000 pairs in 1955 (Ruttledge 1966); 2,000 pairs 1966 (Lovegrove in prep.)
Inishvickillaun, Kerry	Order 5	7,600 pairs estimated in 1953 (Ruttledge 1966); 10,000 pairs 1966 (Lovegrove in prep.)
Inishnabro, Kerry	Order 3	c. 1,000 pairs in 1955 (Ruttledge 1966)
Inishtearaght, Kerry	Order 5	Vast numbers (Kennedy et al. 1954); thought to exceed 10,000 pairs (Irish Bird Report 1967); over 20,000 pairs 1968 (Lovegrove in prep.)

Table 4 continued

Table 4 continued

Colony	Status in 1969/70	Previous history when known
Great Blasket, Kerry	Suspected – Sight	Not known
Inishtooskert, Kerry	Order 4	3,000–5,000 pairs in 1955 (Ruttledge 1966)
Illaunimmil, Kerry	Suspected – Smell	Not known
Illaunturlough, Kerry	Order 2	Not known
Gurrig, Kerry	Order 2	Not known
Brannock Island (Aran Is.), Galway	Suspected – Sight	Does not breed in Aran Islands (Kennedy *et al.* 1954; Ruttledge 1966)
Caher, Mayo	Order 2	Less than 100 pairs (Ruttledge 1966)
Clare Island, Mayo	Suspected – Sight	A few possibly breeding (Kennedy *et al.* 1954)
Blackrock, Mayo	Order 1	Ceased to nest (Kennedy *et al.* 1954)
Inishglora Mayo	Breeding	500 pairs (Kennedy *et al.* 1954)
Rathlin O'Birne, Donegal	Order 3	Large colony (Kennedy *et al.* 1954)
Inishkeeragh, Donegal	Suspected – Sight and Sound	Not known
Tory Is., Donegal	Breeding	Small numbers breeding (Kennedy *et al.* 1954); *c.* 20 pairs in 1962 (Ruttledge 1966)
Icho Tower Reef, Channel Islands	Order 1	Breeding in 1935, max. 4 pairs 1936–46 (Dobson 1952)
Godin, Channel Is.	Suspected – Sight	Not known
Burhou, Channel Islands	Order 4	Breeding since 1830 (Dobson 1952)

TABLE 5. *Storm Petrel colonies in Britain and Ireland not surveyed in 1969–70*

Colony	Past history
Argyll – Mull, Iona and islands	Breeding 1850, 1871, 1891 and 1917 (Baxter and Rintoul 1953)
Skye	Said to nest sparingly in Ascrib Islands (Harvie-Brown and Macpherson 1904); nesting on islands off Skye (Baxter and Rintoul 1953)

Colony	Past history
Outer Hebrides – Flannan Isles	Clarke (1905) found them very numerous; in 1951 between 10 and 40 pairs (Andrew and Sandeman 1953); small numbers seen and three breeding pairs located in 1959 (Anderson *et al.* 1961)
Orkney	Breeding Pentland Skerries, Faray Holm (Balfour 1968); breeding Sanday in 1885 (Baxter and Rintoul 1953)
Shetland	Breeding Lady's Holm, Colsay, Hilda, Unst, Uyea, Out Skerries, Whalsay, West Linga, Wether Holm and Bressay (Venables and Venables 1953)
Devon	Breeding Thatcher Rock, 1874 and 1950 (Moore 1969)
Cornwall	Breeding Gull Rock, Falmouth 1866 and Gulland Rock 1920s, 1960s (Penhallurick 1969); Carters Rock – old egg found in 1967 (Phillips 1968)
Isles of Scilly	Breeding Rosevean 1948, Rosevear 1962, Mellegdon 1961, Castle Bryher 1961, Scilly Rock 1960, Menavaur 1960 and Round Island where breeding at least until 1951 but not found in 1961 and 1962 (Penhallurick 1969)
Co. Kerry	Illaunboy and Beginish – a few pairs in 1953 (Ruttledge 1966)
Co. Clare	Breeding Mattle Island and Mutton Island (Ruttledge 1966)
Co. Galway	High Island – up to 40 pairs in 1943 and Corrigeenagowlra – up to 15 pairs in 1942 (Ruttledge 1966); Inishshark – breeding (Ruttledge 1957), a considerable colony (Ruttledge 1966); Inishbofin – thought to be breeding (Ruttledge 1957), a few pairs (Ruttledge 1966)
Co. Mayo	Duvillaun Beg – up to 150 pairs in 1942; Duvillaun More, Inishdalla, Kid Island, Stags of Broadhaven and Carrickawilt – all less than 100 pairs (Ruttledge 1966)
Co. Donegal	Roaninish – 250–350 pairs in 1953, 1955 and 1957; Inishduff – 20–30 pairs in 1960; Inishbeg – has bred; Torglass – one or two pairs; Umfin – one or two pairs (Ruttledge 1966)
Channel Islands	Breeding Grand Amfroque (Herm) 1903, 1905, 1914, 1946. Les Etacs (Alderney) *c.* 1900, Great Casquet (Alderney) 1938 and islets of Sark 1878, 1903, and 1946 (Dobson 1952)

TABLE 6. *Gannetries in Britain and Ireland: pairs occupying nests in 1968–70 and past history*

Counts during 1968–70 apply to 1969 except for the Bass Rock (1968) and Bull Rock (1970), and the census techniques are shown by initials as follows: LC = made by observer on land; SC = made by observer at sea; AP = photographed from the air; SP = photographed from sea

Colony	When founded or first recorded	1887–1913 (Gurney 1913 as amended by Fisher and Vevers 1943)	1914–35 (Wynne-Edwards et al. 1936)	1939 (Fisher & Vevers 1943)	1949 (except Noss) (Fisher & Vevers 1951)	1955–66 (sources cited)	1968–70 and census techniques (see key)
Scar Rocks	Breeding in 1883	—	—	Recolonised 2–6	100	167 (1960) (Young 1968)	450 LC
Ailsa Craig	Breeding by 1526	3,250 (1905)	7,000 (1935)	5,419	4,947	9,390 (1959) (J. Gibson *in litt.*)	13,054 LC, SC
St Kilda	Occupied by 9th cent. (arch. ev.)	14,750 (1902)	16,500 (1931)	16,900	17,035	44,526 (1959) (Boyd 1961)	c. 52,000 AP
Flannan Islands	First reported 1969	—	—	—	—	—	16 CS
Sula Sgeir	Breeding by 1549	5,000 (1887)	5,000 (1933)	3,970	6,182	c. 5,000 (1965) (Fisher papers)	8,964 AP
Sule Stack	Breeding by 1710	4,000 (1904)	4,000 (1914)	3,490	2,010	2,900 (1960) (Fisher papers)	4,018 AP
Hermaness	Founded 1917	—	1,000 (1935)	2,611	3,750	4,500 (1965) (Fisher papers)	5,894 LC, AP
Noss	Founded 1914	—	800 (1935)	1,830	3,150 (1946)	Not counted	4,300 LC, SC

Colony	When founded or first recorded	1887–1913 (Gurney 1913 as amended by Fisher and Vevers 1943)	1914–35 (Wynne-Edwards et al. 1936)	1939 (Fisher & Vevers 1943)	1949 (except Noss) (Fisher & Vevers 1951)	1955–66 (sources cited)	1968–70 and census techniques (see key)
Bass Rock	Breeding by 1521	3,000 (1904)	4,147 (1929)	4,374	4,820	6,908 (1962) (Nelson 1966)	8,977 LC, SC
Bempton Cliffs	Founded 1937	—	—	4	2	6 (1959) (H. O. Bunce in litt.)	18 LC
Grassholm	Founded 1820–60	275 (1904)	4,750 (1933)	5,875	9,200	15,528 (1964) (Barrett and Harris 1965)	16,128 AP
Great Saltee	Founded 1929	—	1 (1935)	0	2	125 (1964) (Irish Bird Report)	155 LC
Bull Rock	Founded 1850s	300 (1908)	400 (1930)	575	295	500 (1955) (Kennedy 1961)	c. 1,500 LC, SC
Little Skellig	Breeding by 1700	17,500 (1906)	10,000 (1930)	9,500	12,000	17,700 (1966) (Irish Bird Report)	c. 20,000 SP
Les Etacs	Founded early 1940s	—	—	—	418	1,010 (1960) (Fisher papers)	c. 2,000 LC, SC
Ortac	Founded 1940	—	—	—	225	925 (1960) (Fisher papers)	c. 1,000 SC
TOTALS		48,075	53,598	54,548	64,136	109,115 (excl. Noss)	138,474
Number of colonies		8	11	12	15	15	16

TABLE 7. *North Atlantic gannetries: year of foundation and most recent census figures* (*pairs occupying nests*)

Historical information from Fisher and Vevers (1943), Monnat 1969 (France), Dobson and Lockley 1946 (Channel Islands), Brun 1972 (Norway), Gibbs and Mawby 1968 (Faeroes), Reinsch 1969 and Dr F. Gudmundsson *in litt.* (Iceland), Canadian Wildlife Service *in litt.* (Newfoundland and Quebec)

	Colony	When founded or first recorded	Pairs occupying nests and census year		TOTALS
France	Rouzic, Sept Iles, Brittany	1939	2,500	1967	2,500
Channel	Ortac, Alderney	1940	1,000	1969	
Islands	Les Etacs, Alderney	c. 1940	2,000	1969	3,000
Ireland	Great Saltee, Wexford	1929	155	1969	
	Bull Rock, Cork	1850s	1,500	1970	
	Little Skellig, Kerry	by 1700	20,000	1969	21,655
Wales	Grassholm, Pembrokeshire	1820–60	16,128	1969	16,128
England	Bempton Cliffs, Yorkshire	1937	18	1969	18
Scotland	Scar Rocks, Wigtownshire	1939	450	1969	
	Ailsa Craig, Ayrshire	by 1526	13,054	1969	
	St Kilda, Outer Hebrides	by 9th cent.	52,000	1969	
	Flannan Isles, Outer Hebrides	1969	16	1969	
	Sula Sgeir, Outer Hebrides	by 1549	8,964	1969	
	Sule Stack, Outer Hebrides	by 1710	4,018	1969	
	Hermaness, Unst, Shetland	1917	5,894	1969	
	Noss, Shetland	1914	4,300	1969	
	Bass Rock, East Lothian	by 1521	8,977	1968	97,673
Norway	Runde, Möre og Romsdal	1946	383	1971	
	Mosken, Lofoten Islands	1965	77	1971	
	Nordmjele	1967	65	1971	
	Syltefjord	1961	44	1971	569
Faeroes	Mykinesholm	by 1673	1,081	1966	1,081
Iceland	Vestmannaeyjar	c. 1700	5,315	1960	
	Eldey	by 1821	15,000	1962	
	Raudinupur	1944	34	1959	
	Stóri Karl	1955	63	1961	
	Skrúdur	1943	314	1961	
	Máfadrangur	1962	100	1962	20,826
EASTERN ATLANTIC TOTAL					163,450
Newfound-	Cape St Mary's	1897	c. 3,000	1969	
land	Baccalieu Island	c. 1901	351	1969	
	Funk Island	1936	2,987	1971	6,338
Quebec	Anticosti Island	1919	144	1969	
	Bonaventure	1860	21,215	1966	
	Bird Rocks	by 1534	3,353	1969	24,712
WESTERN ATLANTIC TOTAL					31,050
GRAND TOTAL					194,500

TABLE 8. *Numbers of pairs of Cormorants and Shags breeding in Britain and Ireland in 1969–70*

	Cormorant	Shag		Cormorant	Shag
Kirkcudbrightshire	140	8	Glamorgan	10	2
Wigtownshire	360	130	Pembrokeshire	380	150
Ayrshire	100	180	Cardiganshire	180	45
Buteshire	14	26	Merioneth	45	—
Argyll	60	2,080	Caernarvonshire	415	200
West Inverness	180	1,840	Anglesey	390	170
West Ross	80	540	TOTAL WALES	1,420	567
West Sutherland	105	2,050			
Outer Hebrides	380	2,790	Co. Dublin	320	270
Orkney	590	3,580	Co. Wicklow	—	5
Shetland	460	8,600	Co. Wexford	390	340
Caithness	850	1,560	Co. Waterford	65	90
East Ross	200	25	Co. Cork	30	140
Morayshire	1	—	Co. Kerry	130	370
Banffshire	—	50	Co. Clare	100	35
Aberdeenshire	—	250	Co. Galway	150	150
Kincardineshire	—	40	Co. Mayo	160	115
Angus	—	15	Co. Sligo	120	20
Fife	—	880	Co. Donegal	290	850
East Lothian	150	440	Co. Antrim	110	200
Berwickshire	1	125	Co. Down	—	25
TOTAL			TOTAL		
SCOTLAND	3,671	25,209	IRELAND	1,865	2,610
Northumberland	215	165	Jersey	55	275
Co. Durham	25	—	Guernsey	—	45
Yorkshire	60	20	Herm	5	145
Isle of Wight	185	10	Sark	—	40
Dorset	120	50	Alderney	2	65
South Devon	200	65	TOTAL CHANNEL		
Cornwall	170	740	ISLANDS	62	570
Isles of Scilly	50	1,000			
North Devon	20	70			
Somerset	40	—			
Cumberland	1	—			
Isle of Man	30	550			
TOTAL ENGLAND	1,116	2,670	GRAND TOTALS	8,134	31,626

TABLE 9. *Changes in numbers of breeding pairs of Great Skuas at sites in Shetland for which past information is available (sites listed from north to south)*

Data from Baxter and Rintoul (1953), Davis (1965), Dott (1967), Jackson (1966), Low (1879), Venables and Venables (1955)

	pre-1940	1941–68	1969–70
Hermaness, Unst	Max. 23 in 1897, 42 in 1907, 80–100 in 1926	300–350 incl. non-breeders in 1949, 286 in 1965	300
Saxa Vord, Unst	1 in several years from 1890, flourishing in 1938	45 in 1949	80
Uyea, off Unst	—	Few in 1950	4
Urie Lingey	—	2 in 1950	2–3
Fetlar	Colonised in early 1900s	Less than 30 in 1946, 15–25 in 1950–52	275
Hascosay	Breeding in 1913, 60–70 in 1932	30–40 in 1947–49, 75 in 1952	40
Yell	Colonised during 1887–96, 56 in 1932	96 in 1946, decreasing in 1951	125
Uyea Is., off Mainland	—	2–3 in 1952	2
Ronas Hill, Mainland	Up to 16 in late 19th century, 2–3 in 1900s	28 in 1952	79
Yell Sound islands	1 on Bigga in 1896	20 in 1950	7
Gluss Isle, Mainland	—	2 in 1952	1
West Linga, off Whalsay	—	1 in 1952	Nil
Vaila	—	2 in 1948–51	6
Foula	6 in 1774, max. 120 in 1892, 300 incl. non-breeders in 1938	400–500 incl. non-breeders in 1948, 900 in 1963	1,780
Bressay	First nested in 1913	20 in 1946	92
Noss	2 in 1910, 8 in 1922, 14 in 1923, 30 in 1929, 50 in 1932, 90–100 in 1939	113 in 1946, 165 in 1952	210
Trondra	—	1 in 1951–52	Nil
Mousa	Few in 1928	3–4 in 1949–51	12
Fitful Head, Mainland	Seen, breeding not proved, in 1925	3 in 1948, 4–5 in 1952	13
Fair Isle	Probably breeding in 1804, 1 in 1921, 3 in 1930	4 in 1949, 10 in 1952, 30 in 1963; shot by islanders	10

TABLE 10. *Number of pairs of Great Skuas and Arctic Skuas breeding in Scotland in 1969–70*

	Great Skua	Arctic Skua
Shetland	3,060	770
Orkney	90	230
Outer Hebrides	18	40
Sutherland	4	1
Caithness	—	20
Argyll	—	25
TOTALS	3,172	1,086

TABLE 11. *Number of pairs of Black-headed Gulls breeding in coastal colonies in Britain and Ireland in 1969–70*

Kirkcudbrightshire	300	Northumberland	2,310
Wigtownshire	260	Lincolnshire	4,220
Ayrshire	780	Norfolk	1,310
Buteshire	125	Suffolk	3,330
Argyll	550	Essex	3,820
West Inverness	1	Kent	3,240
West Ross	135	Sussex	260
West Sutherland	50	Hampshire	22,060
Outer Hebrides	800	Isle of Wight	260
Orkney	4,490	Dorset	21
Shetland	530	Cheshire	100
Caithness	75	Lancashire	1,730
Morayshire	400	Cumberland	10,360
Aberdeenshire	1,100	Isle of Man	50
Perthshire	500	TOTAL ENGLAND	53,071
Fife	8,000		
TOTAL SCOTLAND	18,096	Co. Wexford	500
		Co. Kerry	30
Pembrokeshire	22	Co. Galway	290
Merionethshire	700	Co. Mayo	125
Anglesey	115	Co. Sligo	5
TOTAL WALES	837	Co. Donegal	280
		Co. Antrim	33
		Co. Down	1,360
		TOTAL IRELAND	2,623
		GRAND TOTAL	74,627

TABLE 12. *Numbers of pairs of Black-headed Gulls breeding in coastal colonies in England and Wales in 1938, 1958 and 1969–70*

Figures in brackets denote number of colonies. The large colony on Havergate Island (Suffolk) has been controlled since 1960

	1938		1958		1969–70	
Northumberland	?	(1)	440	(2)	2,310	(4)
Lincolnshire	15	(1)	540	(3)	4,220	(5)
Norfolk	?	(4)	1,280	(9)	1,310	(5)
Suffolk	12+	(1)	5,070	(3)	3,330	(12)
Essex	1,500	(6)	4,260	(7)	3,820	(7)
Kent	360	(3)	2,510	(3)	3,240	(3)
Sussex	—		155	(1)	260	(1)
Hampshire	125	(2)	5,890	(5)	22,060	(4)

Table 12 continued

Table 12 continued

	1938		1958		1969–70	
Isle of Wight	50	(1)	50	(1)	260	(1)
Dorset	1,300	(2)	—		21	(1)
Devon	4	(1)	—		—	
Glamorgan	—		50	(1)	—	
Carmarthenshire	56	(1)	—		—	
Pembrokeshire	—		—		22	(1)
Merionethshire	214	(3)	225	(1)	700	(1)
Anglesey	300	(2)	310	(2)	115	(1)
Flintshire	15	(1)	—		—	
Cheshire	30	(1)	20	(1)	100	(1)
Lancashire	1,650	(2)	95	(2)	1,730	(3)
Cumberland	10,270	(7)	14,570	(5)	10,360	(6)
Isle of Man	—		—		50	(1)
TOTALS	15,901	(39)	35,465	(46)	53,908	(57)

TABLE 13. *Number of pairs of Common Gulls breeding in coastal colonies in Britain and Ireland in 1969–70*

Kirkcudbrightshire	95	Norfolk	2
Ayrshire	50	Kent	4
Buteshire	1,690	Sussex	1
Argyll	1,520	Cumberland	1
West Inverness	290	TOTAL ENGLAND	8
West Ross	290		
West Sutherland	240	Anglesey	6
Outer Hebrides	640	TOTAL WALES	6
Orkney	4,850		
Shetland	1,380	Co. Cork	4
Caithness	30	Co. Kerry	70
East Sutherland	150	Co. Galway	60
East Ross	265	Co. Mayo	200
East Inverness	10	Co. Sligo	4
Morayshire	80	Co. Donegal	400
Banffshire	12	Co. Antrim	7
Aberdeenshire	4	Co. Down	45
Kincardineshire	25	TOTAL IRELAND	790
TOTAL SCOTLAND	11,621	GRAND TOTAL	12,425

TABLE 14. *Numbers of pairs of Lesser Black-backed Gulls, Herring Gulls and Great Black-backed Gulls breeding on the coasts of Britain and Ireland in 1969–70*

	L.B.-b. Gull	Herring Gull	G.B.-b. Gull		L.B.-b. Gull	Herring Gull	G.B.-b. Gull
Kirkcudbrightshire	570	5,200	60	Northumberland	1,400	450	—
Wigtownshire	5	1,070	16	Co. Durham	—	80	—
Ayrshire	430	1,160	29	Yorkshire	—	3,300	—
Buteshire	2,280	2,860	180	Suffolk	150	150	—
Argyll	2,640	8,050	540	Kent	2	630	—
West Inverness	210	4,600	360	Sussex	1	860	—
West Ross	250	1,900	180	Hampshire	—	3	—
West Sutherland	320	6,670	1,960	Isle of Wight	1	1,250	5
Outer Hebrides	500	3,610	2,610	Dorset	1	2,200	17
Orkney	810	7,800	6,000	South Devon	—	7,180	36
Shetland	570	10,150	2,490	Cornwall	14	9,800	260
Caithness	16	19,500	1,100	Isles of Scilly	2,500	1,000	1,200
East Sutherland	—	180	3	North Devon	100	5,450	69
East Ross	3	10,100	500	Somerset	800	8,200	58
East Inverness	—	3	1	Gloucestershire	7	50	—
Morayshire	50	1,160	22	Lancashire	17,500	17,000	10
Banffshire	14	4,600	16	Cumberland	700	3,000	16
Aberdeenshire	2	28,000	8	Isle of Man	53	9,900	280
Kincardineshire	3	11,000	22	TOTAL ENGLAND	23,229	70,503	1,951
Angus	—	4,300	1				
Fife	2,210	16,060	4				
Midlothian	5	30	—				
East Lothian	330	7,300	1	Monmouthshire	10	200	33
Berwickshire	6	1,500	—	Glamorgan	1,100	1,500	2
TOTAL SCOTLAND	11,224	156,803	16,103	Carmarthenshire	—	180	—
				Pembrokeshire	5,700	12,700	680
				Cardiganshire	9	3,000	50
Co. Dublin	43	4,800	160	Merionethshire	—	300	—
Co. Wicklow	—	370	6	Caernarvonshire	6	1,900	17
Co. Wexford	470	6,600	500	Anglesey	3,700	29,900	160
Co. Waterford	9	4,000	45	Denbighshire	9	700	—
Co. Cork	120	3,400	320	TOTAL WALES	10,534	50,380	942
Co. Kerry	590	4,100	520				
Co. Clare	60	1,700	140				
Co. Galway	70	2,200	380	Jersey	13	1,240	50
Co. Mayo	50	2,290	500	Guernsey	11	460	10
Co. Sligo	16	680	80	Herm	40	640	55
Co. Donegal	34	5,380	250	Sark	125	1,310	40
Co. Londonderry	—	250	—	Alderney	115	320	45
Co. Antrim	65	9,300	90	TOTAL CHANNEL IS.	304	3,970	200
Co. Down	160	6,900	150				
TOTAL IRELAND	1,687	51,970	3,141	GRAND TOTALS	46,978	333,626	22,337

TABLE 15. *Changes in numbers of breeding pairs of Lesser Black-backed Gulls at colonies for which past information is available.*

	Before 1930	1930–68	1969–70
Arran, Buteshire	Very common (Gray 1871), ceased to nest by end of century (Paterson 1901)	Two small colonies in 1944 (Gibson 1955)	570
Inchmarnock, Buteshire	15 in 1916, 200 in 1924 (McWilliam 1938)	300 in 1937 (McWilliam 1938), 200 in 1953, 400 in 1958, 700 in 1964 (Gibson 1969)	1,000
Tiree, Argyll	Bred before 1899	Several in 1955 (Boyd 1958)	50
Coll, Argyll	Bred before 1899	Several hundred at one site in 1955 (Boyd 1958)	55
Raasay, West Inverness	Numbers breeding during 1896–1902 (Collier 1904)	A few in 1936–37 (Temperley 1938)	Nil
Priest Island, West Ross		120 birds in 1937 (Darling 1940)	13
Eilean Mhuire, Shiant Is., Outer Hebrides	40 in 1888, still present 1910 (Baxter and Rintoul 1953)	—	Nil
Flannan Isles, Outer Hebrides	Several hundred in 1881 (Harvie-Brown 1882)	6 breeding, not proved, in 1937 (Atkinson 1938)	Nil
St Kilda, Outer Hebrides	Breeding in 1847 and 1884, 1 in 1911	1 in 1931, 15 in 1947, 100 in 1957 (Williamson 1958)	292
North Rona, Outer Hebrides	Breeding in 1886–87 (Harvie-Brown and Buckley 1888), large colony in 1910	6 in 1936 (Ainslie and Atkinson 1937), 2–3 in 1958, but breeding not proved (Bagenal and Baird 1959)	Nil
Hoy, Orkney	—	300 in north of island (Meinertzhagen 1939), large colonies (Lack 1942–43)	1

	Before 1930	1930–68	1969–70
Walls, South Hoy and Rousay, Orkney	Numerous (Buckley and Harvie-Brown 1891)	—	Nil
Egilsay, Gairsay, Sweyn Holm and the Green Holms, Orkney	All occupied in 1907 (Baxter and Rintoul 1953)	—	Nil
Shetland	Huge reduction in numbers during present century, with colonies which once contained several hundred pairs now deserted or nearly so (Venables and Venables 1955)		520
Isle of May, Fife	—	First nested in 1930, 15 in 1938, 73 in 1946, 100 in 1948, 115 in 1951, 165 in 1952, 175 in 1953, 200 in 1954, 250–300 in 1955 (Eggeling 1960)	2,000
Lundy, Devon	?	350 in 1939, 100 in 1953 (Davis 1954), 69 in 1962 (*Lundy Bird Report 1962*)	100
Flat Holm, Glamorgan	—	First nested in 1954, 218 in 1957, 455 in 1960, 450 in 1961, 550 in 1962, 616 in 1964, 1,000 in 1966 (Heathcote et al. 1967)	1,100
St Margarets Island, Pembrokeshire	?	17 in 1949 (Fursdon 1950), 2 in 1962 (Sutcliffe 1963)	Nil
Skomer Island, Pembrokeshire	?	1,000 in 1946 (Buxton and Lockley 1950), 1,400 in 1962 (Harris 1962a), 3,150 in 1966 (Saunders 1967)	3,500
Newborough Warren, Anglesey	?	300 in early 1960s (Hope Jones 1965)	2,100
Walney Island, Lancashire	—	First nested in 1930s (Oakes 1953), 9,000 during 1962–65 (Brown 1967)	17,500

TABLE 16. *Changes in numbers of breeding pairs of Herring Gulls at colonies for which past information is available*

	Before 1930	1930–68	1969–70
Little Ross, Kirkcudbright	1 in 1920 (Baxter and Rintoul 1953)	?	570
Inchmarnock, Buteshire	15 in 1916, 50 in 1924 (McWilliam 1938)	300 in 1937 (McWilliam 1938), 350 in 1953, 650 in 1958, 850 in 1964 (Gibson 1969)	1,250
Ceann a' Mhara, Tiree, Argyll	Bred in 19th century	100–150, including Lesser Black-backed Gulls, in 1955 (Boyd 1958)	365
Canna, West Inverness	?	335+ in 1963 (Evans and Flower 1967)	1,600
Handa, Sutherland	?	150 in 1959 (Dickinson and Harris 1960)	360
Fair Isle, Shetland	?	140 in 1959 (Davis 1965)	315
River Esk, Kincardineshire	—	First nested in 1952 (*Scottish Birds* 2: 490)	189
Tentsmuir, Fife	—	First nested in 1955 (Grierson 1962)	55
Isle of May, Fife	First nested in 1907 (Eggeling 1955)	455 in 1936, 760 in 1947, 1,750 in 1952, 3,000 in 1954–55 (Eggeling 1960)	15,000
Orford Ness, Suffolk	?	2–3 in 1963 (*Suffolk Bird Report 1963*)	150
Dungeness, Kent	First nested in 1908	700 in late 1930s, 45 in 1955 (Axell 1956)	17
Steep Holm, Somerset	?	700 in 1930s, 3,600 in 1956 (Palmer and Ballance 1968)	5,070
Stert Island, Somerset	?	100 in 1946 (Palmer and Ballance 1968)	3,120
Denny Island, Monmouthshire	?	8 in 1961 (Humphreys 1963)	95

	Before 1930	1930–68	1969–70
Flat Holm, Glamorgan	—	First nested in 1954, 73 in 1957, 89 in 1959, 181 in 1960, 225 in 1961, 352 in 1962, 275 in 1963, 381 in 1964, c. 600 in 1966 (Heathcote et al. 1967)	920
Skokholm Island, Pembrokeshire	?	570 in 1949 (*Skokholm Bird Observatory Report for 1949*)	1,350
Skomer Island, Pembrokeshire	?	700 in 1946 (Buxton and Lockley 1950), 1,070 in 1962 (Harris 1962a), 1,650 in 1966 (Saunders 1967)	2,200
Newborough Warren, Anglesey	?	2,000–3,000 in early 1960s (Hope Jones 1965)	4,780
Puffin Island, Anglesey	?	20,000 in 1960 (Harris unpubl. thesis)	15,500
Walney Island, Lancashire	Attempted to nest in 1904, established in 1928 (Oakes 1953)	120 in 1947 (Oakes 1953), 9,000 during 1962–65 (Brown 1967)	17,000
St Bees Head, Cumberland	?	1,670 in 1956 (Stokoe 1962)	3,000
Irelands Eye, Dublin	?	490 in 1961 (O. J. Merne pers. comm.)	1,250
Great Saltee, Wexford	?	2,000 in 1960 (Ruttledge 1966)	3,600
Inishmurray, Sligo	?	50 in 1955, 150 in 1961 (Cabot 1962)	310

TABLE 17. *Number of pairs of Great Black-backed Gulls breeding in England and Wales in 1930, 1956 and 1969–70*

Brackets indicate incomplete coverage

	1930	1956	1969/70
Isle of Wight	—	6	5
Dorset	1	4	17
South Devon	31	30	36
Cornwall	80	120–150	260
Isles of Scilly	600–800	(370)	1,200
North Devon	64	42	69
Somerset	2	80	58
Gloucestershire	—	1	—
Monmouthshire	—	4	33
Glamorgan	5	4	1
Pembrokeshire	180	500	680
Cardiganshire	7	15	50
Caernarvonshire	10	55	17
Anglesey	(20)	150	160
Lancashire	—	1	10
Cumberland	4	2	16
Isle of Man	6	210	280
TOTALS	1,000–1,200	1,594–1,624	2,892

TABLE 18. *Changes in numbers of breeding pairs of Great Black-backed Gulls at certain colonies*

Figures in the right-hand column apply to 1969 unless otherwise stated. Numbers on Skokholm and Skomer have been controlled since 1959 and 1960 respectively.

	Before 1930	1930–68	1969–70
Ailsa Craig, Ayrshire	None by 1900, re-established 1922	12 in 1940s (Gibson 1951)	18
Tiree, Argyll		First nested 1949 (Boyd 1958)	82
Canna, West Inverness		10 in 1930s, 17 in 1963 (Evans and Flower 1967)	61
Am Balg, Sutherland	1 in 1927	150 in 1947 (Fisher and Piercy 1950)	c. 300
North Rona, Outer Hebrides	Largest colony in British Isles (Harvie-Brown 1888)	700–1,000 in 1939 (Darling 1943)	1,800
Hoy, Orkney		Serle (1934), Meinertzhagen (1939) and Lack (1942–43) mentioned only occasional pairs well inland	2,530; large colonies up to 2½ miles inland
Fair Isle, Shetland	'Numerous'	12–20 in 1930s, 40 in 1959 (Davis 1965)	55
Lyra Stack, Papa Stour, Shetland	30 in 1890 (Raeburn 1891)	30 in 1951 (Venables and Venables 1955)	85 in 1970
Isle of May, Fife		First nested 1962 (Gordon 1963)	4
Enys Dodman, Cornwall		16 in 1931, 28 in 1945 (Ryves 1948), 20 in 1951, 6 in 1953 (Davis 1958)	3
Mullion Island, Cornwall		Not mentioned in any previous surveys	150; largest colony in Cornwall

Table 18 continued

Table 18 continued

	Before 1930	1930–68	1969–70
Bedruthan Steps, Cornwall		20 in 1931, 6 in 1953 (Davis 1958)	3
Lye Rock, Cornwall		15 in 1956 (Davis 1958)	3
Lundy, Devon	6–7 in 1900 (Blathwayt 1900)	50 in 1930 (Harrisson and Hurrell 1933), 57 in 1937 (Perry 1940), 32 in 1956 (Davis 1958)	50
Stert Island, Somerset		2 in 1956, first record (Davis 1958)	17
Steep Holm, Somerset	First nested 1923 (Ingram and Salmon 1923)	12 in 1946, 74 in 1956 (Davis 1958), 49 in 1962 (*Lundy Bird Report 1962*)	41
Denny Island, Monmouthshire		First nested 1954 (Davis 1958)	33
Worms Head, Glamorgan	Nesting in 1898	Maximum 25 in 1941 (Heathcote *et al.* 1967)	None
St Margarets Island, Pembrokeshire		36 in 1956 (Davis 1958)	169
Grassholm, Pembs.		18 in 1956 (Davis 1958)	50
Skokholm, Pembs.		44 in 1947, 72 in 1949, 45 in 1954, 39 in 1959 (*Skokholm Bird Observatory Reports*)	12
Skomer, Pembrokeshire		60 in 1946 (Buxton and Lockley 1950), 220–250 in 1956 (Davis 1958), 283 in 1961 (Saunders 1962)	160

Table 18 continued

	Before 1930	1930–68	1969–70
Walney Is., Lancashire		First recent nesting in 1952, 1 in 1956 (Davis 1958)	10
Rockcliffe Marsh, Cumberland		1 in 1956 (Davis 1958)	14
Little Saltee, Wexford		12 in 1943 (Davis 1958), 200 in 1963 (Rutt-ledge 1966)	250
Great Saltee, Wexford		75 in 1943 (Davis 1958), 89 in 1959, 150 in 1964 (Ruttledge 1966)	200
High Island, Galway		50 in 1943 (Ruttledge 1966)	100
Inishkea Island, Mayo		Several in 1940, 100 in 1961 (Cabot 1963)	150
Inishmurray, Sligo		Several in 1955, 35 in 1961 (Cabot 1963)	38 in 1970
Inishduff, Donegal		30 in 1961 (Cabot 1962)	60
South Minnis Is., Down		49 in 1956 (Ruttledge 1966)	16
Drummond Is., Down		40 in 1956 (Ruttledge 1966)	20

TABLE 19. *Number of pairs of Kittiwakes breeding in Britain and Ireland in 1969–70*

Kirkcudbrightshire	30	Glamorgan	560
Wigtownshire	670	Pembrokeshire	2,960
Ayrshire	7,740	Cardiganshire	60
Argyll	3,990	Caernarvonshire	2,230
West Inverness	2,060	Anglesey	940
West Sutherland	17,240	TOTAL WALES	6,750
Outer Hebrides	25,380		
Orkney	128,680		
Shetland	42,770		
Caithness	52,340	Co. Dublin	3,850
East Ross	400	Co. Wicklow	20
Morayshire	430	Co. Wexford	3,750
Banffshire	11,320	Co. Waterford	2,960
Aberdeenshire	13,920	Co. Cork	2,830
Kincardineshire	38,060	Co. Kerry	4,840
Angus	1,650	Co. Clare	4,380
Fife	3,280	Co. Galway	820
East Lothian	1,070	Co. Mayo	3,270
Berwickshire	19,200	Co. Sligo	1,000
TOTAL SCOTLAND	370,230	Co. Donegal	10,610
		Co. Antrim	4,550
		Co. Down	3
Northumberland	2,990	TOTAL IRELAND	42,883
Durham	3,400		
Yorkshire	36,880		
Norfolk	3	Alderney	12
Suffolk	30	TOTAL CHANNEL ISLANDS	12
Kent	50		
Isle of Wight	10		
Dorset	260		
Devon	2,230		
Cornwall (including Scilly Is.)	2,280+		
Cumberland	1,470		
Isle of Man	910		
TOTAL ENGLAND	50,513	GRAND TOTAL	470,388

TABLE 20. *Numbers of pairs of Sandwich Terns, Roseate Terns, Common Terns, Arctic Terns and Little Terns breeding on the coasts of Britain and Ireland in 1969–70.*

	Sandwich	Roseate	Common	Common or Arctic	Arctic	Little
Kirkcudbrightshire	1	—	350	—	30	2
Wigtownshire	—	—	50	—	15	1
Ayrshire	190	12	160	—	60	6
Buteshire	—	—	150	—	110	—
Argyll	—	3	820	—	1,700	60
West Inverness	—	—	70	—	280	—
West Ross	—	—	340	—	200	—
West Sutherland	—	—	70	—	400	—
Outer Hebrides	—	—	76	—	1,200	66
Orkney	290	3	200	—	12,300	—
Shetland	—	—	390	—	7,660	—
Caithness	—	—	50	—	60	3
East Sutherland	—	—	20	—	180	6
East Ross	1,000	—	30	—	210	—
East Inverness	—	—	110	—	6	—
Morayshire	—	—	500	—	90	10
Banffshire	—	—	15	—	—	—
Aberdeenshire	740	—	490	—	320	24
Kincardineshire	—	—	5	—	7	40
Angus	—	1	4	—	70	10
Fife	—	—	260	—	20	10
Midlothian	50	50	100	—	—	—
East Lothian	225	55	420	—	40	13
TOTAL SCOTLAND	2,496	124	4,680	—	24,958	251
Northumberland	2,270	315	1,700	—	4,100	15
Co. Durham	—	—	30	—	—	2
Yorkshire	—	—	—	—	—	4
Lincolnshire	—	—	95	—	—	60
Norfolk	3,950	—	1,900	—	4	416
Suffolk	160	—	310	—	—	70
Essex	17	—	65	—	—	130
Kent	—	—	390	—	—	55
Sussex	—	—	150	—	—	160
Hampshire	220	2	260	—	—	80
Isle of Wight	—	—	1	—	—	5
Dorset	—	—	155	—	—	120
Isles of Scilly	—	20	150	—	—	—
Cheshire	—	—	40	—	—	—
Lancashire	160	1	730	—	120	35
Cumberland	460	—	140	—	80	70
Isle of Man	—	—	1	—	30	20
TOTAL ENGLAND	7,237	338	6,117	—	4,334	1,242

Table 20 continued

Table 20 continued

	Sandwich	Roseate	Common	Common or Arctic	Arctic	Little
Merionethshire	—	—	—	—	—	7
Caernarvonshire	—	—	—	—	—	7
Anglesey	2	200	280	—	440	7
Flintshire	—	—	10	—	—	4
TOTAL WALES	2	200	290	—	440	25
Co. Dublin	—	60	70	—	120	13
Co. Wicklow	—	—	16	—	—	50
Co. Wexford	250	1,200	840	60	50	100
Co. Cork	—	10	570	5	140	2
Co. Kerry	60	—	500	65	1	11
Co. Clare	—	—	20	—	5	—
Co. Galway	215	—	300	105	210	60
Co. Mayo	190	—	130	20	130	12
Co. Sligo	—	—	100	—	—	2
Co. Donegal	200	3	170	45	170	40
Co. Londonderry	—	—	—	—	—	6
Co. Antrim	—	190	390	—	40	—
Co. Down	1,210	250	400	1,060	175	—
TOTAL IRELAND	2,125	1,713	3,406	1,360	1,041	296
Jersey	—	—	100	—	—	—
Guernsey	—	—	7	—	—	—
TOTAL CHANNEL ISLANDS	—	—	107	—	—	—
GRAND TOTALS	11,860	2,375	14,700	1,360	30,773	1,814

TABLE 21. *Changes in numbers of breeding pairs of Little Terns in certain counties of England and Scotland and in north and south Wales*

County/ area	History	1967 Cols.	Pairs	1969–70 Cols.	Pairs
Fife	Increased at Tentsmuir until over 30 in 1905. Decreased on north shore from 16 in 1924 to few and finally none by 1953. At Shelly Point 70 in 1953, 40 in 1954, 35 in 1955, 20 in 1959 (Grierson 1962), nil in 1969	3	7	3	8
Yorkshire	Teesmouth colony now deserted. At Spurn Point 100 in early part of century and 1930s; declined late 1940s to 60 in 1950 (Chislett 1952), 15 in 1961, 10 in 1963 (*Yorkshire Bird Reports*), 4 in 1969	2	11	1	4
Lincolnshire	—	5	32	5	60

Table 21 continued

Table 21 continued

County/ area	History	1967 Cols.	1967 Pairs	1969–70 Cols.	1969–70 Pairs
Norfolk	Total 160–230 in late 1950s and early 1960s; 170 in 1963, 265 in 1965 (Seago 1967)	11	304	11	417
Suffolk	Max. 150 in late 1950s. At Walberswick one chick reared from 50 pairs in 1950 (Payn 1962); 6 pairs there in 1969	9	71	10	69
Essex	Seven colonies holding 160–180 (Hudson and Pyman 1968) including (1969 figs. in brackets) Little Oakley 20–30 (9), Naze 15–20 (1), Leewick 12–15 (15), Goldhanger 1–3 (nil), Foulness up to 95 (84)	7	152	9	130
Kent	70–140 during 1954–65 (*Kent Bird Reps.*)	9	92	4	55
Sussex	Increased 1939–45 to 200 (des Forges and Harber 1963); 80–100 in 1960, 71 in 1962, 31 in 1963, 50 in 1965, 90 in 1966 (*Sussex Bird Reports*)	6	102	7	158
Hampshire	60 in 1958 but only 18–46 during 1959–64 (*Hampshire Bird Reports*)	7	59	9	80
Dorset	Main colony rarely completely counted: 60 in 1918, 70 in 1934 (Blathwayt 1934); 100 in 1964 (Moule 1965)	1	200	1	100+
Lancashire	Mainly on Furness coast, formerly also near Lytham St Anne's and Fleetwood. Walney Island, 40 in 1949 (Oakes 1953), 18 in 1969. Foulney Island, 36 in 1961 (*Lancashire Bird Report*), 4 in 1969	5	18	4	35
Cumberland	Colonies once all the way from Lancashire border to Grune Point, where 100 in 1917, 20 in 1954 (Stokoe 1962), only 2 in 1969	4	41	6	67
North Wales	Colonies once all the way from Dyfi estuary to Pwllheli, now only two there. Seven colonies in Caernarvonshire included one near Criccieth with 50 pairs (Forrest 1907), now the only one remaining, with 7 pairs in 1969. Aber Menai Point (Anglesey), 40 in 1946 (North et al. 1949), 2 in 1969	8	35	7	25
South Wales	Nested in north Cardiganshire until 1940s (Peach and Miles 1961). Two colonies in Glamorgan, one with 30 pairs in 1910, both deserted since 1930s (Heathcote et al. 1967)	Nil		Nil	

TABLE 22. *Numbers of pairs of Razorbills and Guillemots breeding in Britain and Ireland in 1969–70*

	Razorbill	Guillemot		Razorbill	Guillemot
Kirkcudbrightshire	130	280	Glamorgan	70	140
Wigtownshire	150	1,900	Pembrokeshire	3,300	6,200
Ayrshire	2,280	4,200	Cardiganshire	170	570
Argyll	2,190	4,500	Caernarvonshire	700	5,200
West Inverness	1,170	2,400	Anglesey	700	1,900
West Ross	3	—	TOTAL WALES	4,940	14,010
West Sutherland	14,200	49,300			
Outer Hebrides	22,200	65,000	Co. Dublin	1,760	11,500
Orkney	8,500	129,800	Co. Wicklow	4	—
Shetland	8,900	77,400	Co. Wexford	5,900	9,700
Caithness	19,000	62,200	Co. Waterford	1,140	390
East Ross	60	750	Co. Cork	1,970	4,800
Banffshire	640	8,500	Co. Kerry	2,800	3,800
Aberdeenshire	410	5,100	Co. Clare	1,650	8,500
Kincardineshire	5,800	33,000	Co. Galway	317	1,500
Angus	130	180	Co. Mayo	2,105	3,200
Fife	350	9,000	Co. Sligo	55	2,000
East Lothian	60	1,200	Co. Donegal	27,160	10,950
Berwickshire	260	6,700	Co. Antrim	3,500	22,300
TOTAL SCOTLAND	86,433	461,410	TOTAL IRELAND	48,361	78,640
Northumberland	7	2,900	Jersey	5	—
Yorkshire	1,740	12,600	Herm	15	25
Isle of Wight	6	65	Sark	10	30
Dorset	22	530	Alderney	12	35
South Devon	8	430	TOTAL CHANNEL		
Cornwall	620	580	ISLANDS	42	90
Isles of Scilly	400	60			
North Devon	1,000	1,900			
Cumberland	55	2,600			
Isle of Man	570	1,100			
TOTAL ENGLAND	4,428	22,765	GRAND TOTALS	144,204	576,915

TABLE 23. *Changes in numbers of breeding pairs of Razorbills at certain colonies* (1967 information from 'Seafarer' pilot survey and BTO auk survey)

	Before 1930	1930–68	1969–70
Scar Rocks, Wigtownshire		15 in 1943, 50 in 1953 (Young 1968)	74
Ailsa Craig, Ayrshire		2,160 in 1950 (Gibson 1951); 2,310 in 1964, 2,020 in 1967 (Gibson 1970)	2,280
Glunimore, Argyll		Colonised mid-1920s, about 50 in 1950 (Gibson 1970)	156
Sheep Island, Argyll		Colonised late '20s, at least 50 in 1950 (Gibson 1970)	250
Mull, Argyll	Numerous on south and west cliffs in 1850s and 1860s (Graham 1890)	—	Nil
Tiree, Argyll		80 birds in 1952 (Boyd 1958)	125
Eagamol, Inverness	Few in 1889 (Evans and Flower 1967)	Few in 1934, increasing in 1966 (Evans and Flower 1967)	150
Rhum, Inverness		A few colonies up to 25, plus c. 200 in 1960 (Evans and Flower 1967)	410
Skye (north-west mainland)	Great numbers (Harvie-Brown and Macpherson 1904)	—	Nil
Summer Isles, West Ross		Breeding on three islands in late 1930s; less than 10 pairs on Priest Island (Darling 1940)	Only on Priest Is. 3
Handa, Sutherland		5,340 in 1962 (R. H. Dennis *in litt.*)	8,370
North Rona, Outer Hebrides		1,500 in 1939 (Baxter and Rintoul 1953); 2,000 in 1958 (Dennis and Waters 1962)	330 (913 in 1972- P. Evans)
Hoy, Orkney		Tens of thousands in 1933 (Serle 1934)	360
Fair Isle, Shetland		No evidence of any marked change: 750–1,000 (Davis 1965); 1,100 in 1966 (R. H. Dennis *in litt.*)	1,200
Noss, Shetland	Immense colonies in 1880s (Raeburn diaries)		3,100
Papa Stour, Shetland	Considerable numbers in 1880s (Raeburn diaries)		50
Isle of May, Fife		500 in 1936 (Southern 1938); 375 in 1952 (Eggeling 1955)	350
Bass Rock, E. Lothian	200 in 1928 (Baxter and Rintoul 1953)		Less than 20

	Before 1930	1930–68	1969–70
Bempton Cliffs, Yorkshire		2,130 in 1964 (Williams and Kermode 1968)	1,730
Isle of Wight		1,000 in 1937, decreasing in 1947, 60 in 1958 (Cohen)	6
Purbeck Cliffs, Dorset		130 in 1932, 100–250 in 1948 (*Dorset Bird Reports*); scores in mid-1950s (Dr W. Bourne pers. comm.)	15
Bats Head, Dorset		20 in 1932, 18 in 1955 (*Dorset Bird Reports*)	1
Portland Bill, Dorset		20 in 1932, 12 in 1951, 40 in 1958 (*Dorset Bird Reps.*)	6
Berry Head, Devon		30 in 1941, 40 in 1952, 10 in 1962 (*Devon Bird Reps.*)	6
Scabbacombe, Devon		10 in 1948, 5 in 1962 (*Devon Bird Reports*)	2
Lundy, Devon		10,500 in 1939 (Perry 1940); max. 2,600 in 1954 (Davis 1954)	580
Isles of Scilly	Colonies on many islands; largest Rosevear where 'hundreds' if not 'thousands' nested until 1914–15 (Penhallurick 1969)	1946 – still abundant, but considered to have greatly decreased during past 40 years. May 1961 – only 75 birds seen in whole of Scilly (Penhallurick 1969)	c. 400
Worms Head, Glamorgan	250 in 1925 (Heathcote *et al.* 1967)	60 in 1948 (Heathcote *et al.* 1967)	70
St Margarets Is., Pembrokeshire		158 in 1962 (Sutcliffe 1963)	104
Skokholm Island, Pembrokeshire	800 in 1928 (*Skokholm Bird Obs. Reports*)	670 in 1947, 343 in 1963 (*Skokholm Bird Obs. Reps.*)	675
Middleholm, Pembrokeshire		180 in 1933, 85 in 1966 (Lockley and Saunders 1967)	78
Skomer Island, Pembrokeshire		2,170 in 1966 (Saunders 1967); 1,700 in 1967	1,490
Bardsey, Caernarvonshire	20 in 1913 (Norris 1953)	20 in 1930, increased (Norris 1953)	162
Great Saltee, Wexford		10,000 in 1960 and 1964 (Ruttledge 1966); 8,000 in 1967	5,800
Cape Clear, Cork		260 in 1963, 180 in 1967 (Sharrock and Wright 1968)	180
Tory Island, Donegal		750 in 1954 (Redman 1964)	710
Sheep Island, Antrim		155 in 1967 ⎫ Seafarer	60
Muck Island, Antrim		80 in 1967 ⎬ Pilot	180
The Gobbins, Antrim		265 in 1967 ⎭ survey	80

TABLE 24. *Changes in numbers of breeding pairs of Guillemots at certain colonies*
1967 information from 'Seafarer' pilot survey and BTO auk survey.

	Before 1930	1930–68	1969–70
Scar Rocks, Wigtownshire	Abundant in 1869 (Young 1968)	1,500 in 1943, 750 in 1965 (Young 1968)	1,200
Ailsa Craig, Ayrshire	50,000 in 1910 (Gibson 1951)	5,380 in 1950 (Gibson 1951); 5,130 in 1964, 4,200 in 1967	4,180
Mull (mainland), Argyll	Myriads in 1867 (Graham 1890)	Some present in 1948 (Baxter and Rintoul 1953)	Nil
Tiree, Argyll	400 in 1891 (Boyd 1958)	Present in 1920, ceased breeding by 1942 (Boyd 1958)	Nil
Sanday, Inverness		90 in 1963 (Evans and Flower 1967)	146
Muck, Inverness	None in 1889 (Evans and Flower 1967)	Breeding in 1934, decreasing recently (Evans and Flower 1967)	515
Rhum, Inverness	Many in 1910 (Baxter and Rintoul 1953)	Several colonies of up to 25 and several up to 250 in 1950s, 250 in 1960 (Evans and Flower 1967)	935
Handa, Sutherland		38,390 in 1962 (R. H. Dennis *in litt.*)	30,790
St Kilda, Outer Hebrides		13,850 in 1959 (Boyd 1960)	21,150
North Rona, Outer Hebrides		5,000 in 1958 (Dennis and Waters 1962)	6,810
Sule Stack, Outer Hebrides		Few thousand in 1939 (James Fisher papers)	200
Fair Isle, Shetland		1,500–2,000 in 1959 (Davis 1965); 5,640 in 1966	10,000
Isle of May, Fife	300 in 1888 (Baxter and Rintoul 1953)	2,080 in 1938, 2,000 in 1954–55 (Eggeling 1955)	9,000
Craigleith, E. Lothian		First nested in 1934 (Baxter and Rintoul 1953)	620
Bass Rock, E. Lothian	250 in 1928 (Baxter and Rintoul 1953)		500
St. Abb's Head, Berwickshire	550 in 1885 (Baxter and Rintoul 1953)		6,000
Bempton Cliffs, Yorkshire	130,000 eggs said to have been taken in a year (Nelson 1907)	12,950 in 1964 (Williams and Kermode 1968)	12,600
Isle of Wight		3,000 in 1937, 1,200 in 1946, 80 in 1962 (Cohen 1963)	10
Purbeck Cliffs, Dorset		3,000 in 1932, 500 in 1948, 250 in 1962 (*Dorset Bird Reports*)	500
Bats Head, Dorset		200 in 1932 (*Dorset Bird Report*)	3

	Before 1930	*1930–68*	*1969–70*
Portland Bill, Dorset		100 in 1932 (*Dorset Bird Report*)	35
Berry Head, Devon		500 in 1941 (*Devon Bird Report*)	420
Scabbacombe, Devon		60 in 1950 (*Devon Bird Report*)	6
Carn les Boel, Cornwall		100 in 1942 (Penhallurick 1969)	Nil
Morvah, Cornwall		50 in 1942 (Phillips 1968)	14
Lundy, Devon		19,000 in 1939 (Perry 1940); 5,000 in 1951 (Davis 1954); 3,560 in 1962 (Moore 1969)	1,647
Isles of Scilly	Considered to be outnumbered by Razorbills by 25 to 1 but nested in great profusion becoming scarce late 19th cent. Only sites early 20th cent. Menavaur, Hanjague (Penhallurick 1969)	1946 and 1947 colonies too large to estimate noted on Gorregan. 1967 17 pairs Gorregan, 8 Scilly Rock and c. 25 Menavaur (Penhallurick 1969)	c. 60
Worms Head, Glamorgan	300 in 1925 (Heathcote et al. 1967)		140
St Margarets Is., Pembrokeshire		97 in 1962 (Sutcliffe 1963)	118
Elegug Stacks, Pembrokeshire		1,750 in 1960 (Lockley 1961)	520
Skokholm Island, Pembrokeshire		220 in 1937, 110 in 1947, 60 in 1963 (*Skokholm Bird Obs. Reports*)	120
Middleholm, Pembrokeshire		250 in 1933, 124 in 1966 (Lockley and Saunders 1967)	60
Skomer Island, Pembrokeshire		5,000 in 1946 (Buxton and Lockley 1950); 4,900 in 1966 (Saunders 1967)	3,920
Bardsey, Caernarvonshire	Some hundreds in 1905 (Norris 1953)	70 in 1961 (*Bardsey Bird Obs. Report*)	30
Great Saltee, Wexford		15,000 in early 1960s (Ruttledge 1966); 14,500 in 1967	9,670
Tory Island, Donegal		165 in 1954 (Redman 1964)	146
Sheep Island, Antrim		130 in 1967 ⎫	100
Carrick-a-rede, Antrim		150 in 1967 ⎪ Seafarer	62
Muck Island, Antrim		300 in 1967 ⎬ Pilot Survey	360
The Gobbins, Antrim		800 in 1967 ⎭	260

TABLE 25. *Number of pairs of Black Guillemots breeding in Britain and Ireland in 1969–70*

Kirkcudbrightshire	4	Anglesey	8
Wigtownshire	20	TOTAL WALES	8
Ayrshire	60		
Buteshire	10	Co. Louth	1
Argyll	710	Co. Dublin	16
West Inverness	420	Co. Wicklow	40
West Ross	440	Co. Wexford	6
West Sutherland	420	Co. Waterford	90
Outer Hebrides	530	Co. Cork	60
Orkney	2,240	Co. Kerry	40
Shetland	2,330	Co. Clare	20
Caithness	370	Co. Galway	20
Banffshire	1	Co. Mayo	140
TOTAL SCOTLAND	7,555	Co. Sligo	15
		Co. Donegal	160
Cumberland	2	Co. Antrim	110
Isle of Man	40	Co. Down	20
TOTAL ENGLAND	42	TOTAL IRELAND	738
		GRAND TOTAL	8,343

TABLE 26. *Number of Puffin colonies (in Orders of Abundance) in Britain and Ireland in 1969–70*

	Order 1 1–9 pairs	Order 2 10–99 pairs	Order 3 100–999 pairs	Order 4 1,000– 9,999 pairs	Order 5 10,000– 99,999 pairs
Wigtownshire	2				
Ayrshire		1			
Argyll	4	6	1	1	
West Inverness	8	4	3		
West Sutherland		1	4		1
Outer Hebrides (a)	2	3	2	5	2
St Kilda					4
Orkney	12	20	6	1	1
Shetland	19	23	8	6	3
Caithness	1	1	4	4	1
Banffshire (b)			1		
Aberdeenshire (b)			2		
Kincardineshire	1	2			
Angus			1		
Fife		1		1	
East Lothian	2	1	1		
Berwickshire		2			
TOTAL SCOTLAND	51	65	33	18	12

Table 26 continued

	Order 1 1–9 pairs	Order 2 10–99 pairs	Order 3 100–999 pairs	Order 4 1,000–9,999 pairs	Order 5 10,000–99,999 pairs
Northumberland		1	2	2	
Yorkshire			1		
Isle of Wight	1				
Dorset	1	1			
Cornwall	1	3	1		
Isles of Scilly	5	1			
North Devon		1			
Cumberland	1				
Isle of May	2	3			
TOTAL ENGLAND	11	10	4	2	
Pembrokeshire	4	1	1	2	
Caernarvonshire			1		
Anglesey	2	1			
TOTAL WALES	6	2	2	2	
Co. Dublin	1	1			
Co. Wexford		1	1		
Co. Cork	1		2		
Co. Kerry			2	3	
Co. Clare			1		
Co. Mayo(c)		3	2	1	
Co. Donegal			2	1	
Co. Antrim	2		1		
TOTAL IRELAND	4	5	11	5	
Channel Islands	3	5	1		
GRAND TOTAL	75	87	51	27	12

Notes (a) The colony on Haskeir was not visited in 1969–70; 50 pairs nested in 1953 (Parslow 1967)

(b) The colony on the Aberdeenshire–Banffshire border at Lion and Pennan Heads has been shown as two colonies, one in each county.

(c) The colony on Bills Rocks was not visited in 1969–70; 1,900 pairs nested in 1967 (Cabot 1967).

TABLE 27. *Changes in numbers of breeding pairs of Puffins at certain colonies*

	Up to 1930	1931–68	1969–70
Ailsa Craig, Ayrshire	Immense numbers (Gray 1871); decrease first noted 1900 (McWilliam 1936)	Practically extinct 1934 (McWilliam 1936). 30 birds 1947 (Gibson 1948), 12 in 1961 and 1967 (Gibson 1969)	20
Sheep Is. & Glunimore, Argyll	Colonised 1920s (Gibson 1969)	Numbers fluctuate due to rock falls. (Gibson 1969)	95 Sheep Is. 125 Glunimore
Sanda, Argyll	—	First colonised 1940s, deserted some years; maximum 25 (Gibson 1969)	None
Eigg, West Inverness	—	Several hundred 1934, none by 1953 (Evans and Flower 1967)	None
Rhum, West Inverness	—	Several hundreds in early 1950s (Bourne 1957a), decreased to 100 by 1960 (Evans and Flower 1967)	70
Ascrib Islands, Skye	Large numbers (Gray 1871; Harvie-Brown & Macpherson 1904)	—	10
Fladda-chuain, Skye	Large colony (Wilson 1842)	Great colony (Baxter and Rintoul 1935)	200
Summer Is., West Ross	Fairly common in 1887 (Dobbie 1898)	20 in late 1930s (Darling 1938), none in 1952 (Fisher papers)	None
Eilean Mhuire, Shiant Is., Outer Hebrides	Whole 3 mile perimeter occupied in 1888 (Harvie-Brown and Buckley 1888)	Every rock niche occupied, all grass slopes riddled with burrows (Baxter and Rintoul 1953)	c. 15,000 in four colonies but much unoccupied ground

Table 27 continued

	Up to 1930	1931–68	1969–70
North Rona, Outer Hebrides	Very large colony. (Swinburne 1884; Harvie-Brown & Buckley 1888)	100,000 in 1939 (Darling 1940), 8,000 in 1958 (Dennis and Waters 1962). In 1966 some deserted colonies (Robson 1969)	Some colonies noted in 1958 deserted or reduced
Fair Isle, Shetland	—	20,000 (Davis 1965)	15,000
Papa Stour, Shetland	None (Raeburn 1891)	Scattered pairs 1945–53 (Venables 1955)	100
Troup Head, Banffshire	Thousands (Harvie-Brown & Buckley 1895)	Still plentiful (Baxter and Rintoul 1953)	270
Penman Head, Aberdeenshire	—	Large colonies (Baxter and Rintoul 1953)	140
Isle of May, Fife	20 in 1880	50 in 1936 (Baxter and Rintoul 1953)	2,500
Inchkeith, Fife	—	First nested 1965 (Smith 1966)	80
Lye Rock, Cornwall	—	1,000+ in 1940s (Penhallurick 1969)	110
Annet, Isles of Scilly	Large numbers (Penhallurick 1969), 100,000 birds in 1908 (Parslow 1967)	25 in 1945 (Penhallurick 1969)	50
Lundy, Devon	Large numbers (D'Urban & Mathew 1892)	3,500 in 1939, 400 in 1953 (Davis 1954), 92 in 1962, 60 in 1966 (Moore 1969)	41
Grassholm, Pembs.	Very large colony, said to be half million birds in 1890 (Lockley et al. 1949), 200 in 1928 (Lockley 1957)	50 in 1946 (Lockley 1957)	2

Table 27 continued

	Up to 1930	1931–68	1969–70
Skokholm I., Pembs.	—	20,000 in 1930s, 5,000–10,000 in 1953 (Conder 1954), 6,000 in 1958 (Dickinson 1959)	2,500
Skomer I., Pembrokeshire		50,000 in 1946 (Lockley 1958)	7,000
St Tudwal's Islands, Caernarvonshire	Very large colony (Forrest 1908)	Several thousand in 1935, none in 1951 (Thearle et al. 1951)	None
Puffin Island, Anglesey	2,000+ in 1907 (Forrest 1908)	Several hundred in 1946 (Campbell et al. 1949)	80
Lambay Island, Co. Dublin	—	1,000 in 1939 (Lockley 1953)	100
Ireland's Eye, Co. Dublin	—	100 in 1939 (Lockley 1953)	8
Great Saltee, Co. Wexford	Many thousands (Ussher and Warren 1900)	3,000 in 1949, 1,500 in 1965 (Ruttledge 1966)	750
Great Skellig, Co. Kerry	—	5,000 in 1966 (Ruttledge 1966)	6,600
Puffin Is., Co. Kerry	—	20,000 in 1965 (Ruttledge 1966)	3,700
Rathlin Is., Co. Antrim	—	Densely populated colony (Kennedy et al. 1954) 2,200 in 1967 ('Seafarer' Pilot Survey)	850

References

ACLAND, C. M., and SALMON, H. M. 1924. 'The Grassholm Gannets in 1924 – a great increase.' *Brit. Birds*, 18: 178–85.

AINSLIE, J. A., and ATKINSON, R. 1937. 'Summer bird notes from North Rona.' *Scot. Nat.* (1937): 7–13.

ALEXANDER, M. 1968. 'Breeding Birds 1967.' *Calf of Man Rep. 1966/67*: 3–9.

ALEXANDER, S. M. D. 1954. 'The birds of the Blasket Islands.' *Bird Study*, 1: 148–68.

ANDERSON, A., BAGENAL, T. B., BAIRD, D. E., and EGGELING, W. J. 1961. 'A description of the Flannan Isles and their birds.' *Bird Study*, 8: 71–88.

ANDREW, D. G. 1963. 'Review of ornithological changes in Scotland in 1962. First breeding records for areas and counties. Common Gull *Larus canus*.' *Scot. Birds*, 2: 349.

— 1964. 'Review of ornithological changes in Scotland in 1963. First breeding records for areas and counties. Common Gull *Larus canus*.' *Scot. Birds*, 3: 176.

— and SANDEMAN, G. L. 1953. 'Notes on the birds of the Flannan Isles.' *Scot. Nat.*, 65: 157–66.

ARMSTRONG, E. A. 1940. *Birds of the Grey Wind*. Oxford and London.

ASH, J. S., and ROOKE, K. B. 1954. 'Balearic Shearwaters off the Dorset coast in 1953.' *Brit. Birds*, 47: 285–96.

ASHMOLE, N. P. 1963. 'The regulation of numbers of tropical oceanic birds.' *Ibis*, 103b: 458–73.

— 1971. 'Sea bird ecology and the marine environment.' In *Avian Biology*, vol. 1, edited by D. S. Farner and J. R. King. New York and London. pp. 223–86.

ATKINSON, R. 1938. 'Natural history notes from certain Scottish islands – North Rona, the Flannan Isles, Handa Island.' *Scot. Nat.* (1938): 145–7.

— and AINSLIE, J. A. 1940. 'The British breeding status of Leach's Fork-tailed Petrel.' *Brit. Birds*, 34: 50–5.

— and ROBERTS, B. 1955. 'Leach's Fork-tailed Petrel (*Oceanodroma leucorhoa*) in the Flannan Isles and Loch Roag.' *Scot. Nat.*, 67: 109–10.

AXELL, H. E. 1956. 'Predation and protection at Dungeness Bird Reserve.' *Brit. Birds*, 49: 193–212.

BAGENAL, T. B., and BAIRD, D. E. 1959. 'The birds of North Rona in 1958, with notes on Sula Sgeir.' *Bird Study*, 6: 153–74.

BALFOUR, E. 1968. 'Breeding birds of Orkney.' *Scot. Birds*, 5: 89–104.

—, ANDERSON, A., and DUNNET, G. M. 1967. 'Orkney Cormorants – their breeding distribution and dispersal.' *Scot. Birds*, 4: 481–93.

BANNERMAN, D. A. 1959. *The Birds of the British Isles*. Edinburgh and London. vol. 8.

— 1962. *The Birds of the British Isles*. Edinburgh and London, vol. 11.

— 1963. *The Birds of the British Isles*. Edinburgh and London, vol. 12.

— 1963–8. *Birds of the Atlantic Islands*. Edinburgh and London.

BARNES, J. A. G. 1952. 'The status of the Lesser Black-backed Gull.' *Brit. Birds*, 45: 3–17.

— 1961. 'The winter status of the Lesser Black-backed Gull, 1959–60.' *Bird Study*, 8: 127–47.

BARRETT, J. H., and HARRIS, M. P. 1965. 'A count of the Gannets on Grassholm in 1964.' *Brit. Birds*, 58: 201–3.

BARRINGTON, R. M. 1890. 'A list of birds observed in Shetland, June 1890.' *Zoologist* (1890): 345–8.

BARTH, E. K. 1952. 'Incubation period and loss of weight of eggs of the Common Gull, and of the Lesser Black-backed Gull.' *Pap. Game Res.*, 8: 111–21.

— 1955. 'Egg-laying, incubation and hatching of the Common Gull (*Larus canus*).' *Ibis*, 97: 222–39.

BAXTER, E. V. 1957. 'Review of ornithological changes in Scotland in 1955. Breeding records. Common Gull *Larus canus*.' *Scot. Nat.*, 69: 44.

— 1958. 'Review of ornithological changes in Scotland in 1957. Breeding records. Common Tern *Sterna hirundo*.' *Scot. Birds*, 1: 32–3.

— and RINTOUL, L. J. 1953. *The Birds of Scotland: Their History, Distribution and Migration*. Edinburgh and London.

BAYES, J. C., DAWSON, M. J., and POTTS, G. R. 1964. 'The food and feeding behaviour of the Great Skua in the Faroes.' *Bird Study*, 11: 272–9.

BELOPOL'SKII, L. O. 1961. *Ecology of Sea Bird Colonies of the Barents Sea*. Translated by the Israel Program for Scientific Translations, Jerusalem.

BERRY, R. J., and DAVIS, P. E. 1970. 'Polymorphism and behaviour in the Arctic Skua.' *Proc. Roy. Soc. Lond.*, 175B: 255–67.

BIBBY, C. J. 1972. 'Auks drowned in fish-nets.' *Seabird Rep.* 2: 48–9.

— and BOURNE, W. R. P. 1971. 'More problems for threatened seabirds.' *Birds*, 3: 307–9.

BLATHWAYT, F. L. 1934. 'Notes on birds.' *Proc. Dorset Nat. Hist. Arch. Soc.*, 55: 165–209.

BLEZARD, E. 1943. *The Birds of Lakeland*. Carlisle.

BLUS, L. J. 1970. 'Measurements of Brown Pelican eggshells from Florida and South Carolina.' *BioScience*, 20: 867–9.

BOCHENSKI, Z. 1962. 'Nesting of Black-headed Gull *Larus ridibundus* L.' *Acta Zool. Cracov.*, 7: 87–104.

BONHAM, W. N., and HICKLING, G. 1971. 'The Grey Seals of the Farne Islands: report for the period October 1969 to July 1971.' *Trans. Nat. Hist. Soc. Northumberland Durham Newcastle-upon-Tyne*, 17: 141-162.

BOSWALL, J. 1960. 'Observations on the use by sea-birds of human fishing activities.' *Brit. Birds*, 53: 212–15.

BOURNE, W. R. P. 1955. 'The birds of the Cape Verde Islands.' *Ibis*, 97: 508–56.

— 1957a. 'The birds of the island of Rhum.' *Scot. Nat.*, 69: 21-31.

— 1957b. 'The breeding birds of Bermuda.' *Ibis*, 99: 94–105.

— 1963. 'A review of oceanic studies of the biology of seabirds.' *Proc. Int. Orn. Congr.*, 13: 831–54.

— 1965. 'Birdwatching by submarine. II. A trip to Gibraltar in September.' *Seabird Bull.*, 1: 34–7.

— 1966. 'The plumage of the Fulmars of St. Kilda in July.' *Bird Study*, 13: 209–13.

— 1968a. 'Oil pollution and bird populations.' *Field Studies*, 2: supplement, 200–18.

— 1968b. 'Observation of an encounter between birds and floating oil.' *Nature*, 219: 632.

— 1971. 'Vanishing Puffins.' *New Scientist*, 52 (no. 772): 8–9.

— 1972. 'Threats to seabirds.' *ICBP Bull.*, 11: 200–18.

— and BOGAN, J. A. 1972. 'Polychlorinated biphenyls in North Atlantic seabirds.' *Mar. Poll. Bull.*, 3: 171–5.

— and PATTERSON, I. J. 1962. 'The spring departure of Common Gulls *Larus canus* from Scotland.' *Scot. Birds*, 2: 3–17.

BOYD, H. 1954. 'The "wreck" of Leach's Petrels in the autumn of 1952.' *Brit. Birds*, 47: 137–63.

BOYD, J. M. 1958. 'The birds of Tiree and Coll.' *Brit. Birds*, 51: 41–56, 103–18.

— 1960. 'The distribution and numbers of Kittiwakes and Guillemots on St. Kilda.' *Brit. Birds*, 53: 252–69.

— 1961. 'The gannetry of St. Kilda.' *J. Anim. Ecol.*, 30: 117–36.

BRITISH ORNITHOLOGISTS' UNION 1971. *The Status of Birds in Britain and Ireland*. Oxford.

BROOKE, M. de L. 1972. 'The Puffin population of the Shiant Islands.' *Bird Study*, 19: 1–6.

BROWN, R. G. B. 1967. 'Species isolation between the Herring Gull *Larus argentatus* and Lesser Black-backed Gull *L. fuscus*.' *Ibis*, 109: 310–17.

— 1968. 'Sea birds in Newfoundland and Greenland waters.' *Canadian Field Nat.*, 82: 88–102.

— 1970. 'Fulmar distribution: a Canadian perspective.' *Ibis*, 112: 44–51.

BRUCE, S. 1952. 'Leach's Fork-tailed Petrel on Whalsay, Shetland.' *Brit. Birds*, 45: 421.

BRUN, E. 1960. 'The breeding birds of the Calf of Man in 1959.' *Peregrine*, 3: 42–8.

— 1969. 'Utbredelse og hekkebestand av lomvi (*Uria aalge*) i Norge.' *Sterna*, 8: 209–24.

— 1972. 'Establishment and population increase of the Gannet *Sula bassana* in Norway.' *Orn. Scand.*, 3: 27–38.

BUCKLEY, T. E., and HARVIE-BROWN, J. A. 1891. *A Vertebrate Fauna of the Orkney Islands*. Edinburgh.

BUNCE, H. O., and FENTON, K. 1956. 'The status of the Shag (*Phalacrocorax aristotelis*) on the chalk cliffs of the East Riding.' *Naturalist* (1956): 109–12.

BURTON, P. J. K., and THURSTON, M. H. 1959. 'Observations on Arctic Terns in Spitsbergen.' *Brit. Birds*, 52: 149–61.

BURTON, R. W. 1970. 'Biology of the Great Skua.' In *Antarctic Ecology*, vol. 1, edited by M. W. Holdgate. London and New York. pp. 561–7.

BUXTON, J., and LOCKLEY, R. M. 1950. *Island of Skomer*. London.

CABOT, D. B. 1962. 'An ornithological expedition to Inishmurray, Co. Sligo.' *Irish Nat. J.*, 14: 59–61.

— 1963. 'The breeding birds of the Inishkea Islands, Co. Mayo.' *Irish Nat. J.*, 14: 113–15.

— 1967. 'The birds of Bills Rocks, Co. Mayo.' *Irish Nat. J.*, 15: 359–61.

CAMPBELL, J. W. 1959. 'Great Skua nesting in Outer Hebrides.' *Scot. Birds*, 1: 156–7.

— 1961. 'Review of ornithological changes in Scotland in 1960.' *Scot. Birds*, 1: 443–6.

CHESTNEY, R. 1970. 'Notes on the breeding habits of Common and Sandwich Terns on Scolt Head Island.' *Trans. Norfolk Norwich Nat. Soc.*, 21: 353–63.

CHISLETT, R. 1952. *Yorkshire Birds*. London and Hull.

CLARK, J., and RODD, F. R. 1906. 'The birds of Scilly.' *Zoologist* (1906): 241–52, 295–306, 335–46.

CLARKE, W. E. 1892. 'Report on the Great Skua in Shetland during the season of 1891.' *Ann. Scot. Nat. Hist.* (1892): 87–92.

— 1905. 'The birds of the Flannan Islands.' *Ann. Scot. Nat. Hist.*, 8-19, 80-86.

COHEN, E. 1963. *The Birds of Hampshire and the Isle of Wight*. Edinburgh and London.

COLLIER, C. 1904. 'The birds of the island of Raasay.' *Ibis* (1904): 490–512.

COLLINGE, W. E. 1924-27. *The Food of Some British Wild Birds: A Study in Economic Ornithology*. York. Revised edition.

— 1926. 'An investigation of the food of terns at Blakeney Point, Norfolk.' *Trans. Norfolk Norwich Nat. Soc.*, 12: 35–53.

CONDER, P. J. 1950. 'On the courtship and social displays of three species of auk.' *Brit. Birds*, 43: 65–9.

— 1954. 'Skokholm Bird Report, 1953.' *Skokholm Bird Obs. Rep. 1953*: 6–14.

CORKHILL, P. 1973. 'Manx Shearwaters on Skomer: population and mortality due to gull predation.' *Brit. Birds*, 66: 136–43.

COULSON, J. C. 1961. 'Movements and seasonal variation in mortality of Shags and Cormorants ringed on the Farne Islands, Northumberland.' *Brit. Birds*, 54: 225–35.

— 1963. 'The status of the Kittiwake in the British Isles.' *Bird Study*, 10: 147–79.

— 1973. 'Changes in the status of the Kittiwake 1959–70.' In press.

— and BRAZENDALE, M. G. 1968. 'Movements of Cormorants ringed in the British Isles and evidence of colony-specific dispersal.' *Brit. Birds*, 61: 1–21.

—, DEANS, I. R., POTTS, G. R., ROBINSON, J., and CRABTREE, A. M. 1972. 'Changes in organochlorine contamination of the marine environment of eastern Britain monitored by Shag eggs.' *Nature*, 236: 454–6.

— and HOROBIN, J. M. 1972. 'The annual re-occupation of breeding sites by the Fulmar.' *Ibis*, 114: 30–42.

—, POTTS, G. R., DEANS, I. R., and FRASER, S. M., 1968. 'Exceptional mortality of Shags and other seabirds caused by paralytic shellfish poison.' *Brit. Birds*, 61: 381–404.

CRAIG, R. E. 1959. 'Hydrography of Scottish coastal waters.' *Mar. Res. Scot.* (1959): no. 2.

CRAMP, S. 1971. 'Gulls nesting on buildings in Britain and Ireland.' *Brit. Birds*, 64: 476–87.

—, CONDER, P. J., and ASH, J. S. 1962. *Deaths of Birds and Mammals from Toxic Chemicals (January–June 1961)*. Roy. Soc. Prot. Birds, Sandy.

CULLEN, E. 1957. 'Adaptations in the Kittiwake to cliff-nesting.' *Ibis*, 99: 275–302.

CULLEN, J. M. 1960. 'Some adaptations in the nesting behaviour of terns.' *Proc. Int. Orn. Congr.*, 12: 153–7.

— 1962. 'An introduction to the behaviour and displays of British terns.' In *The Birds of the British Isles*, vol. 11, by D. A. Bannerman. Edinburgh and London. pp. 80-6.

CUNNINGHAM, W. A. J. 1959. 'Great Skua nesting in Outer Hebrides.' *Scot. Birds*, 1: 124.

CURRY-LINDAHL, K. 1961. *Våra Fåglar i Norden*. Stockholm. Revised edition, vol. 3.

CUSHING, D. H. 1971. 'Upwelling and the production of fish.' *Adv. Mar. Biol.*, 9: 255–334.

DALE, I. M., BAXTER, M. S., BOGAN, J. A., and BOURNE, W. R. P. 1973. 'Mercury in seabirds.' *Mar. Poll. Bull.*, 4: 77–79.

DARLING, F. F. 1940. *Island Years*. London.

— 1943. *Island Farm*. London.

DAVIS, P. E. 1954. *A List of the Birds of Lundy*. Lundy Field Society, Exeter.

— 1957. 'The breeding of the Storm Petrel.' *Brit. Birds*, 50: 85–101, 371–84.

— 1965. 'A list of the birds of Fair Isle.' In *Fair Isle and its Birds*, by K. Williamson. Edinburgh and London. pp. 251–96.

DAVIS, T. A. W. 1958. 'The breeding distribution of the Great Black-backed Gull in England and Wales in 1956.' *Bird Study*, 5: 191–215.

DEANE, C. D. 1954. 'Handbook of the birds of Northern Ireland.' *Bull. Belfast Mus. Art Gallery*, 1: 119–93.

DE NAUROIS, R. 1969. 'Peuplement et cycles de reproduction des oiseaux de la côte occidental d'Afrique.' *Mem. Mus. Nat. Hist. Nat. Series A Zoologie*, 56: 1–312.

DENNIS, R. H. 1966a. 'Notes on the breeding birds, 1966.' *Fair Isle Bird Obs. Bull.*, 5: 201–5.

— 1966b. 'Notes on the breeding biology of the Black Guillemot *Cepphus grylle*.' *Fair Isle Bird Obs. Bull.*, 5: 205–8.

— and WATERS, W. E. 1962. 'Systematic list of the birds of North Rona.' Unpublished.

DES FORGES, G., and HARBER, D. D. 1963. *A Guide to the Birds of Sussex*. Edinburgh and London.

DIAMOND, A. W., DOUTHWAITE, R. J., and INDGE, W. J. E. 1965. 'Notes on the birds of Berneray, Mingulay and Pabbay.' *Scot. Birds*, 3: 397–404.

DICKENS, R. F. 1964. 'The North Atlantic population of the Great Skua.' *Brit. Birds*, 57: 209–10.

DICKINSON, H. 1959. 'Puffins and burrows.' *Skokholm Bird Obs. Rep. 1958*: 27–34.

— and HARRIS, M. P. 1960. 'Handa birds, July 1959.' *Fair Isle Bird Obs. Bull.*, 4: 119–23.

DIXON, T. J. 1973. 'The St. Kilda Gannets and "Operation Seafarer".' *Seabird Rep. 1971*: 5–12.

DOBBIE, J. B. 1898. 'The summer birds of the Summer Islands.' *Proc. R. Phys. Soc. Edin.* 14: 46–57.

DOBBS, A. 1964. 'Lesser Black-backed Gulls breeding in Nottinghamshire.' *Brit. Birds*, 57: 516–17.

DOBIE, W. H. 1894. 'Birds of west Cheshire, Denbighshire, and Flintshire.' *Proc. Chester Soc. Nat. Sci.*, 4: 282–351.

DOBSON, R. 1952. *The Birds of the Channel Islands*. London.

— and LOCKLEY, R. M. 1946. 'Gannets breeding in the Channel Islands: two new colonies.' *Brit. Birds*, 39: 309–12.

DORWARD, D. F. 1963. 'The Fairy Tern *Gygis alba* on Ascension Island.' *Ibis*, 103b: 365–78.

DOTT, H. E. M. 1967. 'Numbers of Great Skuas and other seabirds of Hermaness, Unst.' *Scot. Birds*, 4: 340–50.

DUFFEY, E. 1951. 'Field studies on the Fulmar.' *Ibis*, 93: 237–45.

DUNN, E. K. 1972. 'Studies on terns with particular reference to feeding ecology.' Ph.D. thesis, University of Durham.

DUNN, R. 1837. *The Ornithologist's Guide to the Islands of Orkney and Shetland*. Hull.

DUNNET, G. M., ANDERSON, A., and CORMACK, R. M. 1963. 'A study of survival of adult Fulmars with observations on the pre-laying exodus.' *Brit. Birds*, 56: 2–18.

D'URBAN, W. S. M., and MATHEW, M. A. 1895. *The Birds of Devon*. London. Second edition.

EGGELING, W. J. 1955. 'The breeding birds of the Isle of May.' *Scot. Nat.*, 67: 72–89.

— 1960. *The Isle of May*. Edinburgh and London.

ERDMAN, D. S. 1967. 'Sea birds in relation to game fish schools off Puerto Rico and the Virgin Islands.' *Caribb. J. Sci.*, 7: 79–85.

ERSKINE, A. J. 1963. 'The Black-headed Gull (*Larus ridibundus*) in eastern North America.' *Audubon Fld. Notes*, 17: 334–8.

EVANS, A. H., and BUCKLEY, T. E. 1899. *A Vertebrate Fauna of the Shetland Islands*. Edinburgh.

EVANS, P. G. H. 1972a. 'The south-west Irish seabird populations.' *Seabird Report*, 2: 35–40.

— 1972b. 'Seabirds at Faraid Head, north Sutherland, and on North Rona and Sula Sgeir in 1971.' *Seabird Report*, 2: 41.

EVANS, P. R., and FLOWER, W. U. 1967. 'The birds of the Small Isles.' *Scot. Birds*, 4: 404–45.

FISHER, J. 1940. *Watching Birds*. Harmondsworth, Middlesex.

— 1948. 'St. Kilda a natural experiment.' *New Nat. J.*, 1: 91–108.

— 1952a. *The Fulmar*. London.

— 1952b. 'A history of the Fulmar *Fulmarus* and its population problems.' *Ibis*, 94: 334–54.

— 1966a. *The Shell Bird Book*. London.

— 1966b. 'The Fulmar population of Britain and Ireland, 1959.' *Bird Study*, 13: 5–76.

— and LOCKLEY, R. M. 1954. *Sea-Birds*. London.

— and PIERCY, K. 1950. 'Notes on Eilean Bulgach, Sutherland.' *Scot. Nat.*, 62: 26–30.

— and VEVERS, H. G. 1943. 'The breeding distribution, history and population of the North Atlantic Gannet (*Sula bassana*). Part I. A history of the Gannet's colonies, and the census in 1939.' *J. Anim. Ecol.*, 12: 173–213.

—— 1944. 'The breeding distribution, history and population of the North Atlantic Gannet (*Sula bassana*). Part II. The changes in the world numbers of the Gannet in a century.' *J. Anim. Ecol.*, 13: 49–62.

—— 1951. 'The present population of the North Atlantic Gannet (*Sula bassana*).' *Proc. Int. Orn. Congr.*, 10: 463–7.

— and WATERSTON, G. 1941. 'The breeding distribution, history and population of the Fulmar (*Fulmarus glacialis*) in the British Isles.' *J. Anim. Ecol.*, 10: 204–72.

FLEGG, J. J. M. 1972. 'The Puffin on St Kilda 1969–71.' *Bird Study*, 19: 7–17.

FORREST, H. E. 1907. *The Vertebrate Fauna of North Wales*. London.

— 1919. *A Handbook to the Vertebrate Fauna of North Wales*. London.

FREEMAN, R. B. 1940. 'On the birds of the islands of Oigh-Sgeir and Causamul, North Uist.' *Brit. Birds*, 33: 330–2.

FURSDON, J. 1950. 'Bird protection, Pembrokeshire, 1949.' *Ann. Rep. West Wales Fld. Soc.*, 12: 14–15.

GIBBS, R. G., and MAWBY, P. J. 1968. 'Ornithological observations in the Faroes, 1966.' *Dansk Orn. Foren. Tidsskr.*, 62: 137–40.

GIBSON, J. A. 1950. 'Methods of determining breeding-cliff populations of Guillemots and Razorbills.' *Brit. Birds*, 43: 329–31.

— 1951. 'The breeding distribution, population and history of the birds of Ailsa Craig.' *Scot. Nat.*, 63: 73–100, 159–77.

— 1955. 'The birds of the island of Arran.' *Trans. Butesh. Nat. Hist. Soc.*, 14: 87–114.

— 1969. 'Population studies of Clyde seabirds.' *Trans. Butesh. Nat. Hist. Soc.*, 17: 79–95.

— 1970. 'Population studies of Clyde seabirds.' *Trans. Butesh. Nat. Hist. Soc.*, 18: 21–30.

GOETHE, F. 1964. 'Lenkung der Möwenbestände an der deutschen Nordseeküste mit Hilfe der Einschläferung erwachsener Möwen durch Glukochloralose-α.' *Int. Rat. Vogelschutz Deutsche Sektion*, 4: 53–7.

GOODBODY, I. M. 1955. 'The breeding of the Black-headed Gull.' *Bird Study*, 2: 192–9.

GORDON, N. J. 1963. 'Isle of May Bird Observatory and Field Station Report for 1962.' *Scot. Birds*, 2: 278–86.

GRAHAM, H. D. 1890. *The Birds of Iona and Mull.* Edinburgh.

GRANT, P. J., and SCOTT, R. E. 1969. 'Field identification of juvenile Common, Arctic and Roseate Terns.' *Brit. Birds*, 62: 297–9.

GRAY, R. 1871. *The Birds of the West of Scotland, including the Outer Hebrides.* Glasgow.

GREENWAY, J. C., JR. 1958. *Extinct and Vanishing Birds of the World.* New York.

GREENWOOD, J. 1964. 'The fledging of the Guillemot *Uria aalge* with notes on the Razorbill *Alca torda*.' *Ibis*, 106: 469–81.

GREENWOOD, J. J. D., DONALLY, R. J., FEARE, C. J., GORDON, N. J., and WATERS-TON, G. 1971. 'A massive wreck of oiled birds: northeast Britain, winter 1970.' *Scot. Birds*, 6: 235–50.

GREGORY, T. C. 1948. 'Colony of tree-nesting Cormorants in Kent.' *Brit. Birds*, 41: 185–6.

GRIBBLE, F. C. 1962. 'Census of Black-headed Gull colonies in England and Wales, 1958.' *Bird Study*, 9: 56–71.

GRIERSON, J. 1962. 'A check-list of the birds of Tentsmuir, Fife.' *Scot. Birds*, 2: 113–64.

GROSS, A. O. 1955. 'Changes of certain sea bird populations along the New England coast of North America.' *Proc. XI Intern. Orn. Congr.*, 446–9.

GUDMUNDSSON, F. 1954. 'Islenzkir fuglar. IX. Skumur (*Stercorarius skua*).' *Náttúrufraeðingurinn*, 24: 132–6.

GURNEY, J. H. 1913. *The Gannet. A Bird with a History.* London.

GURNEY, R. 1919. 'Breeding stations of the Black-headed Gull in the British Isles.' *Trans. Norfolk Norwich Nat. Soc.*, 10: 416–47.

HAFTORN, S. 1971. *Norges Fugler.* Oslo.

HAMILTON, F. D. 1962. 'Census of Black-headed Gull colonies in Scotland, 1958.' *Bird Study*, 9: 72–80.

HARRIS, M. P. 1962a. 'The *Larus* gulls breeding on Skomer, Skokholm and Grassholm Islands.' *Nat. in Wales*, 8: 56–8.

— 1962b. 'Migration of the British Lesser Black-backed Gull as shown by ringing data.' *Bird Study*, 9: 174–82.

— 1962c. 'Recoveries of ringed Great Black-backed Gulls.' *Bird Study*, 9: 192–7.

— 1964. 'Aspects of the breeding biology of the gulls *Larus argentatus*, *L. fuscus* and *L. marinus*. *Ibis*,' 106: 432–56.

— 1965a. 'Puffinosis among Manx Shearwaters on Skokholm.' *Brit. Birds*, 58: 426–34.

— 1965b. 'The food of some *Larus* gulls.' *Ibis*, 107: 43–53.

— 1966a. 'Breeding biology of the Manx Shearwater *Puffinus puffinus*.' *Ibis*, 108: 17–33.

— 1966b. 'Age of return to the colony, age of breeding and adult survival of Manx Shearwaters.' *Bird Study*, 13: 84–95.

HARRISON, J. M. 1953. *The Birds of Kent.* London.

HARRISSON, T. H., and HURRELL, H. G. 1933. 'Numerical fluctuations of the Great Black-backed Gull (*Larus marinus* Linn.) in England and Wales.' *Proc. Zool. Soc. Lond.*, 103: 191–209.

HART, T. J., and CURRIE, R. I. 1960. 'The Benguela Current.' *Discovery Rep.*, 31: 123–298.

HARVIE-BROWN, J. A. 1888. 'Further notes on North Rona.' *Proc. Roy. Phys. Soc. Edinb.*, 9: 284–98.

— 1912. 'The Fulmar: its past and present distribution as a breeding species in the British Isles.' *Scot. Nat.*, 97–102, 121–32.

— and BUCKLEY, T. E. 1888. *A Vertebrate Fauna of the Outer Hebrides.* Edinburgh.

— and MACPHERSON, H. A. 1904. *A Fauna of the North-West Highlands and Skye.* Edinburgh.

HEATHCOTE, A., GRIFFIN, D., and SALMON, H. M. 1967. *The Birds of Glamorgan.* Cardiff Naturalists' Society.

HEWITSON, W. C. 1831–42. *British Oology.* Newcastle-upon-Tyne.

HICKLING, R. A. O. 1954. 'The wintering of gulls in Britain.' *Bird Study*, 1: 129–48.

— 1967. 'The inland wintering of gulls in England, 1963.' *Bird Study*, 14: 104–13.

HILLIS, J. P. 1967. 'Cliff nesting site of the Common Gull *Larus canus* L.' *Irish Nats. Journ.*, 15: 273.

— 1971. 'Sea-Birds scavenging at trawlers in Irish waters.' *Irish Nats. Journ.*, 17: 129–32.

HINDE, R. 1951. 'Further report on the inland migration of waders and terns.' *Brit. Birds*, 44: 329–46.

HOLDGATE, M. W. 1971. *The Seabird Wreck of 1969 in the Irish Sea.* Natural Environment Research Council, London.

HOLGERSEN, H. 1961. 'Norske Lomviers vandringer' (English summary: 'On the movements of Norwegian *Uria aalge* (Pont.)'). *Sterna*, 4: 229–40.

HOLLOM, P. A. D. 1940. 'Report on the 1938 survey of Black-headed Gull colonies.' *Brit. Birds*, 33: 202–21, 230–44.

HOPE JONES, P. 1965. 'Birds recorded at Newborough Warren, Anglesey, June 1960–May 1965.' *Nat. in Wales*, 9: 196–215.

—, HOWELLS, G., REES, E. I. S., and WILSON, J. 1970. 'Effect of "Hamilton Trader" oil on birds in the Irish Sea in May 1969.' *Brit. Birds*, 63: 97–110.

HOROBIN, JEAN M. 1969. 'The breeding biology of an aged population of Arctic Terns.' *Ibis*: 111, 443.

HUDSON, R. 1968. 'The Great Skua in the Caribbean.' *Bird Study*, 15: 33–4.

— 1971. 'Recoveries in Great Britain and Ireland of birds ringed abroad.' *Brit. Birds*, 64: 488–501.

— and PYMAN, G. A. 1968. *A Guide to the Birds of Essex.* Essex Bird-Watching and Preservation Society.

HUDSON, W. H. 1898. *Birds in London.* London.

HUMPHREYS, G. R. 1937. *A List of Irish Birds.* Dublin.

HUMPHREYS, J. N. 1962. 'The Second census of birds nesting on the Medway and Swale Islands.' *Kent Bird Report for 1961*, 10, 42–51.

HUMPHREYS, P. N. 1963. New revised edition of *The Birds of Monmouthshire* by G. C. S. Ingram and H. M. Salmon. Newport, Mon.

INGHAM, M. C., and MAHNKEN, C. V. W. 1966. 'Turbulence and productivity near St Vincent Island, B.W.I. A preliminary report.' *Caribb. J. Sci.*, 6: 83–7.

JACKSON, E. E. 1966. 'The birds of Foula.' *Scot. Birds*, 4: supplement.

JARVIS, M. J. F. 1970. 'Interactions between man and the South African Gannet *Sula capensis*.' *Ostrich*, supplement 8: 497–513.

JENSEN, S., JOHNELS, A. G., OLSSON, M., and OTTERLIND, G. 1969. 'DDT and PCB in marine animals from Swedish waters.' *Nature*, 224: 247–50.

JOENSEN, A. H. 1963. 'Ynglefuglene på Skúvoy, Færøerne, deres udbredelse og antal.' *Dansk Orn. Foren. Tidsskr.*, 57: 1–18.

JOHANSEN, H. 1959. 'To interessante ringfund.' *Dansk Orn. Foren. Tidsskr.*, 53: 40–1.

JOURDAIN, F. C. R. 1918. 'The first nesting record of the Great Skua in the Orkneys.' *Brit. Birds*, 12: 50–2.

— 1919. 'Further notes on the breeding of the Great Skua in the Orkneys.' *Brit. Birds*, 12: 170–1.

KADLEC, J. A., and DRURY, W. H. 1968. 'Structure of the New England Herring Gull population.' *Ecology*, 49: 644–76.

KENNEDY, P. G. 1961. *A List of the Birds of Ireland.* Dublin.

—, RUTTLEDGE, R. F., and SCROOPE, C. F. 1954. *The Birds of Ireland.* Edinburgh and London.

KOEMAN, J. H. 1971. *Het Voorkomen en de Toxicologische Betekenis van Enkele Chloorkoolwaterstoffen aan de Nederlandse Kust in de Periode van 1965 tot 1970.* University of Utrecht.

—, TEN NOEVER DE BRAUW, M. C., and DE VOS, R. H. 1969. 'Chlorinated biphenyls in fish, mussels and birds from the River Rhine and the Netherlands coastal area.' *Nature*, 221: 1126–8.

KOOYMAN, G. L., DRABEK, C. M., ELSNER, R., and CAMPBELL, W. B. 1971. 'Diving behavior of the Emperor Penguin, *Aptenodytes forsteri*.' *Auk*, 88: 775–95.

KURODA, N. 1954. *On the Classification and Phylogeny of the Order Tubinares, particularly the Shearwaters (Puffinus) with Special Consideration of their Osteology and Habit Differentiation.* Tokyo.

— 1967. 'Morpho-anatomical analysis of parallel evolution between Diving Petrel and Ancient Auk, with comparative osteological data of other species.' *Misc. Rep. Yamashina Inst. Orn. Zool.*, 5: 111–37.

LACK, D. 1942–43. 'The breeding birds of Orkney.' *Ibis*, 84: 461–84; 85: 1–27.

— 1945. 'The ecology of closely related species with special reference to Cormorant (*Phalacrocorax carbo*) and Shag (*P. aristotelis*).' *J. Anim. Ecol.*, 14: 12–16.

276   REFERENCES

— 1967. 'Interrelationships in breeding adaptations as shown by marine birds.' *Proc. Int. Orn. Congr.*, 14: 3–42.

LANGHAM, N. P. E. 1968. 'The comparative biology of terns.' Ph.D. thesis, University of Durham.

— 1971. 'Seasonal movements of British terns in the Atlantic Ocean.' *Bird Study*, 18: 155–75.

LIND, H. 1963. 'Nogle sociale reaktioner hos terner' (English summary: 'Notes on social behaviour of terns'). *Dansk Orn. Foren. Tidsskr.*, 57: 155–75.

LIVERSIDGE, R. 1959. 'The place of South Africa in the distribution and migration of ocean birds.' *Ostrich*, supplement 3: 47–67.

LLOYD, D. A. B. 1968. 'The use of inland habitats by gulls *Larus* spp. in the Ythan valley, Aberdeenshire.' M.Sc. thesis, University of Aberdeen.

LOCKIE, J. D. 1952. 'The food of Great Skuas on Hermaness, Unst, Shetland.' *Scot. Nat.*, 64: 158–62.

LOCKLEY, R. M. 1932. 'On the breeding habits of the Storm-Petrel, with special reference to its incubation and fledging-periods.' *Brit. Birds*, 25: 206–11.

— 1942. *Shearwaters*. London.

— 1953a. *Puffins*. London.

— 1953b. 'On the movements of the Manx Shearwater at sea during the breeding season.' *Brit. Birds*, 46: supplement.

— 1957. 'Grassholm: some facts and a legend.' *Nat. in Wales*, 3: 382–8.

— 1958. 'Sea birds and their protection.' *Bird Notes*, 28: 380–3.

— 1961. 'The birds of the south-western peninsula of Wales.' *Nat. in Wales*, 7: 124–33.

— and SAUNDERS, D. R. 1967. 'Middleholm (Midland Isle), Pembrokeshire.' *Nat. in Wales*, 10: 146–50.

LOCKWOOD, W. B. 1954. 'Linguistic notes on "Fulmar".' *Brit. Birds*, 47: 336–9.

LOVEGROVE, R. R. 1973. 'The birds of the Kerry islands.' in prep.

—, BYRNE, E. J., and REAR, D. 1965. 'Notes on a visit to the Great Skellig Rock, Co. Kerry.' *Irish Nat. J.*, 15: 47–9.

LOW, G. 1879. *A Tour through Orkney and Schetland in 1774*. Kirkwall.

LOYD, L. R. W. 1925. *Lundy, its History and Natural History*. London.

LUMSDEN, W. H. R., and HADDOW, A. J. 1946. 'The food of the Shag (*Phalacrocorax aristotelis*) in the Clyde sea area.' *J. Anim. Ecol.*, 15: 35–42.

MACAN, T. T., and WORTHINGTON, E. B. 1951. *Life in Lakes and Rivers*. London.

MCWILLIAM, J. M. 1936. *The Birds of the Firth of Clyde including Ayrshire, Renfrewshire, Buteshire, Dunbartonshire and South Argyllshire*. London.

— 1938. 'The birds of Inchmarnock, a Clyde island.' *Trans. Butesh. Nat. Hist. Soc.* (1938): 1–17.

MAKATSCH, W. 1952. *Die Lachmöwe*. Leipzig.

MANIKOWSKI, S. 1971. 'The influence of meteorological factors on the behaviour of sea birds.' *Acta Zool. Cracov.*, 16: 581–667.

MARCHANT, S. 1952. 'The status of the Black-headed Gull colony at Ravenglass.' *Brit. Birds*, 45: 22–7.

MARPLES, G., and MARPLES, A. 1934. *Sea Terns or Sea Swallows*. London.

MATHEW, M. A., 1894 *The Birds of Pembrokeshire and its Islands*. London.

MATTHEWS, G. V. T. 1953. 'Navigation in the Manx Shearwater.' *J. Exp. Biol.*, 30: 370–96.

— 1955. 'An investigation of the "chronometer" factor in bird navigation.' *J. Exp. Biol.*, 32: 39–58.

MAYAUD, N. 1961. 'Sur les migrations de la Mouette de Sabine *Xema sabini* (Sabine) et la question de ses zones d'hivernage.' *Alauda*, 29: 165–74.

— 1965. 'Sur la zone d'hivernage atlantique de la Mouette de Sabine *Xema sabini* (Sabine).' *Alauda*, 33: 81–3.

MEAD, C. J. in press. 'The results of ringing auks in Britain and Ireland.' *Bird Study*.

MEIKLEJOHN, M. F. M. and PALMER C. E. 1958. 'Report on birds of the Clyde area 1956. Common Tern *Sterna hirundo*.' *Scot. Birds*, 1:7.

MEINERTZHAGEN, R. 1925. 'The distribution of the phalaropes.' *Ibis*, 67: 325–44.

— 1939. 'A note on the birds of Hoy, Orkney.' *Ibis*, 81: 258–64.

MILLS, D. H. 1964. 'The ecology of the young stages of the Atlantic Salmon in the River Bran, Ross-shire.' *Freshwat. Salm. Fish. Res.*, no. 32. H.M.S.O.

— 1965. 'The distribution and food of the Cormorant in Scottish inland waters.' *Freshwat. Salm. Fish. Res.*, no. 35. H.M.S.O.

— 1969a. 'The food of the Shag in Loch Ewe, Ross-shire.' *Scot. Birds*, 5: 264–8.

— 1969b. 'The food of the Cormorant at two breeding colonies on the east coast of Scotland.' *Scot. Birds*, 5: 268–76.

MONNAT, J.-Y. 1969. 'Statut actuel des oiseaux marins nicheurs en Bretagne. VI: Haut-trégor et Guelo (de Trébeurden à Paimpol).' *Ar Vran*, 2: 1–24.

MONTAGU, G. 1802. *Ornithological Dictionary; or, Alphabetical Synopsis of British Birds*. London.

— 1813. *Supplement to the Ornithological Dictionary, or Synopsis of British Birds*. London.

MOORE, N. W., and TATTON, J. O'G. 1965. 'Organochlorine insecticide residues in the eggs of sea birds.' *Nature*, 207: 42–3.

MOORE, R. 1969. *The Birds of Devon*. Newton Abbot.

MOUGIN, J.-L. 1967. 'Etude écologique des deux espèces de Fulmars: le Fulmar atlantique (*Fulmarus glacialis*) et le Fulmar antarctique (*Fulmarus glacialoides*).' *Oiseau*, 37: 57–103.

MOULE, G. W. H. 1965. 'A revised list of the birds of Dorset up to 1962.' *Proc. Dorset Nat. Hist. Archaeol. Soc.*, 86: 66–85.

MURPHY, R. C. 1936. *The Oceanic Birds of South America*. New York.

— and HARPER, F. 1921. 'A review of the diving petrels.' *Bull. Amer. Mus. Nat. Hist.*, 44: 495–554.

MYRBERGET, S. 1962. 'Contribution to the breeding biology of the Puffin *Fratercula arctica* (L.)'. *Papers Norwegian State Game Res. Inst.*, 2nd series No. 11.

— JOHANSEN, V., and STORJORD, O. 1969. 'Stormgvater (Family Hydrobatidae) i Norge.' *Fauna*, 22: 15–26.

MYRES, M. T. 1963. 'Observations with radar of the feeding flights of Kitti-wakes.' *Bird Study*, 10: 34–43.

NEHLS, H. W. 1969. 'Zur Umsiedlung, Brutortstreue und Brutreife der Brand-seeschwalbe (*Sterna sandvicensis*) nach Ringfunden auf Langenwerder.' *Vogelwarte*, 25: 52–7.

NELSON, J. B. 1964a. 'Some aspects of breeding biology and behaviour of the North Atlantic Gannet on the Bass Rock.' *Scot. Birds*, 3: 99–137.

— 1964b. 'Fledging in the Gannet.' *Scot. Nat.*, 71: 47–59.

— 1965. 'The behaviour of the Gannet.' *Brit. Birds*, 58: 233–88, 313–36.

— 1966. 'The breeding biology of the Gannet *Sula bassana* on the Bass Rock, Scotland.' *Ibis*, 108: 584–626.

— 1967. 'Colonial and cliffnesting in the Gannet.' *Ardea*, 55: 60–90.

— 1970. 'The relationship between behaviour and ecology in the Sulidae with reference to other sea birds.' *Oceanogr. Mar. Biol. Ann. Rev.*, 8: 501–74.

NELSON, T. H. 1907. *The Birds of Yorkshire*. London.

NETTLESHIP, D. 1972 'Breeding success of the Common Puffin (*Fratercula arctica* L.) on different habitats at Great Island, Newfoundland.' *Ecol. Monog.*, 42: 239–68.

NORMAN, R. K., and SAUNDERS, D. R. 1969. 'Status of Little Terns in Great Britain and Ireland in 1967.' *Brit. Birds*, 62: 4–13.

NORRIS, C. A. 1953. 'The birds of Bardsey Island in 1952.' *Brit. Birds*, 46: 131–7.

— 1954. 'Further notes on the birds of Bardsey Island.' *Brit. Birds*, 47: 206–7.

NORTH, F. J., CAMPBELL, B., and SCOTT, R. 1949. *Snowdonia*. London.

OAKES, C. 1953. *The Birds of Lancashire*. Edinburgh and London.

OLIVER, P. J. and DAVENPORT, D. L. 1972. 'Large passage of seabirds at Cap Gris Nez.' *Seabird Rep.* 2: 16–24.

ONSLOW, G. HUGHES 1943. 'Scarce birds in Ayrshire.' *Brit. Birds*, 36: 241–2.

PALMER, E. M., and BALLANCE, D. K. 1968. *The Birds of Somerset*. London.

PALMER, RALPH S. 1962. *Handbook of North American Birds*. New Haven and London Vol. I.

PALMER, R. S. 1941. 'A behavior study of the Common Tern (*Sterna hirundo hirundo* L.).' *Proc. Boston Soc. Nat. Hist.*, 42: 1–119.

PARMELEE, D. F., and MACDONALD, S. D. 1960. 'The birds of West-Central Ellesmere Island and adjacent areas.' *Bull. Nat. Mus. Canada*, no. 169.

PARSLOW, J. L. F. 1965. 'Great Black-backed Gulls preying on Storm Petrels.' *Brit. Birds*, 58: 522–3.

— 1967. 'Changes in status among breeding birds in Britain and Ireland. Parts 1 and 3.' *Brit. Birds*, 60: 2–47, 177–202.

—, JEFFERIES, D. J., and FRENCH, M. C. 1972. 'Ingested pollutants in Puffins and their eggs.' *Bird Study*, 19: 18–33.

PASHBY, B. S., and CUDWORTH, J. 1969. 'The Fulmar "wreck" of 1962.' *Brit. Birds*, 62: 97–109.

PAYN, W. H. 1962. *The Birds of Suffolk*. London.

PEACH, W. S., and MILES, P. M. 1961. 'An annotated list of some birds seen in the Aberystwyth district, 1946–56.' *Nat. in Wales*, 7: 11–20.

PEARSON, T. H. 1968. 'The feeding biology of sea-bird species breeding on the Farne Islands, Northumberland.' *J. Anim. Ecol.*, 37: 521–52.

PENHALLURICK, R. D. 1969. *Birds of the Cornish Coast.* Truro.

PENNIE, I. D. 1948. 'Summer bird notes from Foula.' *Scot. Nat.*, 60: 157–63.

— 1953a. 'The Arctic Skua in Caithness.' *Brit. Birds*, 46: 105–8.

— 1953b. 'Great Skuas on the Scottish mainland.' *Brit. Birds*, 46: 262–3.

— 1962. 'A century of bird-watching in Sutherland.' *Scot. Birds*, 2: 167–92.

PERDECK, A. C. 1960. 'Observations on the reproductive behaviour of the Great Skua or Bonxie, *Stercorarius skua skua* (Brünn.), in Shetland.' *Ardea*, 48: 111–36.

PERRINS, C. M. 1966. 'Survival of young Manx Shearwaters *Puffinus puffinus* in relation to their presumed date of hatching.' *Ibis*, 108: 132–5.

— 1967. 'The numbers of Manx Shearwaters on Skokholm.' *Skokholm Bird Obs. Rep. 1967*: 23–9.

PERRY, R. 1940. *Lundy, Isle of Puffins.* London.

PETTITT, R. G. 1972. 'A comparison of auk movements in spring in north-west Spain and western Ireland.' *Seabird Rep. 1970*: 9–15.

PHILLIPS, J. H. 1963. 'The pelagic distribution of the Sooty Shearwater *Procellaria grisea*.' *Ibis*, 105: 340–53.

PHILLIPS, N. R. 1968. 'After the Torrey Canyon.' *Ann. Rep. Cornwall Bird-Watch. Pres. Soc.*, 37 (1967): 90–129.

PIGGINS, D. J. 1959. 'Investigations on predators of salmon smolts and parr.' Appendix 1 to *Report and Accounts, Salmon Research Trust for Ireland Incorporated.*

PLUMB, W. J. 1965. 'Observations on the breeding biology of the Razorbill.' *Brit. Birds*, 58: 449–56.

POLLOCK, K. 1963. 'Great Skua breeding on St Kilda.' *Scot. Birds*, 2: 427.

POST, P. W. 1967. 'Manx, Audubon's, and Little Shearwaters in the north-western North Atlantic.' *Bird-Banding*, 38: 278–305.

POTTHOF, J., and RICHARDS, W. J. 1970. 'Juvenile Bluefin Tuna *Thannus thannus* (Linnaeus) and other Scombrids taken by terns at the Dry Tortugas, Florida.' *Bull. Mar. Sci.*, 20: 389–413.

POTTS, G. R. 1967. 'Winter breeding of Shags.' *Brit. Birds*, 60: 214–15.

— 1968. 'Success of eggs of the Shag on the Farne Islands, Northumberland, in relation to their content of dieldrin and pp 'DDE.' *Nature*, 217: 1282–4.

— 1969. 'The influence of eruptive movements, age, population size and other factors on the survival of the Shag, *Phalacrocorax aristotelis*.' *J. Anim. Ecol.*, 38: 53–102.

— 1971. 'Moult in the Shag *Phalacrocorax aristotelis*, and the ontogeny of the "Staffelmauser".' *Ibis*, 113: 298–305.

PRESTT, I., JEFFERIES, D. J., and MOORE, N. W. 1970. 'Polychlorinated biphenyls in wild birds in Britain and their avian toxicity.' *Env. Poll.*, 1: 3–26.

— and RATCLIFFE, D. A. 1972. 'Effects of organochlorine insecticides on European birdlife.' *Proc. Int. Orn. Congr.*, 15: 486–513.

RADFORD, M. C. 1960. 'Common Gull movements shown by ringing returns.' *Bird Study*, 7: 81–93.

— 1962. 'British ringing recoveries of the Black-headed Gull.' *Bird Study*, 9: 42–55.

RAE, B. B. 1969. 'The food of Cormorants and Shags in Scottish estuaries and coastal waters.' *Mar. Res.*, no. 1. H.M.S.O.

RAEBURN, H. 1891. 'The birds of Papa Stour, with an account of the Lyra Skerry.' *Zoologist* (1891): 126–35.

RAITT, D. F. S., LOSSE, G. F., SCHMIDT, W., and HOFF, I. 1970. 'Preliminary results of acoustic/fishing surveys in West African coastal waters.' FAO Technical Conference on fish finding, purse seining and aimed trawling, Reykjavik, 24–30 May 1970. Agenda item 1/2.2.1. FII: FF/70/31. p. 16.

RANKIN, M. N., and RANKIN, D. H. 1943. 'The status of the Fulmar Petrel in north-east Ireland.' *Irish Nat. J.*, 8: 49–54.

REDMAN, P. S. 1964. 'Tory Island – the breeding birds.' *Rep. Tory Island Bird Obs.*, 5: 26–9.

REINSCH, H. H. 1969. *Der Basstölpel.* Wittenberg Lutherstadt.

RISEBROUGH, R. W. 1971. 'Effects of environmental pollutants upon animals other than Man.' Sixth Berkeley Symposium of Mathematical Statistics and Probability, Berkeley.

—, RIECHE, P., PEAKALL, D. B., HERMAN, S. G., and KIRVEN, M. N. 1968. 'Polychlorinated biphenyls in the global ecosystem.' *Nature*, 220: 1098–102.

ROBERTSON, W. B., JR. 1964. 'The terns of the Dry Tortugas.' *Bull. Florida State Mus.*, 8: 1–94.

— 1969. 'Transatlantic migration of juvenile Sooty Terns.' *Nature*, 222: 632–4.

ROBINSON, H. W. 1934. 'First nesting of Leach's Fork-tailed Petrel in Orkney.' *Scot. Nat.* (1934): 93.

ROBSON, M. J. H. 1968. 'The breeding birds of North Rona.' *Scot. Birds*, 5: 126–55.

— and WILLS, P. 1963. 'Notes on the birds of Bearasay, Lewis.' *Scot. Birds*, 2: 410–14.

ROGERS, A. E. F. 1965. 'The changing status of the Fulmar in Northern Ireland.' *Bird Study*, 12: 34–45.

ROOTH, J., and JONKERS, D. A. 1972. 'The status of some piscivorous birds in the Netherlands.' *TNO – nieuws*, 1972: 551–5.

RUTTLEDGE, R. F. 1957. 'The birds of Inishbofin, Co. Galway, with some notes on those of Inishshark.' *Bird Study*, 4: 71–80.

— 1966. *Ireland's Birds.* London.

RYVES, B. H. 1948. *Bird Life in Cornwall.* London.

— and QUICK, H. M. 1946. 'A survey of the status of birds breeding in Cornwall and Scilly since 1906.' *Brit. Birds*, 39: 3–11, 34–43.

SAGE, B. L. 1970. 'The winter population of gulls in the London area.' *London Bird Rep.*, 33: 67–80.

— and KING, B. 1959. 'The influx of phalaropes in autumn 1957.' *Brit. Birds*, 52: 33–42.

— and PENNIE, I. D. 1956. 'Great Skuas on the Scottish mainland.' *Brit. Birds*, 49: 284.

SALMON, H. M. 1958. 'Lesser Black-backed and Herring Gulls nesting on a factory-roof inland in Glamorgan.' *Brit. Birds*, 51: 399–401.

SALOMONSEN, F. 1965. 'The geographical variation of the Fulmar (*Fulmarus glacialis*) and the zones of marine environment in the North Atlantic.' *Auk*, 82: 327–55.

— 1967. 'Migratory movements of the Arctic Tern (*Sterna paradisaea* Pontoppidan) in the Southern Ocean.' *Biol. Meddr. Dansk Vid. Selsk.*, 24: 1–42.

— 1972. 'Zoogeographical and ecological problems in arctic birds.' *Proc. Int. Orn. Congr.*, 15: 25–77.

SANDEMAN, G. L. 1963. 'Roseate and Sandwich Tern colonies in the Forth and neighbouring areas.' *Scot. Birds*, 2: 286–93.

SAUNDERS, D. R. 1962. 'The Great Black-backed Gull on Skomer.' *Nat. in Wales*, 8: 59–66.

— 1967. 'Skomer report for 1966.' *Nat. in Wales*, 10: 159–69.

SAXBY, H. L., and SAXBY, S. H. 1874. *The Birds of Shetland*. Edinburgh.

SCHACHTER, O., and SERWER, D. 1971. 'Report on marine pollution problems and remedies.' United Nations, New York.

SEAGO, M. J. 1967. *Birds of Norfolk*. Norwich.

SERGEANT, D. E. 1952. 'Little Auks in Britain, 1948 to 1951.' *Brit. Birds*, 45: 122–33.

SERLE, W., JR. 1934. 'Notes on the breeding birds on the Island of Hoy, Orkney.' *Scot. Nat.* (1934): 129–36.

SHARROCK, J. T. R. (ed.) 1973. *The Natural History of Cape Clear Island*. Berkhamsted.

— and WRIGHT, P. A. 1968. 'Censuses of the cliff-breeding birds of Cape Clear Island.' *Cape Clear Bird Obs. Rep.*, 9 (1967): 33–47.

SLATER, P. J. B. (ed.) 1965a. 'Current notes.' *Scot. Birds*, 3: 366–77.

— 1965b. 'Current notes.' *Scot. Birds*, 3: 421–31.

SLINN, D. J. 1964. 'Observations on the status of certain sea-birds in the Isle of Man, 1952–61.' *Proc. Isle Man Nat. Hist. Antiq. Soc.*, 6: 597–614.

SMITH, R. W. J. 1966. 'The seabirds of the Forth islands.' *Seabird Bull.*, 2: 58–60.

— 1969. 'Scottish Cormorant colonies.' *Scot. Birds*, 5: 363–78.

SNOW, B. K. 1960. 'The breeding biology of the Shag *Phalacrocorax aristotelis* on the island of Lundy, Bristol Channel.' *Ibis*, 102: 554–75.

— 1963. 'The behaviour of the Shag.' *Brit. Birds*, 56: 77–103, 164–86.

SOUTHERN, H. N. 1938. 'A survey of the vertebrate fauna of the Isle of May (Firth of Forth).' *J. Anim. Ecol.*, 7: 144–54.

— 1939. 'The status and problem of the bridled Guillemot.' *Proc. Zool. Soc. Lond.*, 109: 31–41.

— 1943. 'The two phases of *Stercorarius parasiticus* (Linnaeus).' *Ibis*, 85: 443–85.

— 1951. 'Change in status of the bridled Guillemot after ten years.' *Proc. Zool. Soc. Lond.*, 121: 657–71.

— 1962. 'Survey of bridled Guillemots, 1959–60.' *Proc. Zool. Soc. Lond.*, 132: 455–72.

—, CARRICK, R., and POTTER, W. G. 1965. 'The natural history of a population of Guillemots (*Uria aalge* Pont.).' *J. Anim. Ecol.*, 34: 649–65.

— and REEVE, E. C. R. 1941. 'Quantitative studies in the geographical variation of birds. – The Common Guillemot (*Uria aalge* Pont.).' *Proc. Zool. Soc. Lond.*, 111: 255–76.

SPENCER, R. 1959. 'Report on bird-ringing for 1958.' *Brit. Birds*, 52: 441–92.

— 1962. 'Report on bird-ringing for 1961.' *Brit. Birds*, 55: 493–543.

— 1963. 'Report on bird-ringing for 1962.' *Brit. Birds*, 56: 447–540.

— 1965. 'Report on bird-ringing for 1964.' *Brit. Birds*, 58: 533–83.

— 1967. 'Report on bird-ringing for 1966.' *Brit. Birds*, 60: 429–75.

— 1969. 'Report on bird-ringing for 1968.' *Brit. Birds*, 62: 393–442.

— 1971. 'Report on bird-ringing for 1969.' *Brit. Birds*, 64: 137–86.

STANFORD, W. P. 1953. 'Winter distribution of the Grey Phalarope *Phalaropus fulicarius*.' *Ibis*, 95: 483–91.

STARK, D. M. 1967. 'A visit to Stack Skerry and Sule Skerry.' *Scot. Birds*, 4: 548–53.

STEVEN, G. A. 1933. 'The food consumed by Shags and Cormorants around the shores of Cornwall (England).' *J. Mar. Biol. Assoc.*, 19: 277–92.

STOKOE, R. 1962. 'The birds of the Lake Counties.' *Trans. Carlisle Nat. Hist. Soc.*, 10: 1–137.

STRESEMANN, E., and STRESEMANN, V. 1966. 'Die Mauser der Vögel.' *J. Orn.*, 107: supplement.

STUART, D. 1948. 'Vital statistics of the Mochrum Cormorant colony.' *Brit. Birds*, 41: 194–9.

STUBBS, F. J. 1917. 'The London gulls.' *Trans. Lond. Nat. Hist. Soc.* (1916): 37–41.

SUMMERS-SMITH, J. D. 1963. *The House-Sparrow.* London.

SUTCLIFFE, S. J. 1963. 'A survey of the breeding birds of St. Margaret's Island, South Pembrokeshire.' *Nat. in Wales*, 8: 126–7.

SWENNEN, C., and SPAANS, A. L. 1970. 'De Sterfte van zeevogels door olie in Februari 1969 in het Waddengebiet.' *Vogeljaar*, 18: 239–45.

SWINBURNE, J. 1884. 'Notes on the islands of Sula Sgeir or North Barra, and North Rona, with a list of the birds inhabiting them.' *Proc. Roy. Phys. Soc. Edinb.*, 8: 51–67.

TAVERNER, J. H. 1965. 'Observations on breeding Sandwich and Common Terns.' *Brit. Birds*, 58: 5–9.

— 1970. 'Further observations on the breeding behaviour of Sandwich Terns.' *Seabird Rep. 1969*: 46–7.

TEMPERLEY, G. W. 1938. 'The birds of Raasay.' *Scot. Nat.* (1938): 11–27.

— 1951. 'A history of the birds of Durham.' *Trans. Nat. Hist. Soc. Northumberland Durham Newcastle-upon-Tyne*, 9: 1–296.

TEWNION, A. 1958. 'Great Skua breeding on Papa Westray, Orkney.' *Scot. Birds*, 1: 14–15.

THEARLE, R. F., HOBBS, J. T., and FISHER, J. 1953. 'The birds of the St. Tudwal Islands.' *Brit. Birds*, 46: 182–8.

THOM, V. M. 1968. 'Common Gulls using man-made nest sites.' *Scot. Birds*, 5:218.

THOMSON, A. L. 1939. 'The migration of the Gannet: results of marking in the British Isles.' *Brit. Birds*, 32: 282–9.

— 1943. 'The migration of the Sandwich Tern.' *Brit. Birds*, 37: 62–9.

— 1962. 'Migration of the Sandwich Tern.' In *The Birds of the British Isles*, vol. 11, by D. A. Bannerman. Edinburgh and London. pp. 142–5.

— 1965. 'The transequatorial migration of the Manx Shearwater (Puffin des Anglais).' *Oiseau*, 35: supplement, 130–40.

— 1966. 'An analysis of recoveries of Great Skuas ringed in Shetland.' *Brit. Birds*, 59: 1–15.

THRELFALL, W. 1968. 'The food of Herring Gulls in Anglesey and Caernarvonshire.' *Nat. in Wales*, 11: 67–73.

TIMMERMAN, G. 1938–49. 'Die Vögel Islands.' *Visindafélag Íslendinga*, 21: 1–109; 24: 111–238; 28: 239–524.

TINBERGEN, N., and MOYNIHAN, M. 1952. 'Head flagging in the Black-headed Gull; its function and origin.' *Brit. Birds*, 45: 19–22.

TONG, M. 1967. 'Winter breeding of Shags.' *Brit. Birds*, 60: 214.

TSCHANZ, B. 1959. 'Zur Brutbiologie der Trottellumme (*Uria aalge aalge* Pont.).' *Behaviour*, 14: 1–100.

TUCK, L. M. 1960. *The Murres*. Ottawa.

— and SQUIRES, H. J. 1955. 'Food and feeding habits of Brünnich's Murre (*Uria lomvia lomvia*) on Akpatok Island.' *J. Fish. Res. Bd. Can.*, 12: 781–92.

TULL, C. E., GERMAIN, P., and MAY, A. W. 1972. 'Mortality of Thick-billed Murres in the West Greenland Salmon Fisheries.' *Nature*, 237: 42–4.

USPENSKI, S. M. 1958. 'The bird bazaars of Novaya Zemlya.' *Transl. Russ. Game Rep.* (Canadian Wildlife Service), 4: 1–159.

USSHER, R. J., and WARREN, R. 1900. *The Birds of Ireland*. London.

VANDE WEGHE, J.-P. 1966. 'La Sterne Pierregarin *Sterna hirundo* et la Sterne Arctique *Sterna paradisea*. Identification et passage en Belgique.' *Aves*, 3: 1–5.

VAURIE, O. 1965. *The Birds of the Palearctic Fauna. Non-Passeriformes*. London.

VENABLES, L. S. V., and VENABLES, U. M. 1955. *Birds and Mammals of Shetland*. Edinburgh.

VERNON, J. D. R. 1969. 'Spring migration of the Common Gull in Britain and Ireland.' *Bird Study*, 16: 101–7.

— 1970. 'Feeding habitats and food of the Black-headed and Common Gulls. Part 1. Feeding habitats.' *Bird Study*, 17: 287–96.

— and AVENT, C. 1959. 'Lesser Black-backed Gull nesting on a bush.' *Brit. Birds*, 52: 60.

VINE, A. E., and SERGEANT, D. E. 1948. 'Arboreal nesting of Black-headed Gull colony.' *Brit. Birds*, 41: 158–9.

VOOUS, K. H. 1949. 'The morphological, anatomical, and distributional relationship of the Arctic and Antarctic Fulmars.' *Ardea*, 37: 113–22.

— 1960. *Atlas of European Birds*. London.

— and WATTEL, J. 1963. 'Distribution and migration of the Greater Shearwater.' *Ardea*, 51: 143–57.

WALKER, I. M. 1961. 'Manx Shearwater nestling still unfledged in late November.' *Brit. Birds*, 54: 242–3.

WATERS, W. E. 1964. 'Arrival times and measurements of small petrels on St. Kilda.' *Brit. Birds*, 57: 309–15.

WATERSTON, G. 1965. 'Great Skua breeding in North West Highlands.' *Scot. Birds*, 3: 313.

WATSON, A. 1954. 'Nesting of the Shag in Banffshire and Aberdeenshire.' *Scot. Nat.*, 66: 122–3.

WATT, G. 1951. *The Farne Islands*. London.

WILLIAMS, A. J. 1971. 'Ornithological observations on Bear Island 1970.' *Astarte*, 4: 31–6.

—, and KERMODE, D. 1968. 'A census of the seabird colony at Flamborough, June, 1964.' *Seabird Bull.*, 6: 15–21.

WILLIAMS, J. G. 1966. 'A new cormorant from Uganda.' *Bull. Brit. Orn. Cl.*, 86: 48–50.

WILLIAMSON, K. 1940. 'The Puffins of the Calf of Man – the history of the Manx Shearwater.' *J. Manx Mus.*, 4: 178–80, 203–5.

— 1948. *The Atlantic Islands*. London.

— 1952. 'The incubation rhythm of the Fulmar.' *Scot. Nat.*, 64: 138–47.

— 1954. 'The fledging of a group of young Fulmars.' *Scot. Nat.*, 66: 1–12.

— 1958. 'The menace of the gulls at St. Kilda.' *Bird Notes*, 28: 330–4.

— 1970. *The Atlantic Islands*. London. New edition.

—, RANKIN, M. N., and RANKIN, D. H. 1943. 'Field notes on the breeding of the Roseate Tern.' *North-western Nat.*, 18: 29–32.

WILSON, D. R. 1958. 'Leach's Petrels in Shetland.' *Brit. Birds*, 51: 77–8.

WINN, H. E. 1950. 'The Black Guillemots of Kent Island, Bay of Fundy.' *Auk*, 67: 477–85.

WITHERBY, H. F., JOURDAIN, F, C. R., TICEHURST, N. F., and TUCKER, B. W. 1940–41. *The Handbook of British Birds*. London. vols 4 and 5.

WYNNE-EDWARDS, V. C. 1951. 'Lesser Black-backed Gull nesting in Aberdeenshire.' *Scot. Nat.*, 63: 198–9.

— 1955. 'Low reproductive rates in birds, especially sea-birds.' *Proc. Int. Orn. Congr.*, 11: 540–7.

— 1962. *Animal Dispersion in Relation to Social Behaviour*. Edinburgh and London.

—, LOCKLEY, R. M., and SALMON, H. M. 1936. 'The distribution and numbers of breeding Gannets (*Sula bassana* L.).' *Brit. Birds*, 29: 262–76.

YOUNG, J. G. 1968. 'Birds of the Scar Rocks – the Wigtownshire gannetry.' *Scot. Birds*, 5: 204–8.

YTREBERG, N. J. 1956. 'Contribution to the breeding biology of the Black-headed Gull (*Larus ridibundus* L.) in Norway. Nest, eggs and incubation.' *Nytt Mag. Zool.*, 4: 5–106.

ZOUTENDYK, P. 1968. 'The occurrence of Sabine's Gull *Xema sabini* off the Cape Peninsula.' *Ostrich*, 39: 9–11.

Index to Species

Numbers in **bold** type refer to principal entries

The Seabird Group

The Seabird Group was founded in 1956 to promote the development of co-operative research on seabirds and to circulate news of work in progress. It is run by an Executive Committee composed of three members nominated by the British Ornithologists' Union, the British Trust for Ornithology, and the Royal Society for the Protection of Birds, and six elected annually by the members. Its main activities include the study of the behaviour of seabirds as seen from the shore and at sea and, in conjunction with the Royal Society for the Protection of Birds, full and sample breeding counts each year of threatened species and surveys of bird mortality on beaches.

The Group publishes an Annual Report and periodical circulars to members. The Annual General Meeting is normally held at the British Trust for Ornithology's Ringing and Migration Conference in January, and is accompanied by a series of talks by members. Membership is open to all and the full subscription is £1 per annum, full-time students half price. Inquiries to the Secretary, Seabird Group, Zoology Department, Tillydrone Avenue, Aberdeen AB9 2TN